"This book has been an enriching adjunct to my work with singles. Al is extremely personable and instructive in blending theory with the practical nuts and bolts of dating. I highly recommend this book."

—M. *Dorsey Cartwright*, M.Ed., Expressive Therapies Center of Houston, Texas

"I recommend this practical resource for any single person desiring to be in a committed relationship. Al shows how to use past romances and childhood to produce a more fulfilling love life. His concrete examples will assist the reader in recognizing an inner wisdom that will serve them in finding a lifelong partner."

—*Louis W. McLeod*, Ph.D., Atlanta, Georgia

# I'd Rather Be Married

## FINDING YOUR FUTURE SPOUSE

# AL CROWELL, M.S.

NEW HARBINGER PUBLICATIONS, INC.

## Publishers Note

*This publication is designed to provide accurate and authoritative information in regard to the subject matter covered. It is sold with the understanding that the publisher is not engaged in rendering psychological, financial, legal, or other professional services. If expert assistance or counseling is needed, the services of a competent professional should be sought.*

Front cover photograph by Joel Meyerowitz, "The Trellis," 1983.
Text design by Tracy Marie Powell.

Distributed in the U.S.A. by Publishers Group West; in Canada by Raincoast Books; in Great Britain by Airlift Book Company, Ltd.; in South Africa by Real Books, Ltd.; in Australia by Boobook; and in New Zealand by Tandem Press.

Library of Congress Catalog Number: 94-073920

ISBN 1-57224-009-1 paperback
ISBN 1-57224-010-5 hardcover

99  98  97

10  9  8  7  6  5  4  3

For all the women in my life who have loved me and helped me grow: my mother and sisters, my ex-wife, my wonderful lovers during my single years, and especially, Linda.

I am especially indebted to my editor, Diane Frank, who has turned a raw piece of writing into a fine manuscript and taught me much about writing in the process.

# Contents

# Introduction

I recently asked the owner of Great Expectations, a popular dating service, if he could estimate the number of single people in the United States. He said it is difficult to gather that information, but he believes it is between twenty and forty percent of the population. That's a lot of single people! Not that it's wrong to be single. What's wrong is that so many people are unhappy being alone.

When you realize how many single people want to be in relationships, you can't help but feel that something is radically wrong. At a time when therapists' offices are full of attractive, sensible people who can't find a suitable partner, it's clear that we need a new way of relating, communicating, and exploring ourselves. In an era of personal growth seminars, personal ads, singles bars, singles groups, video dating, computer dating, and voice-mail relationship groups, millions of people who want to be coupled are still alone.

I can clearly remember feeling the embarrassment mounting as the years of unsuccessful partner hunting added up and confronted my claim of wanting to settle down in a serious relationship. My new part-time job had become battling off my inner critic's nagging about how defective I was. It was one thing to spend a few years recovering from a divorce, but quite another to be utterly unable to remarry once I had decided that I was ready for a new partner.

Therapists have an occupational hazard of believing that because they know the issues, they don't have to experience them. After several years of unsuccessful relationships, I was suddenly face to face with the truth: **something in me is preventing this from happening**. My own intimacy issues were staring me in the face and demanding attention. For the first time in my life, I couldn't blame anyone else. My usual rationalization, "There just aren't that many great women out there," began to sound simplistic and fatalistic. I had nowhere to look except in the mirror.

That was the beginning of good things for me. It was the initiation of a psychological housecleaning that prepared me for the challenging task of loving and growing in a successful relationship. I began writing this book single, and am now happily in a relationship—a transition that has validated my own process of "cleaning house." It has also inspired me to share my new insights with other single people who desire marriage and are willing to look within themselves for the answers they've been seeking.

When I was searching unsuccessfully for the perfect relationship, I was kidding myself. When I told my friends and lovers, "I really want a serious relationship," I thought it was the whole truth, so help me God. But on the other side of the mirror, there was another veiled truth: "I'm also scared to death of having someone dependent on me and limiting my freedom." Only after I admitted the shadow side of my desire did I make progress. With the help of a good therapist, I began looking at my needs and fears about relationships and the ways that I was dealing with them. The chapters that follow are the gift of my own learning, along with my clients', translated into practical lessons for the reader.

Admitting that I was indeed ambivalent about a serious relationship—something single people have a hard time doing—was momentous. And now that I'm married, being aware of my ambivalence continues to aid my ability to allow more and more closeness in my marriage. Marriage has given stark definition to my ambivalence about being connected with another person. Luckily, I no longer view this ambivalence as something to hide from myself or from my partner.

The central issues that keep people out of relationships revolve around their fears of connectedness, their neglect of safety, and their need to trust themselves and their intuition. Trusting yourself and the intuitive cues you get right from the start of any interaction with another person are probably the best tools to navigate yourself into a situation where you will be comfortable over time, and away from a relationship that will be dangerous or wrong for you in the long run. The truth about any situation is usually deceptively simple and right in front of your face, if you listen.

During the years I searched for a partner, I became tired of three-month relationships that started with fireworks and then fizzled out. I couldn't help realizing that they almost always ended because of qualities or circumstances that I saw on the first date and ignored. But as a therapist, I was possessed with the grand notion of being able to adapt to my partner or change her later. Also, I often used sex to produce an easy intimacy and cover the difficulties. A string of three-month relationships, longer than I'd like to admit, eventually made me sick of this pattern and helped me to start trusting my intuition. I stopped trusting logic, which had fooled me too often. I resolved to "sort" through potential partners and use my intuition to choose or avoid before jumping in and trying to get intimate.

Another major shift that took me a long time to accomplish was a firm commitment to being myself. If you want to be in a committed relationship, don't take this lightly! I was part of what I call the "chameleon complex" group of men. These are men who try hard to please, usually at the expense of their own desires. After trying to please for a while, they tend to resent the effort if they are not getting enough back. It's hard to know what to give back to these men since they can't express very well what they want. They don't understand that not knowing what they want for themselves is the problem.

At this point, I am delighted not to have a "chameleon complex" anymore. My wife is alternately pleased and exasperated with my knowing my own mind. But through the rough times, she is grateful that I have a position and know what I want. She doesn't always give it to me, and she shouldn't, but I like knowing my own desires and wants.

Four important shifts of attitude broke my pattern of attracting unsuccessful relationships:

- Admitting to being scared as well as delighted by connectedness

- Being aware of my need to feel safe in a relationship

- Trusting my intuition

- Learning how to be authentically myself

With these realizations, I was finally able to find and commit myself to the person with whom I am now willing to share my life and my fears.

In this book, I have used my own journey and the journeys of many of my clients to illustrate principles that I believe will be helpful to you.

The client material is presented in a masked way so that no one, including the clients themselves, will ever recognize the actual people.

The book is first of all divided into four parts that reflect the four parts of the process of making a successful relationship with the right partner. First comes cleaning your own house to deal with the blocks preventing you from achieving a good match. The second part contains two chapters on strategies for meeting possible partners. Sorting is the next part to help you to make good choices and learn that sorting and choosing a potentially good partner for you come before intimacy. Finally, "Sharing Intimacy" contains five chapters about growing in intimacy after you have done your sorting.

Relationships are about feelings: having them, wanting them, projecting them, and sharing them with other people. The more skilled you become at knowing your own feelings, the better equipped you will be to navigate the calm and rough waters of a relationship. Besides being interwoven throughout the book, I have devoted an entire chapter to the discussion of feelings because they are the groundwork of learning to put these principles into practice. I have also included many of the exercises I use in my relationship seminars, as well as effective ways to meet available men and women. Yes, there are good men and women out there!

For the serious relationship seeker, I have a strategy for finding your mate. Presented below in a step-by-step list, it may require a sharp change from your current approach. Each step is important, and the chapters that follow describe in detail how you can make the changes and why they are necessary.

## Program for People Seeking a Serious Relationship

1. Have enough potential partners come through your life so that you are not feeling desperate. This is a critical part of the program! Feeling desperate will lead you into many wrong decisions.

2. First dates should always be short—one-half to one hour maximum. They should end at the time agreed. The reason for this is that intimacy needs a foundation on which to build. Time and experiences are that foundation. Talking too intimately on a first date can create the illusion of intimacy too quickly—with no foundation. Spending too much time also builds an intensity for which there is no basis.

3. On that first date, deliberately keep it light—eating or walking make wonderful first dates. The point is to have something you are both focused on, rather than each other. No histories of relationships. No saying what you like or don't about the other person. The only exception is saying, at the end of the date, how you enjoyed the time. What you're doing is seeing how you feel in each other's presence rather than sharing a lot of information.

4. Many people put on special behavior to impress on a first date, but this is usually a mistake. Be the way you like to be on the first date—and all other dates as well. If you are quiet, be quiet. If you are funny, be funny. If you are philosophical, talk philosophy. If you are talkative, talk. In other words, be yourself. The only way you can open your life to someone who loves you the way you are is by being yourself.

5. If you believe that intimacy comes from sharing histories and saying positive things to each other, try to delay that until you are sure this is a person worth going for. That's why the first date should be short with a clear ending. Make it light and enjoyable, focusing on something other than each other. Letting the deeper sharing emerge in its own time creates the strong foundation that intimacy needs to survive and grow.

6. If at all possible, conclude the date by saying, "I'll call you in the next few days." This will give you time to check in with your intuition after you have left each other. You won't have made any commitment other than to call.

7. Keep that commitment, even if you don't want to see the person again. It's a good way to be yourself without apologizing for it. If you want to see the person again, that's great. If not, be honest. Just because you don't think he or she is a good match for you, you have nothing to apologize for. The other person is actually lucky that you are honest enough to free them from waiting for a phone call that never comes.

8. After you have left the date and are alone, ask yourself whether you *want* to see the person again. Notice the word "want." Don't let your intellect interfere at this point. You simply answer yes or no.

9. If the answer to step 8 is no, call your date to say that it doesn't seem like a good match to you for romance, and that you wish him or her luck.

10. If the answer is yes, call and set up another date. This time make it longer, but again one in which you focus on an activity rather than exclusively upon each other. Dancing is very nice because you get to touch and have fun without talking and burdening each other with verbal intimacy.

11. Sorting is the name of the game on these first dates—not building intimacy. In this, your intuition is your main tool. And above all, keep on being yourself. If you want honesty in your relationship, be honest and see how your date responds. If you want a person who can handle personal feelings, talk about some of your feelings and watch the response.

12. As you get to know your new friend, keep on modeling the behavior you desire and then watching the response. In this way, your knowledge of one another will deepen with time and experience.

13. Giving a little of what you want and listening and watching for the response will allow you to see red flags if they arise. Red flags signal qualities that you wouldn't want to live with. If you see them, leave the relationship at the beginning, rather than investing a lot of time in a relationship that won't work down the road.

14. Test as much as you need to until you are sure there are no red flags. If you like what you see in the other person, continue to explore. If red flags come up, move on and look for someone else.

15. It is very important to hold yourself off from building intimacy until you are through the initial sorting. This especially applies to sex. Before getting physically and emotionally over your head, be sure that this is a person *you want* to be involved with.

16. When you have determined that the person you've been dating has no red flags and you always answer yes to "Do I want to see him or her again," it's time to go deeper. When you could see yourself married to this person, then it is time to jump in, experience the person at a deeper level, and build intimacy.

17. The process of sorting shifts to how well you both handle intimacy. How available are each of you? Do you feel safe with this person? Can you trust that he or she will give as much consideration and respect to you as to him- or herself?

18. Finally, watch how hard you are working. The beginning should be easy and fun. Also, both people should be pulling their weight as far as contributing to the intimacy. Hold back if you feel that the closeness is being built mainly by you. Allow the other person to move at their speed, but still keep your intuition open. Make sure you are getting a person who meets you where you are.

Good luck! The following pages will make all of this clear and doable, giving you exercises and insights into how to meet people and date in a manner to be *loved for who you are.*

# Part One

# Getting Ready for a Relationship that Works

# 1

# You Are Your Relationship: Being Loved for Who You Are

You glance around in new social situations trying to spot the right one. At stoplights, you sneak a peek at other drivers. Walking downtown, you are looking, but for whom? How will you know, even if you make contact? You may use yardsticks, such as, "he likes me"; or "she's so attractive, I can't keep my eyes off her"; "I'm really tired of being alone"; or variations of "we think alike, we have similar goals, or he or she challenges me." While all of these might be partial answers, in my practice I seldom hear answers that are based on a tailor-made assessment of relationship qualities and skills uniquely suited to the client.

## Looking for Mr. or Ms. Right

Who is Mr. or Ms. Right for *you*? What do *you* require in a relationship that is unique to you? What qualities deeper than looks, success, and similarities are vital to you? Think about the qualities that really matter in a relationship—willingness to stick around and talk out tiffs, generosity of spirit, emotional health, respect for others, the ability to say I'm sorry, the ability to reach out for help, and other, similar qualities that make a person a good partner.

To attract the best match for you, you need to decide *before anything*, who would be right for *you*. This is the place to start. Finding him or her comes later.

---

What do *you* require in a relationship that is unique to you? What qualities deeper than looks, success, and similarities are vital to you? Do you check for kindness, willingness to stick around and talk out tiffs, generosity of spirit, emotional health, respect for others, the ability to say I'm sorry, the ability to reach out for help, and other qualities?

---

If you were selling a new style chair, your first task would be to know what it can and can't do. You'd want to know its pluses and minuses, and how it differs from its competitors. If you don't know those qualities, you won't aim your advertising at the right audience. The same is true in finding a good mate. Too many people look only at possible mates and not at themselves—what they want, what they need, and what they have to offer. Mr. or Ms. Right has to be right *for you*, because you are a person with a unique collection of conscious and unconscious forces wanting love and being scared by it at the same time.

Knowing yourself is crucial for the simple reason that being with the wrong mate is much worse than being single. While you probably agree that you want to be loved for who you are, you may not realize that achieving that goal requires knowing who you are and what you want. Therefore, the first step in creating a great relationship for yourself is to learn who you are. It is also the most difficult step. Most of us have to overcome a lifetime of conditioning in hiding ourselves, repressing our feelings and desires, and fearing that we won't be loved if we are "found out." However, only when we are genuinely ourselves can we allow someone to love us as we really are.

If you don't understand your needs before you select a mate, you're gambling that you can work it all out within the marriage. Some couples succeed at this; most do not. The theme of this book is that we are all fundamentally ambivalent about being in a serious, committed relationship. This creates difficulties in finding a mate as well as difficulties in making even a good relationship produce the level of intimacy, growth, and enjoyment that people want from a romantic union. Knowing the unconscious forces that pull you toward closeness while simultaneously keeping you away from it is therefore a vital part of finding a good partner. Until you have that knowledge, you cannot be your real self on the dating journey.

That may sound obvious, but the path to this kind of self-knowledge is deceptive and illusive. This book is designed to help you make this journey successfully. It uses two tools: your own reflection and research, life experiments through dating and other social activities.

## Two Forces Are Constantly Pulling You in and out of Relationships

As you try to enter a serious relationship, two powerful forces are working within you. One force is yearning—a deliberately provocative word that implies the search for a hidden quality. You yearn for the goodies of closeness such as partnership, acceptance, belonging, family, or passion. At the same time another force is working to protect you from how a relationship might hurt you—by being taken over or being abandoned once you surrender and begin to enjoy those good feelings.

Until you come to know your particular brand of ambivalence, you are being driven by unconscious forces that work in opposite directions. Once you face it and befriend it, however, you can use your ambivalence as a counselor and friend that will lead you in the direction of a suitable life partner. If you have had a series of relationships that haven't worked, now you know why. Something in you is afraid of a strong connection and has been leading you to relationships that are somehow incomplete because they are safer for your psyche.

So you have a very weird thing going on. While you are trying your best to find a good relationship, the unconscious forces that are scared to death of a good relationship are also working just as hard to keep you out of one. The two forces of ambivalence work together. If you weren't so desirous of closeness and what you want from it, the fears wouldn't be so great. The opposing pulls between the yearning force and the part of you that is afraid are equal in their strength. The more desire, the more fear.

> Until you come to know your particular brand of ambivalence, you are being driven by unconscious forces that work in opposite directions.

Obviously, allowing these forces to secretly pull you in opposite directions isn't going to bring you a satisfying relationship. But you don't have to be paralyzed by these two opposite-pulling forces any longer. The rest of this chapter will use four stories to demonstrate common mistakes people make in dating and illustrate these forces at work. Chapters 2 and 3 will walk you through your ambivalence and help you transform your fears into friendly counselors.

## Trying Too Hard

Marie is thirty-four years old. She married at twenty-three, divorced at twenty-seven, and was quite bitter about men until she turned thirty. Then she had a lot of "fun," as she puts it, dating around until she was thirty-two. But for the last two years, she has wanted to find the right man and settle down.

Marie has learned a lot about herself. She has faced the fact that she used to give her power away to the men she was attracted to. Also, she has seen how often she has reverted to being a little girl to charm her way past the hard spots of her relationships. Before she started dating, she was confident that the mistakes she made in her marriage could be avoided in the future, and she felt more mature and ready for a permanent commitment. But even after all of this preparation, she kept getting into relationships that seemed promising at first but never worked out.

Since the age of thirty-two, Marie has gone out with a string of men with the intention of finding "Mr. Right." She is attractive and outgoing, so it has been easy for her to get dates with lots of men. But Mr. Right has not appeared. Many of the men she has dated have been handsome, successful, and seemed right at first, but something always went wrong over time.

After two years of dating, Marie became obsessed with finding the right man to marry. She asked all of her married friends how to choose a man who wanted commitment. She talked it over with people at work, even with dates. She read *Cosmo*, *New Woman*, *Vogue*, and every book she could get her hands on about relationships; but the answers she was so desperately seeking eluded her.

At first Marie's pattern of relationships was a surprise to me. As her therapist, I felt that she had healed enough from her first marriage to be ready for a new commitment. She was also beyond the bitter stage that many divorced people go through, in which they blame all their problems on their ex-husbands or ex-wives. Because of the psychological insights she had gained about herself during therapy, she was able to admit her own mistakes in the marriage, use them as lessons, and take responsibility for her part in the events that ended her marriage. All in all, she seemed to be a good candidate for a committed relationship.

The leader of one of the workshops Marie attended at that time told her to take a serious look at the qualities she wanted in a man. She made a list of the qualities that appealed to her, and then sorted out whether they were essential or could be compromised. Things like "attractive," "interesting," "smart," "successful," "warm," "honest," and "sensual" were at the top of her list. The more dates she had and the more relationships she went through, the more sophisticated her list became. She began to add relationship skills such as "knows how to talk about feelings," "listens," and "isn't critical."

Even though Marie met men who seemed to fit her list, no one came through for her in the long term. Whenever she started a new relationship, she was excited, infatuated, and would tell her friends that maybe she had found the right one. But her two most important relationships during this period lasted less than five months, and then something crept into them like a wedge that drove her and the man slowly but inexorably apart. In one case she lost interest, and the other time he did. After two years, she began to think that being single was not so bad after all, and that she would rather just not work at this exhausting process anymore. She quit—hopeless and with a wounded heart.

Two months later, at a barbecue for a friend's birthday, she met a man she felt drawn to and started going out with him. Soon, they were seeing each other steadily. A year later, they were married. What happened? There are a lot of opinions about it. Some would say that when she stopped working so hard at finding Prince Charming, everything happened naturally. Others would say that she became more attractive when she stopped being so desperate. I have always had trouble with these answers. Not because I think there is no truth in them, but because it is so difficult to change these aspects of yourself when you want a serious relationship. I would rather take a different approach.

I believe what happened was that Marie relaxed and started acting like herself. She wasn't trying to attract someone and therefore was concentrating on the quality of *her own life*. She was spending time with her friends, enjoying her work, and making time in her life for the activities she enjoyed most. When she went dancing, she did it to feel good. When she went hiking, her purpose was to relax and feel close to nature. Since she wasn't in the market for a husband any longer, she was taking care of herself and finding satisfaction in her own single life. Without even realizing it, she had—for the first time in her life—set herself up to have a good relationship.

## Being Yourself Attracts the Best Partner

I like to define a good relationship as one in which you feel loved for who you are; for being yourself. In fact, the two elements that are crucial to a satisfying relationship over time are *being yourself* and *being loved just for being you*. This is very different from listing qualities and searching for someone who has them. Instead, it relies on how you are feeling in the relationship. It isn't intellectual and analytical. It's intuitive and emotional.

Marie was in a better position to be aware of how she felt because she had turned away from looking for a mate with a certain list of qualities, and was much more interested in living the way she wanted. Since she had made that decision, the new man in her life was an accident, and he fit. They stayed together because Marie and her husband were able to feel loved just for being themselves. This feels so good that both of them refused to give it up.

> The two elements that are crucial to a satisfying relationship over time are *being yourself* and *being loved just for being you.*

By defining a good relationship as one in which I feel loved for who I am, I have also learned the difference between having someone with "all the right qualities" in my life and having someone *who loves me* in my life. In my marriage I am secure in the feeling of being loved for who I am and not for what I am supposed to have or give. But this didn't happen magically overnight.

Meeting my wife was the culmination of three years of working on myself. First I had to learn to be myself—with others as well as alone—and then see if I felt loved by the different women I went out with. It was a long process during which I kept referring back to myself to see if I was in my comfort zone. This process transformed me to the point where I can relax about myself, trust my instincts, admit I'm not perfect, love because I want to, and feel loved simply for being who I am.

## Learning About Yourself Through Your Relationships—The Skill of Sorting

After learning about your personal style of ambivalence, the other major skill in looking for a partner is learning how to sort when you go on dates.

Today, it's common for people to "try on" partners and see how they fit—just like trying on a coat, looking at yourself in the mirror, and returning it to the rack if it doesn't seem right. This works sometimes, but usually not. The "try on" method of dating leaves most people emotionally exhausted and discouraged after a series of relationships lasting three to five months. The fine art of sorting will be discussed more fully in Chapter 6. For now, here are some general ideas about the usefulness of this process in learning to be yourself.

Being yourself involves coming back home to your feelings and learning what pleases you. It also involves living a life that truly expresses who you are "with your shoes off." You aren't working at being yourself in order to please someone else, and you aren't hiding parts of yourself to prevent rejection for being deficient. In the process of learning to live a life in which you are authentically and unapologetically yourself, it's a good idea to practice choosing people who appreciate you. If you can comfortably be yourself with someone you date, keep on exploring the relationship. If you find that you have to hide or suppress important parts of yourself, move on. This is the skill of sorting. At some point, if you keep this up, you are going to attract someone with whom you feel comfortably yourself and feel loved. That's your green light to go forward with the relationship and explore deeper levels of intimacy.

I don't want to pretend this is simple or easy. A sense of yourself emerges over time. It often takes the help of another person, perhaps a therapist, and it usually takes years of experience.

A powerful way of learning about yourself is through relationships. In fact, I believe in the stepping-stone theory of relationships, using dating as a process of learning to be yourself and sorting out people who are inappropriate for you from those who have real potential. If you are aware of your growth as you date, you will, with each relationship, improve both at being your true self and at picking people who nurture that.

The concept of using dating as a sorting tool is one of the central points of my approach. I have carefully divided the sorting section of this book from the section on building intimacy in order to stress the difference between them. Sorting means dating with the idea of separating after a few dates from people who are not right for you. Sorting replaces the too-quick intimacy of sharing feelings, or touch. That is, you should sort until you find a reasonably good prospect for a workable relationship; only then should you attempt to build intimacy. That way you won't waste time and emotional energy with the wrong person, and end up after three months, or three years, with a broken relationship that wasn't right in the first place.

However, while you are in the initial stages of dating, lighten up and consider it practice. You know that you are sincerely looking for the right person, but at the same time, you are still learning to develop your relationship skills. If you make mistakes, it's not such a big deal. Each time, you'll get better and improve your social skills. Ultimately, this will put you in a much better position to succeed at being yourself and being genuinely loving when the right person comes into your life.

## Karen Learns to Sort

Karen knew how to use her sensual looks to attract men, and she spent a large part of her salary on expensive clothes and lingerie. No matter what the occasion, she always dressed in an alluring way that drew men to her. If you asked her what kind of a man she wanted, she would tell you frankly, "a man who makes good money." She certainly could attract them, too.

Another part of Karen's act was creating a sensational beginning to every relationship. She was a gourmet cook and would have her dates over for unusual and exquisite, candlelight dinners. She also had a talent for thinking up and planning romantic excursions. She dressed like a Victoria's Secret model most of the time, and always knocked herself out for her men.

As I got to know Karen, I saw what a quality person she was inside. She was artistically and musically talented, bright, and a genuinely warm and giving person. She wasn't interested in men just for their money. She was clear, however, that she wanted a man with money. She made a good living herself in the design field, and she wanted a man who could match her lifestyle.

Over time, however, Karen reached her own understanding of her problem. "You know, Al, I think I'm beginning to understand the pattern that you have been talking about for weeks now. It finally dawned on me with Phil last night that he is perfectly content to keep receiving from me. Then I thought about some other men that I thought were great for me. I was so wrapped up in doing things for them because I was afraid they would leave me if I didn't do everything.

"For some reason, I never realized that they didn't leave me. I was the one who made the relationships end. I got tired of not feeling loved or cared about. As much as I say I want a man with money, I, even more, want a man who can give to me in other ways. There must be a man out there who has a good career, and who can also be a giving, loving human being!"

This realization was a tremendous breakthrough for Karen. In the months that followed, she began looking for a partner who had the inner qualities she needed along with the external qualities she desired. She realized that she wanted to be taken care of and be given to by a man. Before her breakthrough, she couldn't allow this. Her desire to be loved and taken care of was so strong that she tried to hide it. She did this because she feared that it would turn a man off if he discovered it. After this realization, she began to test relationships more on how she felt she was being treated. This may sound obvious and simple, but Karen had hidden fears that she had never explored, and they kept this bright and charming woman crippled for many years.

During her transition, the hardest part for Karen was to monitor how much she was giving at the beginning of the relationship and allow some of the goodies to come her way from the man. She once told me that the hardest thing she ever did was to leave the planning of a trip to Mexico to Tom. She was sure he would be disappointed if she didn't take care of everything. Also, she worried that Tom would probably find her dull if she didn't perform her usual routine of providing the excitement. At the same time, she realized letting go of her need to control everything and letting Tom give to her was the key to the transformation she was creating for herself.

She realized that creating 100 percent of the romance and excitement is far too much to ask of any one person. During her year of therapy, she also formed a more realistic concept of romance that is possible and sustainable between two people. Karen and Tom are not yet engaged, but they're happy with one another, and they both feel that commitment is a potential.

---

> She realized that creating 100 percent of the romance and excitement is far too much to ask of any one person.

---

## In a Good Relationship, You Feel Loved for Being Yourself

The second part of the definition of a good relationship is to *feel loved for being yourself*. This requires being with someone who loves you as you are. After beginning the process of learning to be relaxed and comfortably yourself, you have to find someone who loves you that way. While sorting skills are of the essence here, there is a block to using them that I want to explain. Some people fall in love with potentials. They like the person's looks and values and forgive that person's depressive behavior, inability to listen, or critical nature with the excuse that these are only temporary and can be changed. But this is the tip of the iceberg that will sink you later on.

If you want a relationship that works, awareness of how you are being treated and loved is crucial. You need to sort for a person who simply loves you the way you want to be loved. It's surprising how many people don't do this.

## Tony's Story

Tony is a successful professional in the computer field. He lived with a woman right after college, but eventually their careers took them to different cities. By then, it felt right to end the relationship anyway. Now, Tony has been out of college for seven years and feels ready to be married. He is confused about his inability to meet the right woman. I will share some of his conversations with me.

"Anne was great at first—she was so entertaining. I loved that about her. I also loved having sex with her. She was creative and funny, would do anything, and was always laughing. I've never been like that. It was like entering another world, another culture. My home life was much more traditional, and my family thought of itself as above the masses. I guess I would have to say that made us stuffy. Anne was always saying crazy things when we went out, and I loved it.

"I remember once at dinner with another couple, she said she was doing research on whether men's cars indicated their penis size. The hotter the car, the smaller the personal equipment. She said things like that all the time. She was always entertaining, and always kept any group we were with laughing.

But I guess it was that same quality that got to me. I started getting snappy about her humor and her pranks. I would accuse her of not taking life seriously. When I thought of having children with her, I would have visions of her leaving them by themselves in the playground while she was entertaining the other mothers on the park benches. The kids were always getting hurt in my visions. She wouldn't take anything seriously."

One month later: "I'm really attracted to this new woman. We've only seen each other three times, but I like her a lot. I can really relax around her. Sometimes it seems that we've known each other forever. You know, that feeling of being in another life together, or something. She's quiet, and I like that after a busy day. We took a walk last weekend, and we didn't need to talk all the time or impress each other. She's the still waters type. You know, 'running deep' and all."

Four months later, Tony came in to tell me about yet another new relationship: "I think I've really met the one this time. She's gorgeous, first of all, but that's not it. She's so much fun. I look forward to being with her hours before the date. The gang at work likes her a whole lot more than Ms. Still Waters. Boy, did she get to be a drip. Monica isn't like her at all. She isn't hyper either, just a lot of fun. She's the one who usually carries the conversation. I can't believe I like that, but I think it's great. She's so well-read. I'm not quite sure what she sees in me, but I'm going for it."

What is happening with Tony? He seems to be swinging like a pendulum between exciting women and restful ones. It's a pattern in which he recovers from his former relationship with the energy of the present one. But at a certain point, the pendulum starts swinging back in the other direction, and Tony becomes restless and dissatisfied. His relationships always seems to start out in a rush of excitement, but they end in a wave of criticism. And regardless of the initial promise that any woman offers, Tony ends up alone after four or five months.

What ultimately helped Tony to become more successful with women was taking a hard look inside himself. An in-depth exploration revealed his own need for excitement versus his need for being quiet and comfortable. To do this, he had to go back to his parents' marriage and extract the messages he received as a child about excitement and boredom. With a closer look at this issue and his ambivalence about serious relationships, he soon realized that he didn't feel comfortable in either camp. He didn't want the excitement of his mother's volatility or the boredom of his father's couch-potato lifestyle.

However, Tony seemed to be paralyzed in between his parents' styles—as if he were caught in a time warp between their fights with no true direction for himself. Therefore, he would find women who represented one parent or the other, and swing back and forth between the two extremes. We worked on that, and gradually he developed his own style of fun and quiet that was much more satisfying. When he did that, his taste in women changed. He didn't rave about how entertaining they were or how restful they were, but rather about whether they matched his own style. Instead of his wild stories from the past, he began to tell me whether he felt comfortable with the women he dated, and whether he could completely be himself.

## Two Half People Don't Make a Whole Relationship

The folk wisdom of many cultures says that opposites attract. On paper it looks great for two people with differing strong and weak points to form a successful partnership. Also, the concept of finding your complement in another person has been popularized in stories—from traditional fairy tales to modern romance magazines. But trying to make yourself whole or complete by finding your complement doesn't work.

Both Tony's and Karen's earlier approaches represent the two-halves-of-a-circle theory. They had been looking for someone else to complete themselves—something was missing, and they were looking for it on the outside. Neither of them felt whole on their own.

This can be represented by a circle cut in half, with two people making up a whole relationship. Each person contributes only half of the total. Neither person feels whole on his or her own, and that is why they are in the relationship—to be rounded out and to become whole.

If you look hard enough, you can find elements of this way of thinking yourself. No matter how independent you are, you probably have some expectation that a relationship will fix your shortcomings, or that having someone in your life will make it more complete or better in some way. I have yet to meet anyone who doesn't have at least some of these expectations.

For example, if you are brainy and serious, you may find yourself attracted to fun-loving people, and vice versa. If you are worried about money and old age, you may have a stable breadwinner in mind for a partner. If you love to process analytical aspects of your relationships, you may be drawn to down-to-earth types who enjoy activity and sensual pleasures.

The people you attract can be a great mirror. One of the best ways to discover areas of incompleteness in yourself is by looking at whom you are drawn to. At the same time, it's important to realize that the person who is responsible for making your life complete is you.

## The Model on Which this Book Is Based

A relationship in which you are loved for who you are is one in which you feel complete in yourself and then, on that basis, enjoy the other person. Your life works on your own terms, and you share it with someone else.

This can be represented by two rings that overlap by about twenty percent. Visualize two whole rings, standing side by side, that have rolled together and are now touching at the center but only merged by about twenty percent. They don't cover each other completely to make one ring, but they're touching and roll together when they want to.

> The person who is responsible for making your life complete is you.

This is the model upon which this book is based: each person working to be whole—dealing with his or her own shortcomings—and then sharing that wholeness with someone else. The two people are not looking for someone else to fix them. As a result, they merge only part of themselves into the relationship.

Of course, everyone has weak and strong points. We all have low self-esteem in certain areas and confidence in others. The point is that the basis of any strong relationship is two mature people standing strong in their own lives, not looking for another person or a marriage to cure them of their problems.

## You Don't Have to Be Perfect to Find a Relationship

I don't know anyone who would be married if they waited for perfection in themselves or in anyone else—and perfectionists are not fun to be with anyway. Who wants to be with someone who's always finding something wrong with you? The differences between people are what make them interesting to each other at first. Yet, later in a committed relationship, these same differences become the material for fights and hurt feelings. This is normal and can produce growth in a long-term relationship; but, at first, the fit should seem much closer and the differences more of enjoying a new "culture" than making you feel whole.

Many people fear that their differences must be wiped away to have a relationship, but I would not want to be married to my female clone. Think about how boring that would be. Our shortcomings, or rough edges, as I like to call them, are also our strengths in other areas. The husband who is bossy at home may be a genius at the office; the woman who can't keep her checkbook balanced may be the one who is warm and calm in a family crisis. Rough edges are the grist that helps polish our lives together into beautiful gems.

The goal I push clients toward is to be unapologetically yourself. This is a matter of accepting yourself as you are, right now. It means not requiring yourself to be perfect or totally together—practically the opposite. So many of the people that my wife and I work with in our Meet Your Mate seminar seem strained with the burden of appearing self-actualized. They are struggling to be more outgoing, more confident, more self-assured, funnier, for example. What is missing is a deep level of self-acceptance. Therefore, they are uncomfortable to be with.

Accepting yourself as you are makes you easy to be with. If you wonder about this, think about the things that make people hard to be around. They talk behind your back, they're defensive, they apologize and self-efface, they blame you, and they are dishonest. All of these habits stem from not being comfortable with who they are.

On the journey to being authentically yourself, the first hurdle to get over is the myth that you have to get rid of your rough edges. You feel you have bad habits, or aren't in perfect shape. You're shy, or bossy, or too assertive, or boring, or all the other reasons you use to condemn yourself. Rooting these qualities out is absolutely not a prerequisite to being comfortable with yourself. Many people believe that they can get rid of their rough edges if they keep polishing. Usually, they have a hidden desire to be liked by everyone, but it just isn't possible.

> The basis of any strong relationship is two mature people standing strong in their own lives, not looking for another person or a marriage to cure them of their problems.

In reality, our strengths and fine qualities are liked by some people and not by others. Similarly, our weaknesses are abhorred by some people, while others find them endearing. You may also want to keep in mind that some of the same qualities that you may not like at first in a friend can become endearing over time.

In this regard, Jack Nicholson, the actor, is a wonderful teacher. I haven't met a woman who doesn't find him lovable and attractive. In many of his films, he portrays the same type of character. What makes him so endearing? It isn't that he is dashing or suave or successful. It isn't because he is sensitive to women or able to communicate his feelings. The primary quality that runs through all of his films—regardless of the character he plays—is that Jack is comfortable with himself. He is the epitome of being unapologetically himself. And this makes him loved by all the women that I have ever asked—feminists or not.

## Overcoming the Chameleon Complex

My client James, however, is a totally different story. He's more apt to commit to a relationship than your typical movie star, he appears to be able to talk about his feelings, and he certainly is sensitive to how other people are feeling. But he isn't getting the women that his less sensitive friends seem to pull in.

James is what women call a nice guy when they describe a person they hang out with—in an unromantic way. "I think I am exactly what women say they want in a man. I take their opinions seriously. I can admit it when I'm wrong, and I'm a good listener. What is wrong with me that I can't make a relationship work?"

In one of our sessions, I asked him to describe a recent date to me: "I was real attracted to this woman and wanted to make a good impression. We had coffee last week after the inevitable phone call that you have to get through when you run a personal ad in the *Bay Guardian*. The great thing was that finally I met a woman who matched in person what I was feeling on the phone. We both felt an electric chemistry and we had a string of common interests. So I asked her to have a casual dinner and go dancing. I have to admit I was nervous and afraid that she wouldn't find me attractive enough or that something would ruin it.

"The first thing I did was ask her where she wanted to go for dinner. She said anything was fine with her. I asked her what kind of food she liked, and she answered that she just liked eating and would be happy with my suggestion. So we went to my favorite Thai place. Over dinner, I asked her about her work, and we had a good conversation about that. Then she asked me about my career, but I hate to talk about it because it's so technical. I changed the subject to relationships and how hard it is to meet people. We spoke about the singles ad process.

"I was careful to listen to her and to be sensitive to her desires. She obviously was a quiet type, so I followed suit. When we danced later, I realized that my leading was a problem and asked her if she would be more comfortable leading herself. When I took her back to her place, I sensed that she didn't want to ask me in, so I didn't suggest it. I told her I had a great time and would call her again. When I did, she told me that it didn't feel right to her, and she would rather not get together again. What happened?"

I call James's problem the "chameleon complex." He's sensitive to whoever he is with, but he isn't as centered inside himself. Although women appreciate his sensitivity and the way he can listen, he doesn't give out his own distinctive stamp. A woman going out with him could easily feel as if she were going out with a duplicate of herself or a computer with a humanistic psychology program—rather than with another whole, different, and interesting human being.

James needs to be more like Jack Nicholson. Jack is just Jack. He doesn't think he is the greatest man on the planet, either. He just is who he is—and he accepts himself as he is. He can even apologize for some of his ways, but that doesn't mean he thinks he can be a different person to fit in better to someone else's life. He's an archetypal bad boy, but women find him lovable.

> I call James's problem the "chameleon complex." He's sensitive to whoever he is with, but isn't centered inside himself. Although women appreciate his sensitivity, he doesn't give out his own distinctive stamp.

In Chapter 11, you'll find practical techniques for accomplishing the illusive goal of accepting yourself. It's a process that you can begin today and keep improving over time.

## A More Enlightened Approach to Relationships

So far, I have been explaining common methods of avoiding good relationships. Marie avoided by searching so hard she lost herself; Tony avoided by alternating different personality types of women; Karen avoided by trying to do everything for the men in her life and thereby control the relationship; and James avoided by attempting to figure out what women really want without disclosing who he is and what he wants. Unconscious ambivalence was running their lives and not permitting them to get into serious relationships.

In therapy, each learned about his or her fears of a committed partner and began to work with them. Marie stopped trying to find a man to make her life better, found herself on her own terms, and then met a man who was a good match for her. On a different path, Tony learned that he needed both rest and excitement and could balance the two within himself. This enabled him to meet a woman who wasn't extreme, but was also balanced within herself. Karen allowed herself to receive love but to choose who she allowed to give it to her; while James discovered his own interests and personality, and then felt strong enough to insist on being loved for who he was.

Usually your fear of getting close expresses itself in trying to find a person who will fix you in some way. My biggest caution for all serious relationship seekers is to beware of trying to find someone or a relationship to fix you. In other words, if you have low self-esteem and get married, you will be a married person with low self-esteem. If you don't have your financial act together and get married, you will be married with financial problems. If you are defensive about your weight or looks or habits and get married, you will be married with all those tender spots.

It's actually worse than that, because you will be married to another person with whom you have to make decisions and deal with conflicts. If you are defensive or have low self-esteem, you carry that into those conflicts, amplifying your personal problems into two lives instead of containing them in one. Furthermore, any expectations that marriage will fix you will serve to depress you further when that doesn't happen.

However, to say that finding a person to complement you in a relationship doesn't work is too simple. That's because no matter how hard you try to find an equal—someone who meets you as you are—you will still have differences. Finding the value in each other's differences is what creates the growth and healing of a relationship. However—and I know I'm repeating myself—it is a mistake to start off with a drastic difference for the sake of fixing yourself. If you see that your life needs fixing in some area, do it on your own terms. You won't get that by finding a relationship.

A relationship unburdened by the expectation of fixing your problems has a chance to grow and evolve into surprises that you couldn't have predicted. Preparing for a great relationship is like learning to float when you first learn to swim. The moment you stop trying so hard and relax, you get it. In the same way, finding a great relationship comes with relaxing, not with struggling harder. This book is designed to help you achieve a relationship in which you can be yourself and be loved for it. You won't have to earn the love, fear making mistakes, worry about being deserted, or exhaust yourself trying to keep your lover's attention.

---

> A relationship unburdened by the expectation of fixing your problems has a chance to grow and evolve into surprises that you couldn't have predicted.

## Exercises in Discovering Who You Are

**Exercise 1.** Get a notebook, title it "My Relationship Journey," and begin doing the exercises in this book.

**Exercise 2.** Examine each of the four stories in this chapter and list what parts you identify with. Think about these things, and then write about how they hinder you in your quest.

**Exercise 3.** Although your ambivalence will be hard to identify before you read the next chapters, you may learn something about the other basic skill—sorting. Do you make decisions about whether another person will treat you well, or are you making decisions based solely on attraction? Go back over your previous relationships and examine this question. Write out how you decided to go out with each person. What was it based on? Try to be as honest with yourself in this private journal as possible. Was it based on looks, similarities, or qualities that were external or internal, for example?

**Exercise 4.** Do you hide from meeting people? What do you fear will happen if you meet someone interesting?

**Exercise 5.** Do you feel you have to respond to any person attracted to you? Why would you think that?

**Exercise 6.** Are you careful to hide certain parts of yourself when you are on a date—your intelligence, aggressiveness, habits, interests, neediness, or loneliness? What do you suppose would happen if you didn't?

The next two chapters are designed to give you much more help with your ambivalence.

# 2

# I Really Want a Serious Relationship . . . or Do I?

OK, you're over thirty, and you're living by yourself. Not exactly what you had planned. The fantasy you've had since childhood of being married or coupled by now has somehow eluded you and slipped out the bedroom window. Your biological clock is ticking like a heart beating in a state of alarm. Most of your life is satisfying, but relationships seem to be the last frontier. You've been honest with yourself—you really want a serious relationship. A committed relationship. But maybe part of you does not.

## The Shock of Discovering that I Was Ambivalent

True confession time: after hearing that yet another relationship of mine was in its final stages, a close friend asked me, "Have you ever thought that perhaps you're ambivalent about having a serious relationship?" Immediately, I could feel a surge of anger come over me. I felt so clear about what I wanted, and he was throwing it all in my face.

"No!" I answered adamantly, "I'm certain that I want a relationship. Look how much work I've put into it."

"Then, how come it hasn't happened when you've met a number of women you've liked?"

> As I explored this issue over time, I realized that my ambivalence could actually be a tool for achieving the committed relationship I'd hoped for.

I had to admit the question was valid and not easy to answer. My neck felt hot, and my stomach was churning in that telltale way of recognizing a truth that makes me nervous. But how could I be ambivalent, I thought, when I've worked at my relationships with such single-mindedness? Being ambivalent sounded so wishy-washy—the exact opposite of how I saw myself. Yet, the more my friend and I talked, the more I could see that not only was I ambivalent, but that I *should be* ambivalent. By the end of the afternoon, I was even admitting to myself that being ambivalent was actually good for me. Then I wondered why I had been blind to this idea for so long.

As I explored this issue over time, I realized that my ambivalence could actually be a tool for achieving the committed relationship I desired.

## Ambivalence as an Asset

Ambivalence is defined as the simultaneous attraction toward and repulsion from an object, person, or action. It means that there are two sides to how a person feels about something. One side says, "Go for it!" and the other flashes, "Caution!" When applied to having a relationship, ambivalence creates a real dilemma. If you pass an ice cream shop and are ambivalent—wouldn't a little dish of that creamy, sweet stuff be good right now, and yet it would put on weight and break that resolution to cut down on fat—you'll feel paralyzed at the door: one foot wanting to march on and the other wanting to step in. Think of the effect ambivalence has on finding a relationship.

It's common today for people to accept themselves as divided. They frequently know that part of them feels one way and part feels another about many of the people or situations in their lives. Yet, when it comes to matters of the heart, ambivalence can be difficult to admit. Despite the cutting level of honesty I usually enjoy about myself, it was hard for me to accept that I felt divided about whether I really wanted a serious relationship or not. My initial response is also typical of my clients when I ask them about their ambivalence. Nobody likes to own up to it.

I find that I usually talk about the fear of relationship as the side of ambivalence that needs the most attention. It is the most hidden, but our desire for closeness and what it will give us is just as big a problem, and also may be hidden. We may want far more out of a relationship than our unconscious thinks we can get. Therefore, it takes charge in order to make sure we don't get into one that is suitable, and therefore, dangerous.

Too often, projects or goals—whether personal or professional—don't work out the way we want them to. Sometimes it even seems that we sabotage their success. But perhaps we sabotage them for good reasons. Something in us may know that the person or the project isn't right for a part of ourselves. We may not have a conscious or logical reason, but somewhere inside, it just doesn't feel right. Knowing this on an unconscious level, we then abort the project or sabotage the relationship in some way other than making a conscious, direct decision. This isn't bad or wrong. It is, however, outside of our conscious control. If, on the other hand, we can get to the bottom of what isn't right about the situation for us, we can make informed decisions and have more control over that project or goal again.

Knowing about your ambivalence can give you more control over every aspect of your life. In this light, ambivalence acts as an early warning signal, if you accept its message. For example, how could it not be right for you to satisfy your needs for deep connection with another person by getting into a serious relationship? Look for the part of you that is scared or has some reservations. Look for the part of you that is nervous when it contemplates being in a long-term relationship. Look for the part of you that has issues about making a commitment. Maybe there's something wrong for you in the person or situation. Or maybe there's some work or growing you need to do yourself. Whatever the case may be, the message is your friend.

## Three Case Histories

Sometimes, asking yourself certain questions can initiate a journey back to your emotional roots. The answers can then reveal areas inside you that need attention. Using this technique, I encourage my clients to ask themselves if there is any fear or dread in the thought of being in a long-term relationship. In every case, their answers have been enlightening and revealing. The knowledge you gain in this process then becomes the springboard for the work you need to do to open yourself in a realistic way to a good relationship.

To share a few examples from my clients ... when I asked Peter if he felt any fear or dread at the thought of being in a long-term relationship, he admitted that he was nervous about being stuck in the wrong relationship. Angela answered that she was afraid of being "taken over." Richard said, "Yeah, I'm afraid I won't be free to do what I want."

Answers like these usually point to the constellation of fears adopted in childhood. For example, as Peter grew up, he saw his father as being more and more unable to live happily with his mother. It's no surprise, then, that he grew up viewing marriage as a trap. Angela saw her mother as having little of her own identity. And Richard came from a family in which both parents—or at least his father—had to be so responsible that there was no time for fun.

## The Three Most Common Fears About Relationships

Most fears about relationships fall into one or more of three general categories: fear of abandonment, fear of engulfment or being taken over, and fear of loss of self-esteem. When I present these core areas of fear to my clients, one of them usually rings a bell more than the others. Suddenly, they realize how they themselves have been sabotaging their quest for a lasting relationship. Or they discover a key they can use in the future for a more realistic and careful attempt at finding a good match for themselves.

> Look for the part of you that is nervous when it contemplates being in a long-term relationship.

The answers of each of my clients in the previous section indicate a fear of engulfment. Concerns about "being stuck in the wrong relationship," being "taken over," or not being "free to do what I want," all fall into this category. If your worst fear of what can happen in a serious relationship is divorce, that indicates a fear of abandonment. If your worst fear is that you won't be respected, that points to a fear of lost self-esteem.

If you think about it for a few minutes, you may be able to answer what you fear most about a serious relationship. However, you might not have called that being ambivalent. In fact, you may not recognize just how powerful a force ambivalence is in your life. To be ambivalent, you may think, you must be torn in two known directions—for example, between wanting to eat that creamy chocolate ice cream cone and not wanting to gain weight. With relationships, however, half of the ambivalence is hidden. It lies deep within you, avoided for years, and often actively denied. Just because you may have denied it, however, doesn't mean that it isn't operating in you all the time—any more than denying that a car that needs oil will keep that from burning itself out.

Starting from simple questions, then, you can find your primary fear or fears. Ask yourself: What are your patterns in relationships? What seem to be the reasons for their endings? What did you have the biggest problem with? And what made you want to run or fight back? What would be the worst thing, even if small, that being in a lifelong relationship would bring to your life?

If your answers to these questions suggest a desire not to be trapped, think about how you can use that knowledge to choose a person who will help with that fear. If your answers point to a fear of being abandoned once a person really gets to know you, pay attention and take care to find a partner who has a high potential for working difficulties out over time. In my practice I find that as my clients grow in self-awareness and pay more attention to patterns that used to lead to failure in their relationships, they are frequently attracted to people with different qualities than the ones they chose before.

## Strategies for Learning How You Are Ambivalent

The search for a good relationship involves looking at your yearnings and your fears. These two are often closely connected, as in the case of Kit, who wants a really passionate connection but hides that from himself and the women he's with. The fear of being trapped with a woman who might not give him that passion is so great that it prevents him from committing. Kit was helped by learning to accept what he wanted, becoming realistic about it, and talking about it with women he was seeing.

Also, our psyche spends a great deal of energy avoiding the feelings that gave birth to our yearnings and fears. If we start seriously working with our fears, we'll have to face certain feelings that are uncomfortable. In the case of relationships, we will have to think about our childhood and our parents. Their relationship could be what scares us most. The way they treated each other, or us, as we were growing up will come to our awareness. Of course, we all know some aspects of our family history. It's the deeper, emotional level that we shield ourselves from.

Many people spend their entire lives trying to detour around early childhood wounds and the painful feelings associated with these wounds. They usually are the last thing we want to reexperience. In fact, we have built up elaborate systems to avoid these early feelings of pain. When experiences remind us of these memories, even in subtle ways, we react strongly but don't understand why. Blaming someone or something else for the reaction is a common way to avoid dealing with these deep feelings inside ourselves.

> Many people spend their entire lives trying to detour around early childhood wounds and the painful feelings associated with them.

Take Esther, for example, a legal secretary whose day is often ruined by a critical remark from the attorney she works for. Even though she is fast, conscientious, and pays exacting attention to detail, her boss takes for granted whatever she does right, and flares up at the one or two things she does wrong. Esther frequently complains to her friends about how insensitive her supervisor is. Curiously, she seems to have run into the problem of critical bosses at all the jobs she's ever held. When she took a close look at the way her life had been going, the recurrent patterns were too unmistakable to result from something "out there."

For the first time in her life, Esther began to gain control over her reactions when therapy helped her to see how her supervisor's remarks instantly triggered the terrible feelings she had while growing up. She allowed herself to reexperience the pain of wanting her father's attention—how she had repeatedly tried to gain his approval by performing well, and how often her performance wasn't "good enough." After working through these early childhood experiences, Esther found that while she was still affected by critical remarks, she had much more control over how she reacted to them. She began to differentiate between helpful criticism and personal attacks. With these new tools, she felt more mature in her way of dealing with powerful or critical people in her life. She faced her yearning for approval as well as her fear of criticism.

## Looking at Your Patterns

Uncovering your primary fears is a fundamental tool for learning how to take care of yourself in a successful relationship. The next step is to study your life for the patterns that have been undermining your success at love. Looking at things that recur in your relationships is the first step, but the best clues may be in other places in your life. Look at everything: your friendships, your work, your family, your childhood. Examine every area of your life that is important to you. Pay attention to the things people say about you as well as your own observations, and the jigsaw puzzle pieces will start fitting into place. If something you see troubles you, don't worry about that. In order to change a pattern that doesn't work for you, you have to see it first.

In this process, it is important to look at parts of yourself that you don't like so much—for example, things about you that your friends have trouble with. Marcia, one of my clients, hears from friends that she frequently cancels dates. After making enough people angry, she has begun to see that it was her way of proving that she wasn't controlled by other people's needs and demands—which is Marcia's deepest fear about relationships.

Steve heard from friends that he made them do most of the work in the relationship. They were always the ones who had to travel to meet him, and it always had to be at his convenience. When he confronted himself with this, Steve began to realize that he was afraid of losing control of his own life when he got close to other people. Steve controlled his relationships so much that he rarely gave his friends choices. But in the process of not allowing himself to feel controlled, he was pushing everyone he wanted to feel close to away.

> In examining the patterns in your life, it's important to look at parts of yourself that you don't like very much—for example, things about you that your friends have trouble with.

After a long sequence of first dates after which she never got called again, Joni found that she had a habit of rushing off at the end of the evening, often leaving the man somewhat startled and confused. He would think she was afraid of sexual advances or just didn't like him, and as a result he wouldn't call her again. Even if a man wasn't put off by Joni's initial abruptness, she still found ways to sabotage her relationships. No matter how much anyone loved her, in time she would find a small excuse and use it as a reason to leave him. Ultimately, Joni realized that it was her fear of being abandoned that drove her to leave the men who loved her. As she became conscious of this pattern, along with the underlying fears that created it, Joni began to open the doors to the deeper areas of her feelings without running away.

## Compensating for Childhood Wounds

Patterns that sabotage our happiness usually stem from reactions to painful feelings from early childhood. Generally, these patterns are compensations for the fears we have about ourselves. I've been told, for instance, that I can be pushy, and I sometimes make sharp-edged statements that are hard on those around me. That has been my way of reacting to my deep fear of engulfment. My method of compensating for feeling that I cannot be my own person is to put on a front of strength.

Another tactic for discovering your primary fears is to watch your parents very closely when you visit them. As an adult, you may find that your parents can often talk more freely about your early years once you're older and more understanding. If they are unavailable, study your memories. Look at pictures of your childhood while paying attention to your thoughts, memories, and intuitions. You'll get a lot of rich psychological material from that process. The following chapter will give many more examples of family influences on your ambivalence.

The process of self-discovery is like personal detective work and requires many of the same techniques of observation and deduction. It may be a wild adventure through the corridors of your family history, but the rewards will last for a lifetime.

## How Informed Ambivalence
## Can Help You

In the process of cleaning house to prepare for a satisfying relationship, truths may surface that you have been hiding for years. Many people discover that they are ambivalent about relationships, that they should be ambivalent, and that it is a positive thing. If you want your relationship to succeed, the fears that are formed early in life have to be taken seriously. They are fears for your survival as an individual. If you know about them and respect them, you can do a much better job of taking care of them without giving up the desire for a relationship.

For example, a man who fears abandonment would be reckless to try to get close to someone who has just accepted an overseas job assignment that starts in two months. If he tries anyway, his ambivalence will probably sabotage the union. He will either invent small reasons to walk away from his partner, without looking at the deeper reason he feels threatened; or the relationship will fizzle in a generalized way, while he walks away believing that relationships just don't work. If he brings his fear of abandonment up to his conscious awareness, he can deal with it in a more productive way and make better choices for himself in the future.

Likewise, a woman who is afraid of being engulfed would be foolish to hook up with a partner whose life is very successful but demands lots of patience, waiting, and tolerance about unexpected changes in plans. If she finds herself in this pattern without looking in the mirror, she might blame her problems on the way "men dominate everything and always expect the woman to be there for them." It would be much more productive for her to become involved with a partner whose lifestyle doesn't make those demands on her.

> If you know about your fears, you can do a much better job of taking care of them without giving up the desire for a relationship.

A woman who has worked hard at building her self-esteem and knows she fears having it taken away would not do well with a partner who seems to have good self-esteem but is also impatient, perfectionistic, and critical. Consistently choosing this type of person could convince her that it is always that way when you fall in love with someone. She would fail to see how her unconscious sets this up to keep her free from losing herself permanently to a man.

Recognizing whether a relationship can be safe for you is the primary benefit of dealing with your ambivalence in a conscious way. It's one of the first steps of the sorting process. When you begin a dating relationship, keep your eyes open to see if your partner's lifestyle and personality traits are comfortable for you. Choose a person who respects your fears and isn't preprogrammed to make your worst fantasies about love come true. This will greatly enhance your chances of being able to commit to each other and enjoy the relationship.

> You may be surprised to find how much more relaxed you can be and how much more joy you can get from a relationship when you respect and value your ambivalence.

The moral of this story is to feel good about being ambivalent. It can actually be an asset. Don't judge yourself as weak when you feel ambivalent. Let your ambivalence become a warning signal that something isn't quite right. Let it show you the way to your hidden fears. This is usually an ongoing process that deepens over time. Once you have a sense of the hidden forces in your life, respect them and become aware of what you need to do to feel safer.

## Exercises to Test Your Ambivalence

**Exercise 1.** Do you think you are affected by one or more of the three fears listed in this chapter? Write this down under a heading of "My Ambivalence" in your notebook.

**Exercise 2.** What would be the worst thing, even if small, that a lifelong relationship would bring to your life? Losing yourself? Being stuck with the wrong person? Not having control over your own life? Being abused? Having to check with someone else about everything? Losing the hunt for new and exciting partners?

**Exercise 3.** From your thoughts so far, what kind of person should you avoid in order to give yourself the best chance of being loved as you are? An insensitive person who is critical or afraid to be personal? A person who lives far away, is very busy and committed to success? How about a person who is wishy-washy, depressed, or a fun-and-games-only type?

**Exercise 4.** What could you admit about your yearning and desires for a relationship that might also teach you something about your fears and how you might sabotage a relationship? For example, you may want to be with someone who is easy—a low-maintenance person—because you are afraid of engulfment and don't want to take care of someone (as you had to take care of your mother or father), so you pick people you can control because you have more personal magnetism. The problem is that you see now that you get bored easily and leave these relationships.

Or, you know that you want love so badly that it brings tears to your eyes, but you don't ever show it for fear of driving someone away. The trouble with that, you now see, is that you never get enough affection or passion from the people you have been choosing.  —

The next chapter will give a more detailed approach to looking at your family and its influence on your yearnings and fears about relationships.

# 3

# Your Parents Are Always with You

You may have left your family and parents in New Jersey, Los Angeles, or Cincinnati, but they are still very close at hand. In the same way a tree grows out of a small seed and takes on all the characteristics implanted in the DNA, we blossom forth from our parents and are shaped by the myriad influences implanted in us by our genes and rearing.

How that affects our relationships in life is the topic of many books, and it's easy to observe with couples. The dynamics between couples almost always reflect early parental influences. The sparks that fly in their tiffs are often familiar embers from childhood—once known, later forgotten, and now rekindled. Herbert can't stand up to his domineering wife any better than he could to his mother. Donna was excited at first by her boyfriend's confidence and take-charge manner, but has felt invalidated by these same forces since they married. Now she remembers that her relationship with her father felt exactly the same way.

The task of observing these hidden dynamics when you're single is more difficult. The sparks that fly for couples aren't ignited yet for a single person. But working at knowing your early childhood influences may yield knowledge that can help you avoid sabotaging your success at finding relationships and thus avoid a bad marriage.

> In the same way a tree grows out of a small seed and takes on all the characteristics implanted in the DNA, we blossom forth from our parents and are shaped by the myriad influences implanted in us by our genes and rearing.

This chapter will help you learn to seek qualities in a partner that go much deeper than looks and excitement. It will help you understand your own childhood deprivations and screen for partners who will heal rather than reenact past wounds. You may learn, for instance, that you should be especially careful to find a partner with gentleness or an ability to talk things out, or someone who can validate your differences or respect your privacy.

## Subterranean Forces

All marriages, no matter how well-chosen, have subterranean forces at work that will well up during the power struggle that every marriage must go through. There is no way to avoid this stage of struggle with its opportunity for growth. However, that doesn't mean you shouldn't increase your knowledge about your upbringing to help you choose as well as possible and give the power struggle stage a chance to heal and form an even better relationship.

Before doing the inner work that led to writing this book, I kept getting into relationships that ended after three to nine months. Either I got scared and ended it, or she did. After working through the principles that I share in this book, I met Linda and wasn't scared—until after we were married. At that point, however, we both wanted the marriage to work, and we put a lot of conscious effort into working out our power struggle.

The difference between my previous dating pattern and being with Linda was my readiness to choose someone with whom I could form a partnership in resolving conflicts, learning to validate each other, and working to understand each other. Before that readiness, I always chose women who excited me, and also in time, scared me. This enabled me to stay away from committed relationships.

All of us have two sets of forces working when we pick people to date: the conscious part is the one we talk about with our friends; the unconscious part is the other side of our ambivalence—the side that is afraid to get connected to anyone. These two forces have very little in common and don't plan strategy together. In fact, they interfere with each other. Before I was ready to meet my wife, my unconscious force kept putting me into situations that always had an exit. It served the part of me that was too afraid to get fully involved with anyone. But this grew tiresome over time.

For a single person, the best reason to examine how your parents determine your relationships is to help you with your ambivalence. It's so frustrating and emotionally exhausting to keep having exciting but short-term relationships which are ultimately destined to keep you from the happiness that a real relationship can bring.

> All marriages, no matter how well-chosen, have subterranean forces at work that will well up during the power struggle that every marriage must go through

## Growing Beyond Appearances

Phyllis, an old friend of mine, knew she wanted a strong man. She was always drawn to confident, good-looking men with stylish ties and expensive suits, but they all seemed to squeeze time with her in between business meetings. She consistently felt like the second priority for these men. Phyllis and her lovers would start wild, romantic affairs that somehow always sputtered out, leaving her emotionally drained and recuperating for months.

After too many of these flash/crash relationships, Phyllis began to realize that her father was like that. As a girl, she had enjoyed expensive lunches with him downtown between his business meetings. She felt special when he showed her around his offices and proudly introduced her to his associates. She also remembered, with help from her therapist, that she hated being fit in between his appointments and never having him at her school plays or even the debating finals that she won. He had his life and she could join it at times, but he seldom fit her successes into his calendar.

This new knowledge helped her understand why she began to have the same feeling of not being appreciated for being her own unique person by the men she dated. She then used this realization to begin choosing men who made time for her and didn't just fit her in. Of course, it wasn't all that simple, because she also had to learn to feel special by herself rather than through these glamorous men. But she did it, and I went with Phyllis and her husband to her son's graduation this summer.

## I Want a Girl Just Like the Girl that Married Dear Old Dad

I know, you're a man or woman of the nineties. You've been around the block a few times, and you like dating people who are exotic. The man you met in Paris last summer seemed different than anyone you had met before—and quite the opposite of your family. But why, after a few months, did you and Jacques break up for the same reason your last three relationships ended?

Many of us consciously pick people with very different traits than our parents, but under the surface, deeper forces are working. Most of us don't believe that we want someone just like our parent of the opposite sex. However, the old song that heads this section betrays an age-old wisdom about picking people who remind us of our parents—even if it's unconscious. After all, regardless of whether their example was positive or negative, our parents are the ones who set our initial prototypes for a mate.

I can remember singing this song spontaneously while thinking how I was feeling comfortable with a new lover because she had some of my mom's characteristics. I also remember thinking that the last thing I wanted was someone just like my mom. Do you recognize the ambivalence? The truth is that like it or not, we are going to pick people who reflect our parents' qualities. We ourselves reflect our parents' qualities!

Harville Hendrix, in *Getting the Love You Want*, has expressed this concept clearly. He uses the word "imago" to describe the configuration of qualities in us that will seek out only certain types of people as love objects. It's almost like a puzzle that is missing one piece—only the right configured piece will fit. This theory departs from our previous understanding by adding that our imago match is made up of characteristics from *both* our parents (or caregivers), not just from the opposite sex parent, as the classic song would have it. I would go further and say that the people we are attracted to can also have characteristics of our brothers and sisters.

Nature seems to force us to keep dealing with the same issues in relationships—first with our parents and then with our love partners. The bad news is that these imago partners will have many of the negative qualities that we wanted to get away from when we left our parents. The good news is that in a committed romantic relationship, we have a chance to empower ourselves by learning how to handle similar conflicts in mature ways.

So what does all this have to do with being single and trying to pick a good partner? I hope it will serve to warn you that your fights with a future mate will remind you of your childhood. Don't be shocked when it starts to happen. However, at this point in your life, I would like this chapter to help you keep your eyes wide open so you won't re-create your childhood sorrows unnecessarily.

Throughout the rest of this chapter, you will reexplore your parents' qualities—the good and the bad. As hard as you try, you will not be able to avoid ending up with someone who carries many of the same frustrating traits. But you don't have to choose the worst of your parents. For instance, if your dad was an alcoholic, you may be attracted to men with addictions. But with your enhanced alertness, you can insist on a man in recovery. If your mom was depressed, you can insist on making sure your future partner, while carrying similar traits, is aware of her tendency toward depression and manages it.

> Nature seems to force us to keep dealing with the same issues in relationships—first with our parents and then with our love partners.

The goal of this chapter and the exercises is self-knowledge to be used in creating a conscious relationship—one in which you are not simply reacting, but are able to make choices about how you are acting.

## Exercise: Traveling Back in Time

To begin exploring the ways your parents, siblings, and others influence your choice of mates, do this exercise. You will need about twenty minutes and your notebook. An excellent way to do it would be to join up with a friend and do it together.

First, take yourself on a guided imagery session back to your early years, into the house of your youth. To do this, relax, close your eyes, breathe until you feel relaxed and at ease. Then use your imagination to re-create your childhood house from an aerial view. Note how the rooms were arranged, where the furniture and appliances were, and how your room was furnished. Now, find your father (or male caretaker if it wasn't your father). Observe him from a distance and notice his qualities. The good and the bad. After you have done that to your satisfaction, go up to him in this totally safe vision and tell him what it was like to grow up with him. You may even tell him something that he should know but you have been afraid to tell him—perhaps what you always wanted from him.

Now, find your mother or female caretaker. Observe her from a distance and notice her qualities. The good and the bad. After you have done that to your satisfaction, go up to her in this totally safe vision and tell her what it was like to grow up with her. You may even tell her something that she should know but you have been afraid to tell her.

Finally, repeat this same process with any influential brother, sister, grandparent, or powerful person in your childhood, like a nanny. One final note: if you can't remember back that far, do exactly the same thing with the time that you can remember even if that is the present.

After you have taken this journey back in time, write down all the qualities that you can remember, both good and bad, of all your parents, caretakers, brothers, or sisters in a section of your notebook entitled "My Imago." Write one-word descriptions of their qualities as you remember them. For instance, you could use words such as "nurturing," "caring," "abusive," "critical," "warm," "gracious," "sharp," "cold," "judgmental," and so on.

After listing all these qualities, write out what it was like to live with that person as a parent, sister, brother, or grandparent, as well as whatever you told them that you had always been afraid to say.

We will use this information in various ways. This exercise provides you with a warehouse full of information about yourself. To make it easier, underline the three most negative qualities from the entire list of adjectives that you have written—mother's, father's, and influential brothers or sisters all combined. Then, circle the three most positive qualities from the entire list. These six qualities will help you see in a few condensed words the most influential qualities that you grew up with. It will give you insight about the people you find yourself attracted to and the qualities that both intrigue and infuriate you. Also, if you use your "qualities" list to think about your partners from the past, you will probably have more insight about what drew you to those people, what you liked about them, and what didn't work for you.

You may also find that you have some of the qualities you have seen in your parents. This is helpful information, as you'll see below.

## The Qualities of Both Parents and Their Relationship

Along with the way the good and bad qualities of both parents influence our selection of a mate, the memory of their marriage keeps steering us in and out of romantic unions. If you take a poll among your friends to see how many of them would like a relationship just like their parents' marriage, the vast majority wouldn't want that at all. In fact, their conscious decisions will try to avoid anything that faintly resembles their parents' marriage. But the unconscious is so tricky that, in mysterious ways, these friends will end up with a relationship in which the issues they fight about will be similar to issues they had with their parents and their parents had with each other. The relationship won't look exactly the same, but the issues will be the same, clothed in a modern wardrobe.

If Lori had her way, she would be with a man who wouldn't leave her emotionally or physically like her father did. She's attracted to calm, confident men who make her feel safe and secure. She wants a man who is steady and reliable, and she looks for these traits in his values about spending money, raising children, or in their hobbies. It has therefore amazed her that so many men who seemed solid and caring in the beginning could turn out, after getting engaged, (this happened twice to her) to withdraw into their own world.

Unfortunately, there are two types of abandonment. The first type is obvious—the person leaves. The second type, which is more subtle, is when a person withdraws emotionally and leaves his or her partner feeling alone despite their physical presence. During her two engagements, Lori felt abandoned in her desires for more time together, more fun, and validation for her opinions when they were different from her fiance's. After making a list of her relationships, she began to see that all of them ended with her feeling emotionally abandoned, just as she did with her father. Further, the issues that came up were the same issues and sometimes even the same words that she remembered hearing her parents use in their quarrels.

I am awed by the complexity of human relationships—the vast array of interconnecting threads that tie us to our parents, our siblings, our spouse, and even to our grandparents. Sorting it all out and making use

> Along with the way the good and bad qualities of both parents influence our selection of a mate, the memory of their marriage keeps steering us in and out of romantic unions.

of our insights may at first seem impossible. However, some fairly simple exercises can help you to gain effective self-knowledge.

**Exercise.** You have listed your parents' and siblings' qualities and some of your early memories of them. I would now like you to make two more lists. First, make a list of the qualities you would like in your ideal partner and call it "My Ideal Partner." Then look at your list and check which of these qualities you think you possess. Have a friend check your list to see if he or she agrees with your assessment. This may test your friend's honesty and your humility, but it will be a very valuable tool in your self-knowledge.

## Early Survival and Defensive Strategies

There are two stages in childhood that have a major impact on our development. The first—from infancy to about eighteen months—has to do with our ability to get close to other people and form attachments. The second, which starts at eighteen months and continues until two or two-and-a-half years or age, involves our sense of self. This includes our likes and dislikes, our personality, and our self-esteem. These two periods of life give us the program by which we will live unless something intervenes to change it. (For a detailed discussion of this topic, see *Keeping the Love You Find* by Harville Hendrix.)

### The First Stage

In the first months of life, nature is busy teaching us about attachment. If an infant is raised in an unfriendly environment, it will be too painful for him or her to hope for closeness later on. At that early point in time, that baby will have to deal with the unfriendly environment by learning how to be independent. Let's say little Suzie was raised in a home in which her mother was constantly overwhelmed and was inconsistent about attending to her. When she did give Suzie attention, it was in the form of teaching her or straightening out her dress, posture, manners, or speech. If Suzie can remember this part of her childhood, she can guess that her earlier years as an infant, which she has no memory of, were the same. The attention was inconsistent, and it was sharp, critical, or cold when present.

How will these early, shaping experiences control her view of getting close to a lover? In two ways. She will have learned a lot about taking care of herself and not being dependent on others, since that approach never worked in her home. Second, she will carry around a deep, but mostly hidden yearning for someone to take care of her in a warm and soft way. This yearning might not be conscious, but it might slip out while watching movies, reading, or seeing little children with their mothers. Suzie might become teary at certain displays of tenderness toward children.

Let's go through a time warp. Suzie, now Suzanne and thirty, meets Roger and is instantly attracted. Can you guess what he will be like? You may have guessed "strong and gentle," and you will be right—those qualities would compensate for her upbringing. Suzanne is probably looking for qualities that she believes will make her feel safe and loved. But you may have missed what her unconscious part would do in this attraction. The hidden agenda of the unconscious is guarding the deep hurt and yearning for consistent loving and warmth that were never there but always longed for.

Letting these yearnings out to express their need in a naked or vulnerable way would be akin to emotional suicide for Suzanne. Her defenses have aided her by burying these frustrated needs and deprivations deep in her unconscious. Thus, in addition to her conscious desires, her unconscious agenda is also helping to choose a mate. What is it looking for in a mate? A person who has difficulty with real closeness. Suzanne's unconscious chose that. Why? Because it will keep the deep yearning, with its fear of ever being hurt again, removed from danger. Her unconscious will choose a man who won't be a good enough partner to allow Suzanne to get too close and dependent—and thereby risk getting hurt in the process.

Pretty complex stuff! And most of it is out of our conscious awareness. If John was raised by a soft, warm, but again, inconsistent mother, he also will have problems with attachment. Yet, he would be looking more to cling to someone who is warm and caring, so he won't be left alone. The attachment stage and its implications on relationships will be discussed further in Chapters 9 and 12.

**Exercise.** The following exercise will help you use your knowledge of the attachment stage and its implications on relationships. There are two major fears about attachment that affect us in forming partnerships as lovers. One is the fear of being abandoned, and the other the fear of being engulfed or taken over. The first makes us want to cling and the second, to isolate.

1. Think about your childhood, your reactions to dating, and your past relationships. Try to get in touch with which of these two major fears is most prevalent for you—the fear of being abandoned or the fear of being engulfed. Write this information under "My Fears of Closeness."

> Her unconscious will choose a man who won't be a good enough partner to allow Suzanne to get too close and dependent—and thereby risk getting hurt in the process.

  a. Do you hate people leaving? Do you often leave first to avoid being left at the end of an evening or fun time together? Now think about your family history. Are there any major leavings like death, divorce, abandonment, or frequent relocations? Is there any other form of abandonment that you had to deal with when you were growing up?

  b. Think about being engulfed and taken over. Are you overly aware of other people's opinions of you? Do you want privacy and control over your own things more than other people you know?

2. When you have explored these fears and have a firmer grasp on how they affect you, use the information to pick a mate who isn't going to reenact your worst fears.

  a. If you fear being abandoned, test for a person who can, above all things, hang in there and talk things out, rather than run away or withdraw. Look for someone who is staying put, and gives you a warning about leaving on trips or work commitments.

  b. If you fear being engulfed or taken over in a relationship, test for someone who can move over and give you room when you need it. Look for someone who has good boundaries—someone who respects privacy, personal belongings, and personal space. Look for someone who is considerate about timing and differences between people.

### The Second Stage

The second major childhood stage is the one in which we develop our personality. It's a time when we gain positive and negative attitudes about ourselves. This stage follows the attachment phase and continues until around two and a half years. At this time children are learning to walk and explore the world, their bodies, and themselves. This brings about personality clashes with parents, whose fears, yearnings, and values are forced out into the open and demonstrated in their approach to child raising.

The big question here is: how were your natural inclinations and curiosities handled by your parents? Were they validated with enjoyment, delight, and room to explore; or were they controlled, criticized, or even handled with violence? The lucky few who were made to feel free and safe with their natural desires and interests will have good self-esteem. For the rest of you, there will be parts of your personalities in which you are vulnerable to criticism and self-doubt. You will have learned to be defensive about those areas at an early age.

These defended enclaves of self-doubt usually center around fears of being lazy, crazy, bad, or stupid. If you fear being called too emotional, your defenses are triggered by any word or issue in the "crazy" category. If being called incompetent or slow-thinking presses your buttons, your defenses center around being called "stupid." If you try especially hard to be good and helpful, you are sensitive to being seen as "bad." If you are sensitive to being called irresponsible or a flake, you may have been accused of being "lazy" when growing up.

These sensitive areas are usually called our "buttons." When someone presses your buttons, you get defensive and feel very young and anxious. Your face can even heat up and get tight or contorted. Your mind races, and you often want to run away or fight back.

**Exercise.** This exercise may seem overly complicated upon reading through all the steps. However, by completing each step, one at a time, you'll get through the maze.

1. Ask yourself which of the following four categories presses your buttons the most. Listed are the four most common negative words and their opposite. You will feel judged by the negative word and desirous of achieving the positive word. For instance, you hate being called lazy and want to impress people with how responsible you are. Write the category that most presses your buttons under "My Vulnerable Area."

   - Lazy/responsible
   - Crazy/sane
   - Stupid/smart
   - Bad/good

To help this process, ask yourself which criticisms bother you the most? What categories are they represented in? More than one? Do you squirm and bite your tongue in order to hide your de-

fensiveness when someone implies that you are lazy, slow, un-
motivated, or sloppy? Or when someone implies you are stupid,
incompetent, intellectually slow, or dense? How about when
someone implies you are crazy, too emotional, or airheaded? Or
bad, stingy, uncaring, or self-centered?

2. Now make a list of qualities you are looking for in a mate. Entitle
it "Desired Qualities List." Use the qualities list in Chapter 6 if
you need ideas. After making your list, go back and try matching
one of the four categories in step 1 to each of the qualities on
your list. For example, the quality of smart falls into the stu-
pid/smart category; the quality of caring is in the bad/good category; and the quality of sexy might be identified with crazy/sane
or for some, bad/good.

3. Underline qualities on this desired list that you think *you* possess.
Ask a friend to check your list to see if he or she agrees with
your assessment. This may test your friend's honesty and your
humility, but it will be very valuable for your self-knowledge. As
an example, you may think you are "understanding," "clear
about feelings," "giving," "sexy," and "smart," and you underlined them. But now, think about your friend's comments. You
*want* to be understanding, but some people may find you abrasive and critical. You *want* to be clear about feelings, but some
people have accused you of being angry and not expressing it or
hurt and not showing it. Take everything into consideration and
underline the qualities you think you possess.

4. Which of the four word categories appears most frequently in the
underlined qualities that you feel you possess: lazy/responsible,
bad/good, stupid/smart, or crazy/sane?

5. What can you learn from this exercise? Let's say that most of the
qualities you listed fall into the bad and crazy categories. Now
you know that you felt judged or misunderstood as a young person when those issues were involved. They are your vulnerability. You want to be yourself but are afraid you will be seen as
bad (not good enough), or crazy (too emotional or needy). You
try hard to look responsible and also hide your needs. This book
will help you work with this knowledge rather than hide your
needs.

6. As an adult looking for a good relationship, you can use this
information in two ways.

a. Make sure that you pick a partner who respects the category that means the most to you:

- If crazy/sane pushes your buttons, you will need a good communicator and a person who is willing to work things out rather than a person who is exciting and fast-paced.

- If lazy/responsible triggers your defenses, you will need a person who stresses living over success; someone who values enjoying life, people, or spiritual qualities over efficiency and success in the world.

- If bad/good is your sensitive area, go for qualities of understanding, caring, and warmth. Look for someone who is supportive rather than demanding and judgmental.

- If stupid/smart is your vulnerable category, find a person who is comfortable with his or her intelligence, someone who isn't judgmental and is patient.

b. The next important thing is to make sure you give what you want to receive. If you want someone gentle, start learning about what it is to be gentle yourself. If you want to be with someone who is kind, practice kindness. If you want to be with someone who is reliable, keep your commitments.

## What We Hide in Ourselves and Seek in a Partner

The main thing to be learned from the previous exercise is an awareness of the areas that are sensitive for you. You then need to take them seriously in selecting a mate.

As part of her personal inventory, Maria worked with this list and realized that her main area of defensiveness was being called crazy or stupid. On her list of desired partner qualities, she had written "exciting, charming, good-looking, successful, can talk intelligently, romantic, patient, sexy, nonjudgmental, loves children, loyal, and fun-loving." However, she noticed that her list contained only a few words that fit her defensive areas.

This led to the realization that she wasn't selecting qualities that would help her take care of herself better. Maria's relationships were exciting but then quickly dissatisfying. After doing this exercise, she decided to focus on four qualities—patient, sexy, talks intelligently, and nonjudgmental—when looking for a potential partner. She decided she would screen for men who truly were patient and nonjudgmental. The reason: men with these qualities would be less likely to live up to her fears by calling her crazy or stupid. They would push these sensitive buttons less often.

At first such men seemed dull to her. She wouldn't have chosen to date them before. However, after a few men of this type that didn't interest her, she met a man who had the qualities she was looking for and also seemed quite exciting. Spending time with him felt different and good. Maria also took seriously the idea about modeling what she wanted. Of course, this turned out to be a major project, but one that produced the most growth, personal power, and sense of wholeness for her. During this process, she started practicing being patient, nonjudgmental, sexy, and talking intelligently. She knew that she would always want to grow in these qualities, but beginning to work on them made her feel more clearly directed and more in charge of her life.

## Changing Patterns in Relationships

Many people are confused about why they are still single after thirty or forty years. They look back at their lives and their choices without understanding why people they were in love with left or why they themselves lost interest over time. The exercises in this chapter are powerful tools to explore previous patterns, overcome them, and make much better choices in the future.

> At first such men seemed dull to her. She wouldn't have chosen to date them before. However, after a few men of this type that didn't interest her, she met a man who had the qualities she was looking for and also seemed quite exciting. Spending time with him felt different and good.

When Lawrence worked with his list of qualities, he told me he didn't get anything out of it except a headache. I asked him to tell me the qualities of the women he usually dated. He mentioned good-looking, great in bed, entertaining, and good dressers. Since these were his first thoughts and maybe the most important to him, I asked him what he didn't like about the relationships and why they ended. Quickly, without thinking, he shot back, "They wanted too much and got really nasty when I wouldn't do everything they wanted."

Then he told me he did learn in the exercise that his strongest defensive button was being called bad. That made me ask him if he used words on his Desired Qualities List that would fit the bad/good category and take care of his needs in that area, like "kind," "warm," "caring," or "nice". He said he did put down "polite." So we started with polite, and he began to emphasize being polite himself and sorting through his dates for politeness.

Two months went by; then he called for an appointment. The first thing I noticed was that he looked younger and dressed in a less polished manner, but seemed much more relaxed. He told me he couldn't believe it, but he wasn't looking for such "hot women" anymore because they didn't seem to be very polite. He was dating women on the basis of politeness, and he was learning that he liked the softer touch they had.

Now Lawrence wanted to talk about adding more qualities to his list that would be important to him. Eventually, we dealt with his own issues about needing to look good and look successful. On the basis of the word "polite," Lawrence realized that he would prefer to spend his life with a woman who was softer and more caring. Thus, he began an inner journey that helped him get love for being himself instead of questing after a good-looking appendage to his self-image.

**Exercise.**  You still have a list of your parents' qualities that we haven't worked with. Look at that list now and see the negative qualities of both your parents and other important people on the list. List them under "Qualities to Avoid" in your notebook. This list can push you into making sure that the qualities you look for in a mate are ones that don't repeat the worst aspects of your parents. Thinking over your experience of these qualities in your childhood is as important as making the list. After all, your childhood experiences are the reference materials for discovering who you are. Screening against these negative qualities will not prevent you, once married, from having to deal with them in your partner. Nature seems to insist that we confront them and learn to deal with them. But consciously sorting them out as best you can will give you a head start.

By looking at these qualities, you can get beyond the external things that you may have been attracted to in the past, such as a way of dressing, looks, sexiness, strength, confidence, and the like. By taking this emotional and nurturing-based approach, you will be emphasizing loving qualities that will become more and more satisfying to you and increase your potential for a lasting and fullfilling relationship. Ultimately, a great relationship consists of feeling accepted, validated, and prized for who you are, and returning the same to your mate.

## Is There Any Hope?

This chapter has helped you clarify the important loving qualities that you in particular need. The chapters that follow will give you methods of making sure you are getting these qualities. As a summary, here are a few examples of the direction this learning can take.

- If you are defensive about being called crazy, you need a good communicator and a person who is willing to work things out.

- If you are defensive about being called lazy, you need a person who stresses living over success. You will want to live with someone who emphasizes enjoying life, enjoying people, or developing spiritual qualities over efficiency and success in the world.

- If "bad" is your defensive word, go for qualities of understanding, caring, support, and warmth.

- If "stupid" sets you off, find a person who is comfortable with his or her intelligence, someone who isn't judgmental and is patient.

- If you fear being engulfed or taken over in a relationship, test for someone who can move over and give you room. Look for someone who has good boundaries and respects privacy, personal belongings, and personal space. Also, make sure your partner is considerate about timing and different ways of doing things between people.

- If you fear being abandoned, test for a person who can, above all, hang in there and talk things out, rather than run away or withdraw. Make sure your potential mate is someone who is staying put geographically and will give you a lot of notice about leaving on trips or work commitments.

This is not to say that other qualities like attractive, fun, and interesting aren't important. These are the things you live with every day and are crucial, but I trust that "chemistry" will take care of you in those areas.

From this chapter you can learn how to make sure you are paying sufficient attention to the softer and deeper qualities that will help you feel accepted and loved. We often hold the mistaken ideal that most people, when in love, will have these kind, warm, communicative, caring qualities; in reality, they are traits that you must identify and search out in the people you meet as potential mates.

Your parents are always with you—their good and bad qualities and your reactions to them. Learn about them so that your choices will be conscious and not knee-jerk reactions that are based solely on chemistry.

# Part Two

# Finding Available Partners

# 4

# Developing a Strategy to Meet Your Mate

Having enough people coming through your life as potential mates is an important part of choosing wisely. If you want to share your life with a lover, husband, or wife, you have to become friends with your ambivalence about commitment—and then meet a person with whom it will work. One without the other doesn't complete the picture. Developing a personal strategy to meet potential mates is a necessary tool for your quest. Before we were married, my wife and I ran singles workshops called Meet Your Mate. This chapter is a condensation of that workshop. After giving practical tips, I will teach you a three-part method for meeting and getting dates with people you find interesting.

> Developing a personal strategy to meet potential mates is a necessary tool for your quest. I will teach you a three-part method for meeting and getting dates with people you find interesting.

## How Much Time to Spend

Let's begin with some practical advice. I recommend that you spend the same amount of time finding potential partners as you plan to spend in the relationship later on. You may be shocked by this and think it means a huge amount of time. However, many people have worked this out to one night during the week and half of the weekend. That averages about eight hours for your own interests per weekend; then spending the rest of the time being social.

As a married person, this makes sense to me. Most people who are married and busy with their careers are lucky to get this much time to enjoy each other. If you decide that one night a week and most of the weekend seems reasonable, then put this amount of time into your strategy. But work out the time commitment for yourself—according to your needs and responsibilities. You may want more or less. Whatever amount of time you want to spend in a relationship is the amount to spend in finding and forming a relationship.

It's surprising how many single people don't think about this. They somehow expect a relationship to come magically flying through their front door. My friend Elena, for example, had six nights a week scheduled with activities that precluded meeting single men. She was in a modern dance ensemble, an ethnic dance troupe, and spent two other evenings volunteering at a hospice program. Despite her artistic charisma and her warm personality, she hadn't had a date for close to four years.

Right before Elena's fortieth birthday, she realized that her life wasn't unfolding the way she had planned. Three weeks later, much to the amazement of her friends, she quit both dance troupes and started spending time in activities where she would meet available men. She began social dancing in groups where she didn't already know everyone, and she joined a singles organization. At this point Elena is still in the sorting stage with her dates, but she's meeting interesting men all the time and feels confident that she will find the relationship she wants in the future.

If finding a relationship is important to you, make this a priority. Give it your time and attention. Put yourself in situations where you will meet people, and then start sorting.

## Where to Meet People

In the introduction to this book, I discussed how our society is full of single people who want to be coupled. The problem is where to meet them. In a society that is isolated, afraid of work entanglements, and terminally busy, you are handicapped. However, the following suggestions are promising avenues to meet other single, available people.

Newspaper personal ads and voice-mail dating services are now much more routine and acceptable for people like you and me. There is an art to using these methods which I will discuss in a separate section. The entertainment section of the Sunday paper also gives many listings of occasions for meeting people at art openings, the theater, workshops, lectures, comedy clubs, and other activities open to the public. Classes for adults are great ways to meet people, whether in the evening division of a local university or at an alternative site. Church groups and bookstores provide good opportunities for socializing. Theater games and tryouts also bring a lot of people together. Hikes and walks scheduled as special events or with an ongoing group, such as Sierra Singles, are also good opportunities to have fun while making yourself available to other single adults.

Social dancing and folk dance groups are also full of single people who want to be in relationships. In fact, many people dance specifically to meet people. In any major city, there are places to dance every night of the week, and rural areas have weekly groups. Usually the evening begins with a dance class for an hour or so, followed by two or three hours of recreational dancing. These occasions are usually set up to facilitate meeting new people.

> If finding a relationship is important to you, make this a priority. Give it your time and attention. Put yourself in situations where you will meet people, and then start sorting.

You can get burned out with any of these activities, so be careful to do the ones that you enjoy and to pace yourself. Going to new places is harder by yourself than with a friend, but it is by far the most effective way of meeting someone new. Also, your search for a partner can be a good excuse to get out of the house and do some of the social and educational activities that you weren't making time for in the past. You do have to get out of your house to meet people.

## Blind Dates

Enlisting others in your search for a partner is efficient but tricky. Despite the bad reputation blind dates have acquired, not everyone who wants to be fixed up is Dracula's nephew. Yes, you might have to spend an hour or two with a toad, but occasionally your friends come up with a prince.

Lisa, a woman in her early thirties, was gently coerced into meeting a friend of a former housemate. When her friend called that evening, Lisa insisted that she wasn't interested in meeting anyone that way, but her friend persisted. "Look, we're having dinner at a cafe a few blocks away from where you live. Just walk down and meet us for a few minutes." Finally she agreed.

When Lisa walked into the cafe and took a look at Scott, the chemistry was instantly electric. In the next few hours, they discovered a number of common interests. He was a filmmaker; she wrote scripts; and both were committed to nonviolence in the film industry. He had a fossil collection, and she already knew the best places to look for fossils in Northern California. He was planning to move to Los Angeles in a few months, which she was also considering as a good move in her career. The evening was a pleasant surprise for both of them, and they dated for several months.

The moral of this story is that blind dates occasionally work. There are fine people like yourself out there who just haven't met the right person yet. If you want to use this method among your other resources, tell all your friends and relatives that you are looking for a relationship and that you're open to meeting anyone they think might be right for you. Thank them for the introduction even if it was a bust. No one really knows how a friend might be on a date. But think about it—meeting someone on a blind date is not so different from meeting a stranger at a dance evening or a party. At least if a friend or relative recommends him or her you will have some kind of pre-screening.

## Working the Ads

Newspaper ads and voice-mail dating services are a great way to get a lot of action going in your life. This sometimes is worthwhile just to get yourself moving and not feeling stuck or desperate. It can also be a successful adventure. In major cities, it is not uncommon to get more than forty responses to a relationship ad. Thousands of people have met partners for long-term relationships, and even marriage, this way.

The art to using these ads successfully is to pace yourself and strictly follow the strategy outlined in the list at the end of this book's introduction. The first common problem with using relationship ads is that people tend to interview a potential partner too much, rather than doing things together and having fun. This leads to the second common problem: trusting intellect more than intuition. The deepest and clearest signals of whether a relationship is right for you *always* come through intuition. Pay attention to those subtle feelings. It would be helpful to reread the introduction's conclusion again before answering or running an ad.

The third common problem with ads is trying to build intimacy before there is any foundation to support it. The first task of dating is the sorting process. If you place a relationship ad or use a dating service, you will meet many people with whom you feel no physical or emotional attraction. When you meet the few people to whom you are attracted, it is much better to slow down and give it a chance. Spending too much time together right away and sharing the intimate details of your life before a foundation of trust is built simply does not work. Also, it is almost always a mistake to share physical intimacy before you know each other quite well, and that takes time. Chapter 6 will also help you in this area.

If you are about to place an ad for the first time, you may make the mistake of not being selective enough about the content of the ad itself. It is easier to use the ads if you receive fewer but more appropriate responses. If you word your ad in a specific way to screen people, you won't have so many nonspecific answers that you get overwhelmed responding to them. Ask for what you, *in particular*, want from a partner. If you ask for things like good communication skills, ability to talk about issues, respectful of women, not bitter toward men, or ability to listen well, you will be able to screen out any responses that don't demonstrate these qualities.

> If you word your ad in a specific way to screen people, you won't have so many nonspecific answers that you get overwhelmed responding to them.

For instance, I ran an ad that asked for a woman interested in an equal relationship. I got lots of replies and had to sort like mad. One person sent me her professional brochure, which included her picture—she was quite attractive—and a tiny note about calling her. I discarded it because my intuition told me this wasn't a woman who wanted an equal relationship. She was relying on her looks and profession. I wanted someone willing to work out a relationship equally, with respect and energy.

## Using the Opportunities in Your Everyday Life

While all of these ideas are valuable to the serious relationship seeker, I still think the most advantageous opportunities come in your everyday life. In your daily routine you have the advantage of seeing potential partners *as they are* in their regular life. You will already know if there is attraction. Personal ads and blind dates don't give you this advantage.

The specific skills for using your everyday life to meet people are described in the sections that follow, but here is an overview. For the best results, establish a routine of going to the same places to shop, eat, clean your clothes, buy pharmaceuticals, get haircuts, and so on. If you take public transportation, you are way ahead of the game, especially if you have a routine and can recognize people who share your schedule. You, of course, can vary your patterns and change your routine if no one interests you over time. It's like digging for diamonds in a mine—if the gems don't emerge, go dig elsewhere.

I call this putting yourself in the path of an interesting person. If the two of you "coincidentally" meet a few times, you can initiate a conversation more easily. I once invented an excuse to have lunch with an interesting woman. I didn't have the nerve to ask her out so I asked if we could share information about a project she was working on over lunch. We enjoyed lunch, talked about the project and then about her relationship with a delightful guy. A rather pleasant way to find out she wasn't available!

A sad fact about this method of meeting people is that the most obvious ways of meeting aren't always ethical or practical. I'm referring to dating your students, clients, or co-workers. The people we see the most frequently are sometimes off-limits, but anyone can take classes! Students can date each other.

The main point here is that the life you live every day is loaded with potential for meeting interesting people. Some of them are bound to be attracted to you, and vice versa. The next time you feel a wave of electricity from someone you see or interact with in the normal life you live, follow up. It could be mutual.

If you use your everyday life as a method for meeting people, you will also have to learn how to refuse the advances of others. Many people feel anxious about rejection, regardless of whether they are giving or receiving it. As a result, they can get razor sharp and hurt the other person's feelings or lose their balance for a few moments. But there are alternatives to these emotional reactions.

The best solution I've found is to develop a good line such as, "Thank you, but I'm involved with someone." The line must be final. Anything else may seem flirtatious, which is exactly what you don't want. If advances continue in the workplace after you've made it clear that you don't want them, you may need to get help through channels that are set up for that.

## How to Meet People for Romance

OK, let's say you've done your homework. You've done the psychological work you need to prepare yourself for a successful relationship. You've spent time dealing with your ambivalence and you understand how to take care of yourself when issues about ambivalence come up. You know what it is you have to offer in a relationship, and you've spent time thinking about what you really want in a partner. All of this is essential preparation. If you haven't done that, you will most likely undermine your success, no matter how many people you meet.

However, if you feel ready for a committed relationship, the next challenge is finding potential partners. While I believe that the preparation is the most important thing you can do, you can't have a relationship without meeting people. So here are some tested and valuable tips for meeting people.

Interestingly enough, your everyday life is the main tool in your search for a mate. There are more opportunities to meet a life partner in what you usually do than anywhere else—if you pay attention.

## The Rule of Three

Meeting people in cities is largely a skill of finding ways to make the encounter feel safe for both people. Although meeting a new person is almost never an anxiety-free situation, there are ways for you to feel more in control. Your task in developing these skills is learning how to make it feel safe for the other person.

Think of meeting people for romance as a dance in three parts—the initiation, the engagement, and the close. If you can't do any one of these three processes, you will not pull off the meeting.

Initiating means breaking the ice. Engaging means getting more personal. Closing is getting a phone number or making plans for a "coffee" date. Remember that all three—in sequence—are essential. If you are great at initiating but not at engaging, you will frighten your new acquaintance off when you try to ask for a phone number or a date. He or she won't

> Your everyday life is the main tool in your search for a mate.
> There are more opportunities to meet a life partner in what
> you usually do than anywhere else—if you pay attention.

feel safe with you unless the conversation has gotten more personal and who you are has emerged more clearly. In the same way, if you are skilled at getting personal and asking for phone numbers but can't work up the nerve to initiate a conversation with someone who interests you, you'll be eating your heart out with all the missed opportunities.

## Breaking the Ice

Another way to look at meeting people is to realize that most people want to be met. This is especially true if they can feel safe while it's happening. However, despite the loneliness that so many people feel, it's important to be realistic enough to know that there is an invisible brick wall between strangers on the street, in elevators, and in lines at the supermarket.

The purpose of initiating a conversation is to soften the bricks into a loose rubble wall. The purpose of engaging is to change the wall to a lace curtain. With this preparation, you have a much better chance of landing on opposite sides of a table in a cafe. Asking for a coffee date without going through the initiating and engaging stages is like running into a brick wall.

Another rule of three is that it generally takes three contacts with someone before a relationship is established. People in sales know that until you've made three contacts, potential buyers don't really feel a kinship with you. You won't stand out in their minds as an individual until that time.

In your search for a loving relationship, realize that if you can make three contacts with someone at your neighborhood market or on a commuter bus or train, you may have the beginning of a relationship. As an example, let's say that Pete sees Marcia on the train platform and is attracted to her. If he catches her eye one day and gives her a smile two days later, he has begun to catch her attention. Later, he will have an easier time initiating with her because it will be the third contact and thus a natural progression. He could simply say that he has noticed her on the train a few times and ask if she works downtown. A whole conversation could flow from there.

Without those three contacts, initiating is harder and takes more nerve, more skill, and occasional gimmicks.

### Gimmicks

Meeting strangers is the art of finding a common ground to break the ice. Asking for information, remarking on a common experience, paying attention to a sudden occurrence, noticing a striking but not too personal feature—a pin, a scarf, an unusual tie or button, a hat, or a dog they are walking—are all examples. The main thing is to find a casual way to catch the other person's attention.

Let's say Pete has caught Marcia's attention and wants to initiate with her. He can stand near her and make brief eye contact. Then he can remark on how hot it is, ask if this bus goes all the way downtown, or say that he couldn't help but notice her political pin and ask why she thinks people should support Joan Good. Marcia, on the other hand, can use all of these methods too. Furthermore, she may be wearing the pin because she knows it's a gimmick to help her break the ice. She wants to meet new people, and she's trying to make it easier.

> Meeting strangers is the art of finding a common ground to break the ice. Ask for information, remark on a common experience, pay attention to a sudden occurrence, notice a striking but not too personal feature—a pin, a scarf, an unusual tie or button, a hat, or a dog they are walking.

In our seminars, my wife and I stress the advantages of using a gimmick or prop to open up pathways for other people to meet you. Think about how easy it is to go up to someone with a puppy or an infant to realize how this works. Imagine how easy it would be to talk to someone holding a bouquet of balloons. Even a medium pizza box on a train or bus can lead to an opening for a conversation.

## Opening Lines

If no prop is available, seize upon any situation that is funny or out of the ordinary. Or ask a question that the person might have the answer to. For instance, standing in line in the supermarket, you may notice the person ahead of you has an inordinate amount of radishes in her cart. You could ask what she intends to do with all those radishes. This actually happened to me! Most shopping carts are full of props to use in striking up a conversation. And that's just one example out of many.

The main thing to remember is that most people do want to be met. The ones who don't make it fairly clear—being sensitive to this is one of the skills you want to pay attention to. When a person does want to be met, a prop or gimmick makes the initiation easy. But if your opening line goes nowhere, just let it pass.

Initiating contact is a skill that needs to be practiced. I suggest trying it out with people who don't intimidate you and in places where you feel comfortable. Good locations to start are lines in stores, subway platforms, bus stops, and small neighborhood shops. Also, some people find it easier to start practicing their lines with people they aren't strongly attracted to because it feels safer to make mistakes. If you really want to date someone, it can be intimidating until you get more practice.

If you don't know what to say, begin by commenting on ties or political buttons. Experiment with wearing props yourself and see what response you get. Ask people for information at bus stops, or ask their advice about using artichokes, which you noticed in jars in their shopping cart. Make jokes about any common situation you both witness. Make eye contact and smile. All of these practice sessions make it easier later when you need these skills to break the ice with someone attractive to you. Also, practicing these skills brings you in contact with peopel and makes you feel less isolated.

### Developing Your Own Style

If you can think of a standard approach for an initiation, you will be much more at ease. For instance, if it suits your personality, you could say after making some eye contact and getting a little encouragement, "All the lines I thought of sounded corny, so I thought I would just say hi." All lines of this type do sound corny and that is taken for granted, but admitting it is unusual.

If you can't think of your own approach, try a few of these for practice: "Hi, my name's, _____. I see you here often and always wish I could think of something to say to meet you. You have a great smile." Or, "I'm terrible at meeting strangers, but I see you here often and have wanted to say hi." Being still after that is the hardest thing because you feel like such an idiot. One of only two things is going to happen. The other person will either indicate they are not interested—and will probably be polite about it—or they will say something that picks up the conversation.

Either response is useful to you because it lets you know where you stand. You either strike out or continue on to the engaging stage. By the way, striking out is part of the game. It's something we all need to accept without being devastated. Later in this chapter, I deal with this at length.

We usually take rejection very personally, and we all need to have a way to keep it from being hurtful. My advice is to see it as a necessary stage of sorting and try not to take it so personally. It's much more helpful to look at responses from other people either as a green light to go ahead to the engaging stage, or a red light to stop and try somewhere else.

Also, try to be realistic in your goals and to take care of yourself as much as possible. If you always set your sights on the most attractive person imaginable, you probably will be intimidated and feel shy, unless you have the charisma of Bette Midler or a face like Robert Redford. If, on the other hand, you go for people who seem friendly, it will be easier, regardless of whether their appearance is flashy or plain.

## Strategies for Engaging

Engaging is the process of getting more personal. It's the art of opening pathways for getting closer. You do this by sharing a common interest or passion, revealing personal feelings of likes and dislikes, and telling personal stories that reveal common understandings or sympathies.

Let's take Pete again on the train platform, now that he has initiated a conversation with Marcia by commenting on her political pin. If Marcia's response has made him feel that she may be receptive to further communication, he could say that he is getting really fed up with male politicians and wants to vote for a woman for a change, but he doesn't think that many women can make it in the crushing political world and hang onto their female values. This statement shares some of his personal attitudes, sympathies, and opinions. It leaves a lot of room for her to respond in an area where she has already demonstrated an interest. Also, it demonstrates the value of having a prop to use for the initial conversation.

Now it's time to look in the mirror. What is it that stands out about you? What makes you interesting? What common interests and sympathies could someone share with you? Are you passionate about something and love to meet people who share that passion? If your answer to all of these questions is nothing, then go get a life for yourself and come back to this project later. But most people have many qualities that are interesting in themselves, along with hobbies, ideas, passions, and talents that would be endearing to a kindred spirit.

So if you're looking for a relationship, the first step is to get in touch with the things about yourself that are special and endearing. This isn't a time to be modest or to take yourself for granted. If you want to attract someone special into your life, the least you can do is allow yourself to be charmed by your own positive qualities. The next step—and this is part of engaging—is to open the door to these aspects of yourself in the presence of another person. It's one of the most effective ways to draw kindred spirits into your life—both for friendships and relationships.

In one of my workshops, James, a man in his thirties, had trouble answering my questions. He was an accountant and he liked his work, but not passionately. "Any hobbies?" I asked. "Movies and going out to dinner, walking through the neighborhoods occasionally." He liked to do lots of things and was open to learning more, but he said he wasn't passionate about any of these. "Volunteer work?" I pursued. He lit up and said he reads to the blind over the radio and sometimes in person. Now that stands out! And it opens a door into an endearing part of his personality.

### Enhancing Your Special Qualities

Why do you need something that stands out? Because we live in a crazy, competitive world with tons of stimuli. You'll be forgotten if you seem bland just because you don't know how to put your most interesting side out there. A freelance writer I know gets a good percentage of her work by talking to everyone she meets about what she does. Strangers on airplanes. People riding on streetcars. Art aficionados at gallery openings and museums. Dance partners. She also gets dates this way because she isn't shy about who she is. And because of her open approach to meeting and engaging with people, the men who ask her out tend to share some common interests.

> Get in touch with the things about yourself that are special and endearing. The next step—and this is part of engaging—is to open the door to these aspects of yourself in the presence of another person.

These same tactics will work for you in your strategy to meet and attract a special person into your life. Think of those things about yourself that make you interesting or mysterious. Then, work out standard ways to get those subjects into conversations. When I was single, I used the fact that I was a priest early in my life if I felt this would be intriguing to certain women. With other women I emphasized my carpentry skills or my folk dancing background.

What is it about you that will help a potential date remember you or want to spend more time with you? What about your life or background might reveal a common ground with another person? Develop some standard lines or approaches to let them know.

### Becoming More Personal

Some people find it easy to open up to new people and engage them in more personal levels of conversation. Other's have trouble with this aspect of the dating process. If this is a major problem for you, it may be wise to spend the time and money for therapy and get through the issues that are standing in your way. Breaking these boundaries may be too difficult on your own, and the results you desire will come much faster with some coaching. If the following suggestions seem frightening or impossible for you to try, get some help.

Once again, having a standard line or approach to becoming more personal quickly will be very useful for you. When she was single, my wife always asked if the person lived in the neighborhood. Then she continued with where she worked and how she liked the area. That led into many other engaging directions. My approach was to share an opinion and ask a question, for example, "I keep thinking that people are feeling less safe and are therefore more protective of themselves on the streets. Have you felt that?" What you want to do is to use a personal part of yourself to engage a personal part of the other person.

To continue with our example, Marcia has found Pete to be interesting and engaging, and she decides to share her political views. They talk for a while, and if all goes well, they will want to have coffee sometime to finish the conversation. That is *the close*—getting a phone number or making plans for a casual date later on.

While there really is no substitute for being an interesting person, not everyone manifests that in the same way. Nor does this have anything to do with shyness. While a shy person may not be a good match for someone looking for a party animal, others will find the shyness, if acknowledged and not apologized for, to be fine. Different qualities, activities, interests, goals, and opinions will all appeal to different people. *Seeing if you match* is the initial step of sorting, which is what dating is all about.

## Closing

At this point, you have worked out how to get your interesting qualities into a conversation quickly and how to be more personal with a new acquaintance. Everything is moving along nicely. But now you are worried because you like this man, and the train is coming to your station. You want to get a date with him or at least give him your phone number. Should you hand him your business card? Stay on the train? Or get off and watch this special opportunity dissolve into the sunset. The train is slowing down, and it's time for a new skill.

Closing is the gentle art of making a connection work for romance. Two mistakes that people frequently make in closing are moving either too slowly or too quickly. Quickly means they skip the engaging stage and go right to closing. This scares the other person and often produces a response that seems hostile when it is really a defense against being invaded and having his or her boundaries crashed.

The other problem, moving too slowly, is much more common. It can be overcome by developing a stock strategy that you can draw upon without having to be too creative on the spur of the moment.

Once you have developed the art of pacing a conversation, you are well on your way to becoming an expert. Again, the skill is putting something out and seeing what you get back. Then you proceed on the basis of that feedback. In this way, you learn to let fruitless conversations die and move on, and to allow more hopeful encounters to develop at a pace that induces a feeling of safety. You now need to invent a line or approach that will work for you when you are ready to ask for a date or a phone number.

You don't have to be original in each situation. Be genuine with your personality and use the same closing line most of the time. Mine was, "I've really enjoyed this conversation. Could we continue it sometime?" Or, "I feel a nice connection with you. Would you like to get together again sometime soon?" My personality is rather blunt, so these blunt lines worked well for the women that I was attracted to and who were attracted to me.

Find an approach that works for your personality. My wife used to use, "I wonder if we could have coffee sometime?" Thus, she was avoiding a direct question but putting the thought out into the airwaves to be pounced upon or not.

I actually used those lines I gave as examples to meet my wife. After we met through her taking a professional photograph of my son, I called her and said that I enjoyed her spirit (which I have grown to adore) and wondered if we could get together sometime. We did.

Unless you develop a close that is comfortable for you, you will find yourself stumbling around at the end of an interesting encounter or avoiding a real ending of the conversation with the person you just met. You won't want it to end because you haven't gotten what you wanted (a date or phone number), and you can't bring it to a close because you can't bring yourself to ask for a date or a phone number. Can you see how this makes you appear to the other person? She or he is probably having the same feelings and difficulty, but of course, will expect you to be the one who knows how to handle it. Thus, when you have a good line ready, it makes it much easier for both of you.

Asking for a first date is difficult for everyone. But more often than you might expect, a person that you are attracted to may also feel a spark for you. When this situation comes up, the person that practices an approach or a line like the ones I have shared above will be able to pull it off.

Now you are worried because you like this man, and the train is coming to your station. You want to get a date with him or at least give him your phone number. Should you hand him your business card? Stay on the train? Or get off and watch this special opportunity dissolve into the sunset?

## Dealing with Rejection

The main reason most of us can't stick our necks out and meet people easily is that we are afraid of making fools of ourselves. In other words, we are afraid of rejection. As I have indicated throughout this book and especially in Chapter 11, if you are fully yourself, you will attract people into your life who will help you feel validated and comfortable. This principle can be a great help in facing your fear of rejection.

If you are rejected, it probably wouldn't have been a good relationship for you anyway. The natural selection process is at work, and it's comforting to remember this. It saves you from spending time where your energy wouldn't bring you what you were looking for, and it frees you up to put your time and attention somewhere more productive.

When I first met her, Daniella, a former client of mine, took every rejection in a relationship as a devastating event. Now, with more self-knowledge and better relationship skills, her approach is completely different. If someone she is attracted to isn't interested, or if a new relationship doesn't pan out in the sorting stage, she feels like she is being saved from something. She just takes it as a signal to move on.

If you find that you are always attracted to people who reject you, then you have to face the fact that on an unconscious level, you don't want a relationship that will validate you and make you feel loved for who you are. If this is your pattern with relationships, again I suggest that you consider therapy to get to the bottom of the issue.

During the sorting process, distortions about your love objects can really get in your way. The first three chapters of this book discussed various aspects of this dilemma. Remember that a relationship consists of a good match between two people. This is not the same thing as being two wonderful, healthy people. We are all wounded and have rough edges. Some people match up better than others. Rejection is part of finding the match for you.

### Three Truths to Help You Through Difficult Times

The emotional issues surrounding fear of rejection are deep and strong. Learning to deal with them is difficult for most people. I can offer some thoughts that may help.

There are three truths that can help you through a paralyzing fear of rejection:

- When you are rejected, it has very little to do with you.

- You wouldn't really want to be with someone who doesn't want to be with you.

- You are probably being saved from something.

**When you are rejected, it has very little to do with you.** This is a simple truth about how people make judgments about other people. We humans do this by reviewing the other person through our own lenses or filters. These in turn have been formed by our history of people similar to the individual now under the magnifying glass, or by situations with people who have created pain in our lives.

---

Some people match up better than others. Rejection is part of finding the match for you.

---

If someone rejects your offer of a date after an initial meeting, remember that they don't know you well enough to do any kind of in-depth evaluation. For instance, the reason why Bob turned you down for a coffee date is because you have brown eyes and pale skin—just like the sister he doesn't get along with. The reason Karen didn't want to give you her phone number was because you are really nice, and she has had bad experiences in her life with her father who seemed nice but was controlling. Thus she fears losing herself to a nice guy. The reason Jess didn't call you back was because he just got out of a relationship, and he's not ready to take another risk right now. These reasons are often unconscious to most people. They just act on them without fully understanding them themselves.

Judy didn't want to go out because you are too good-looking and she was always teased about being fat by her family. She just knows that you'll reject her, and she'd rather not get started. Josh backed off when he found out that you are a recovering alcoholic. When he was growing up, his mother was a sloppy drunk, and he lived his early years terrified of being embarrassed.

The point is that you never really know another person's reasons for rejecting you. In a dating situation, people don't know you well enough to make an informed judgment about what it would be like to be with you. All that anyone can do is use their personal lenses to sort through people as possible mates and find people who seem to fit.

If you don't fit for somebody, it isn't because something is wrong with you. It's just that you don't feel like a good fit to that other person. You, of course, do your own sorting and rejecting too, and it's important that you do. Anyone who wants to be involved with you also gets scrutinized through your personal window of preferences and history. Everyone has his or her ideas about who does and doesn't belong with them, and this has to be respected.

In looking for someone to share their lives with, different people need and want different things. Rejection is the sharp edge of the selection process, but it's a necessary part of dating and sorting for seekers of a serious relationship—even though selecting feels good and rejecting hurts. Until you can face rejection and do some rejecting yourself, you are probably not ready to choose a good mate for yourself.

**You wouldn't want to be with someone who doesn't want to be with you.** This is the second principle about rejection. What creates problems for many people is the longing for attachment at any cost, regardless of the feedback you are getting and what the other person is clearly telling you. However, once you have decided that you only want a relationship in which you can be loved for who you are, better things will come your way. At that point, you will be free to be unapologetically yourself and be loved for it. And if someone doesn't want to be with you as you are, you won't want to be with them.

When you decide that only a person who loves and accepts you is right for you, amazing things happen. You open the door inside yourself for a relationship that will work, and you develop an attitude of detachment about the sorting process. You can let people be who they are—even if they don't fit with you—without taking it personally. It also becomes self-evident why you might *only* want to be with a person whose past history and associations makes them reject you.

Here are several reasons why someone might want to be with someone who rejects them:

- He has something I want and don't have yet.

- She is attractive.

- I feel like a failure if he doesn't accept me.

- I'm lonely.

- She can fix my life.

- He is successful, and I'm poor.

- I would look good with her.

- My biological clock is running out.

None of these are good reasons to get into a relationship. Wait for someone who fits with you and wants to be with you. If events are behind what you or your parents may have wanted, forget about that and take your time anyway. We live in a society of late bloomers, and there are millions of people in their thirties, forties, fifties, and beyond who want relationships. One of the astounding things about nature is how we all can be matched with someone who loves us.

**You are probably being saved from something.** This is the third principle about rejection. Think of rejection—both doing it and having it done to you—as sparing you from being with someone with whom you would be on edge, always worrying and working on being worthy or accepted. There is enough of that when the fit is good. Be grateful for the ability to reject because it helps you go on to a mate who matches you.

There is no substitute for getting out there and being seen and met. Prince Charming may come flying through your window in a lucid dream, but in real life, you have to put yourself in his path. Fear of rejection can be a big deterrent in doing this. Instead, I suggest that you see it as a valuable skill to learn—both in the doing and in the receiving. It's for your own good and for the future of your relationships.

One way to practice rejecting is to run a personal ad. You'll have many responses that aren't right for you and you'll reject them. Also, the first encounters with many people won't feel right, and you'll have to reject them or be stuck with them. In doing all of this, you'll experience doing the rejecting and you'll get used to it as a process rather than a condemnation.

## Exercises to Help You Meet People

The first four exercises will help you form stock phrases you can use for initiating, engaging, and closing; then, we'll address rejection.

**Exercise 1.** Write your responses to these exercises under "My Strategy for Meeting Potential Partners." The first stock phrase that will be handy is something to initiate with. Think of what would fit in many general situations. Questions are good. "Does the bus often come late?" "Have you found this cleaners to be really good?" "How do you prepare those mustard greens, if I might ask?" "Is rain predicted this afternoon, do you know?"

You could make statements of admiration, for example, "I really like that sweater, did you buy it locally?" Notice that a question follows the statement so that a conversation can begin. If you simply say, "I really like your sweater," he'll say thank you, and you'll be back to wondering what to say. Some further examples are, "You seem to be familiar with this train stop, could I ask you something?" or "That purse is outrageous, what made you buy a purse with a clock on the front?" Use props and circumstances, like a near car crash, a dog, a swirl of wind, or bumping into someone to start conversations. Shared experiences bring people together. For example, during times of weather crisis people talk easily to each other. They have a prop, and can act in a less guarded way, which is how they wish they could always live. Be friendly and social, and most people will respond.

Write down a few examples you could use, and then go out today and practice one on someone who looks friendly. Keep practicing until you feel confident. Then, you are ready to spot the man or woman of your dreams and make a connection.

**Exercise 2.** Engaging lines are easier to rehearse than initiating lines. Here's how. In your book, list your interests: surfing, playing tennis, singing, cooking, skiing, hiking, talking politics, investing, working for the environment, reading, going to movies, and so on. Now write what makes you different from most people you know: you hate dogs and cats, you hate television, you work two hours a day, you used to be a biker, you travel to Japan every other month, you tutor disadvantaged children, you write poetry, you visit old people, you used to be a nun. Now list what you strongly believe in and have thought out. This can be political, metaphysical, sociological, or spiritual. Now, write a sentence for each of your strong beliefs by putting it into an "I've been thinking recently that . . . " format. Next, write a sentence about each of your strong interests and things that make you unique. These will be engaging lines to bring out when they fit the occasion. Having practiced a way of saying them will help enormously.

**Exercise 3.** Closing lines can also be stock phrases. To work them out, use the examples I supply and vary them to suit you. "I've really enjoyed this chat, would you be interested in continuing it sometime?"

or, "I have felt a good connection with you, would you like to have coffee sometime?" Such open-ended questions don't ask too much of the other person and make it easier to give a positive response. For instance, if you close with an invitation to dinner, you've raised the ante and might scare her off.

You should now be able to look at your notebook and have some ideas and lines for initiating, engaging, and closing. Practice on easy people first, have fun with this, and then make it work for you.

**Exercise 4.** If you think meeting people in this way will be impossible for you, try rehearsing the meeting through visualization. Imagine you see a person you want to meet, think of the surroundings, and find a prop or conversation starter. Visualize initiating, then engaging, and then asking for a date. This mental practice can be a great help in getting started.

**Exercise 5.** How about rejection? Under "Rejection and Me" write what you fear about rejection. Would you take it to mean that you are ugly, worthless, or incompetent? Look back at the section on rejection and write three other reasons you might have been rejected that don't reflect on you at all. For instance, I know I have not been rejected by everyone, therefore it couldn't be that I'm unattractive, or a terrible person; rather, it could be that she doesn't like short men, or men who talk about feelings, or she isn't ready for a relationship and knows I would get hurt. I could remind her of her older brother, father, boss, or an old lover who abandoned her.

Now write three things you were saved from by being rejected. You were saved from being on edge all the time in the relationship, worrying if you were OK. You were saved from working out a big issue that you triggered in the person. You were saved from having to deal with her projections that weren't really about you. You were saved from the pain of being with a person who wasn't ready for a relationship and knew it, but wasn't telling you. Maybe he was fatally sick, on the run, having an affair and couldn't tell you, and so on.

Think about ways you rejected others and try and put it into the perspective of match rather than judgment. For instance, I rejected women for romance who I thought were wonderful people, but the chemistry wasn't there. I didn't make big judgments about them as people, just as romantic partners. Chemistry is something that we don't know all the components of but still trust as a way of making decisions.

**Exercise 6.** For a more thorough exercise about rejection, run a personal ad and sort through the responses, rejecting some and answering others. You will see how superficial your reasons are for rejecting—you don't even know the people—and how important rejecting is if you are following your intuition. Being on the rejecting side of the picture will push you to understand that being rejected and rejecting are necessary parts of the dating process.

Good luck and be kind to yourself.

# 5

# Specialized and Exotic Techniques for Meeting Partners

If the last chapter wasn't enough for you—you've tried it all before—this chapter is designed to push you into the graduate level of meeting people. You will still use the initiating, engaging, and closing skills but in many more situations—some obvious, others much more creative.

## Some Detective Work

You become a detective and carefully figure out where the type of person you want to meet is likely to hang out. Once you've determined that, you use the three-part method of initiating, engaging, and closing to go after him or her.

First, make a profile of your potential partner. What matters to you? Profession, education, age, parenting status, income, interests, political leanings, awareness of certain issues, and all and any of the other qualities important to you should be listed. If the qualities most important to you are less tangible—for instance, you know that a person who can talk out misunderstandings is high on your list—that is still a quality to put into the profile.

Next, figure out where that person might be found during the week, on weekends, or after work hours. The rest of this chapter describes places that you can consider in this exploration.

> First, make a profile of your potential partner—all and any qualities important to you should be listed, even less tangible ones like the ability to talk out misunderstandings. Then you determine where this person can be found.

## Bookstores

If you want to meet an intelligent, thoughtful person who is a professional, financially able, good-looking, and gracious, start hanging out at the best bookstore in your area, preferably one open late. While hanging out, keep looking for that person by identifying clues like clothes, smiles, way of treating other people, and the sections of the store he or she is drawn to.

If you spot someone you think fits your desires, use a natural and decidedly unflashy line to make the approach. "Excuse me, are you familiar with this author?" Say this as you show him or her a book from a nearby shelf. Or, "Would you be able to help me . . . "; men especially love to help. You might ask for a recommendation or information. You must, of course, follow this initiating line with an engaging line, and follow that, when appropriate, with a closing line.

This will be difficult to do right off. The best way to overcome your barriers is to practice with people of both sexes, especially if you are not attracted to them. Then you'll be ready for the real thing.

## Lectures

Lectures provide a lot of opportunity if you stay on your feet as much as possible. Once you sit down, your scope is limited. Standing and milling is always more inclusive. You are also seen more often, and the rule of three has a chance to create an easier opportunity for making the approach. By the way, I have been told that certain mind-body teachers and spiritual leaders have more men in their audiences than other lecturers.

Once again, know what your initiating line will be so you won't have to think one up on the spot. "I'm enjoying him or her (the speaker) are you?" This is spoken in a matter-of-fact tone. Or, "This is my first chance to hear him or her, have you come before?"

It's crucial that you give yourself the freedom to initiate and move on if there is no interest, or you'll get stuck with someone with whom you aren't engaging but also can't extricate yourself. Milling, saying hello, moving on, returning, and saying hi again work very well.

## Book Signings

Principles about balance of men or women operate here according to the author and topics. If I were a black man and wanted to be in a room full of black women, for example, I would go to a Terry McMillan reading. The women would be feisty but easy to approach with some line like, "Do you really think all black men are like that (or all men in general)?" Or, "Do women really talk that way with each other?"

Although women make up the biggest book market, men go to see certain authors more than others, and I don't mean just fly tying topics. Pick an author and a book topic that will draw the kind of person you want to meet. Make up a few initiating lines and go hang out. Don't sit down too quickly or get bogged down in long, tedious discussions with someone with whom you see no potential.

## The Zoo and Playgrounds

If you are a single parent, the zoo offers a great opportunity to meet other people with children. The zoo also offers you plenty of props, namely the animals and the children, which facilitate the initial contact: "I love these hippos." "Have you ever been here when they feed the lions? Their roars really get the kids entranced."

Playgrounds are the same, except you sit around more and exchange meaningful smiles with the other parents until a conversation buds. Of course, you could train your child to go play with her or his child so you can go make conversation, but even I think that is going too far.

## Political and Other Gatherings

The numerous one-day political, community, and environmental gatherings that occur everywhere are a great opportunity to get to know people while working with them. Props and opportunities to be personal abound. These gatherings might be a cleanup effort on the beach, highway, park, or urban area; or a fund-raising event for a specific group.

Keeping an eye on the paper and an ear tuned to the radio for these events can keep you hopping.

The advantages of working with people and seeing how they interact with others make the time you put in well worth it. Especially since you will probably only want to go to the events you believe in; you'll be doing some good and making new contacts all at once.

**Hint:** Remember that people you get to know at these functions all have friends—some of them single—who they enjoy introducing to other singles. All contacts, therefore, become important for you, not just the single variety. However, you will have to do some low-level advertising, like mentioning your difficulties at finding available men or women who interest you.

## Church and Classes

Again, these two areas, church and classes, give you the opportunity to get to know people while doing things with them. Sometimes a person first spotted doesn't make a big impression, but when you work with them, they begin to shine through. Few situations offer as good a chance for this as church and classes. I remember in graduate school, a small group within a class worked on a presentation together, and we got to know each other. My classmates' beauty and depth really came through over the hours we spent together. Also, you will be relaxed in these settings, taking your time, not feeling like you have to make a move immediately; this helps enormously.

You don't have to be in school; you can go to short term classes to achieve this goal. Picking classes that attract you and a person you want to meet certainly makes the most sense. If you don't like the outdoors, don't go to an outdoors-type class. You'll meet a nice rugged man, fall in love, and then fight for the rest of your lives about his always wanting to run off to the awful outdoors instead of staying home with you. All your interests don't need to be synchronized, but it sure is nice to have major forms of recreation in common.

---

Because people love to hook up single people, all contacts can be fruitful, not just the single variety. However, you do need to do some low-level advertising like mentioning your difficulties at finding available men or women who interest you.

Church offers similar opportunities and the same caveats. If it works for you, you are probably already doing it.

## Computer Fairs

Although computer fairs  are usually expensive to get into, that fact alone may serve as a screen for your search. You will most likely find serious people who have some money. That may be what you are looking for. The other advantage is that there will be props galore to make the initial contact, and plenty of opportunity to engage also. Checking for wedding rings is advisable in scenes such as these.

## Newspaper Stories, Letters to the Editor, or Service Ads with Pictures

Many newspapers contain ads with people's pictures in them. Service directories also frequently publish pictures (these advertise accountants, therapists, dentists, holistic healers, and so on.) There are also interview-type articles in which four or five people are asked a question and the individual responses are given next to a picture.

What to do? If you like the picture and the answers, look up the person's number and call or write a note saying that you found him interesting, and if he is single, you would like to have lunch or something. If this sounds brazen, and you couldn't see yourself doing it, think about the fact that the person who is in the newspaper or in the service ad might be having just as difficult a time meeting interesting and available people. If you can frame your approach as a possible friendship, it makes it easier and expands your possibilities. "I saw your answer in the paper's column and thought it was great, just what I would have said. I'm making a daring step here to see if you would want to get together for lunch sometime. It may seem weird, but I thought, why not." You may be surprised to hear back, "I don't think it's weird, I think it shows a lot of courage and creativity. How about lunch?"

I have used this approach twice and it worked both times. I saw an ad in a directory for services and worked up my courage to call a woman I found very attractive, and I liked what she did for a living. I simply told her all of this and asked if she would be interested in meeting for lunch. She was. We did, and we became friends. Her first comment was to compliment me on such a creative way to meet people, even saying I should write it up somewhere.

Do the same thing with letters to the editor of your local newspaper. I have also done this and it turned into a good friendship. With this method, you can't really know how the person looks or if there will be chemistry before the meeting, but it's a good way to meet interesting and involved people.

## People in the Newspapers

What if you enjoy a writer in your newspaper? Or maybe a person quoted in a paper? You can look up their home or work place number and call them. Tell them that you enjoy their work or what they had to say, and ask if they're single. Why not? It sounds too bold and invasive? It is bold, but maybe you are too. However, it isn't invasive. It's flattering. What married person wouldn't enjoy the brief flirtation of that kind of phone call? It would give them extra points at home at dinner: "I had a call from a man today who liked what I write and wondered if I was single. He wanted to have lunch." Her husband is immediately put on the alert about what an interesting wife he has. A little, safe jealousy could perk up the attention he gives her.

The hard thing about these bold approaches is the initial few calls. After receiving positive feedback for your courage and creativity, you will relax into it, knowing that the worst thing that could happen is the person might say, "I'm not interested." You can handle that! But, I promise you the responses will be much more positive. Here is a sample approach:

"I read your remarks in the paper this morning and wanted to compliment you on them."

"Well, thanks. I guess a lot of people read papers because a number of friends have called."

"I agreed so much with your feelings about _____." At this point, you insert a question about something that you've thought of before making the call. This is the point in the conversation that you engage and become more than just another complimentary call. It might go like this: "What experiences led you to that statement about _____?" Or, "I've been involved with teenagers for four years and came to the conclusion that _____." Or, "I was wondering how you manage to deal with the problem in your comments about _____?"

The point is that you have to engage in the conversation before you can close. If you don't get into a personal conversation of some interest, asking about his or her being single will sound weird and much too forward. But if you have engaged the person first, making a statement afterwards, like, "You sound very interesting, you aren't single are you?"

"No, I'm not but I appreciate your compliments and interest."

"I hope I haven't offended you by asking that?"

"Not at áll. I admire your courage. You know, I have a friend who's single who also works with me on this project. She's a really great person. You two should meet."

"Gee, this is sounding like a dating service, isn't it? Wouldn't it be amazing if we liked each other. We'd have a great story about how we met. I'll give you my number, and if she wants to meet in some place of her choosing, I'll certainly do it."

Nothing may come of this. Or you may meet the friend and have nothing in common. Or, you might. Remember, you are engaged in a numbers game; you will have to meet and sort through a lot of people to find the right one. All the suggestions here are to help you have a lot of people coming through your life.

---

The hard thing about these bold approaches is the initial few calls. After receiving positive feedback for your courage and creativity, you will relax into it.

---

Let's say the answer to your question about whether she is single is yes. Note how scary that question would be if you haven't engaged. The art of engaging is the key to all of these suggestions. If you aren't good at that, do the exercises in the previous chapter. Practice in supermarket checkout lines. You are scary to people if you move from initiating to closing without engaging. Becoming personal is the relationship skill.

In this case, you have had a friendly conversation and the person is feeling good with you and receives your question in that spirit. She says she is single and you say that you are too, and you've enjoyed talking with her so much that you wonder if she would like to have a drink or coffee sometime. She figures it's a public place, what does she have to lose, and agrees to a time and a place.

To get into the mood of these bold approaches, try putting yourself in the other person's place. If they are single and don't want to remain that way, they too are having a hard time meeting the right person. You are giving them an opportunity. Work for a newspaper or being quoted for some work they are doing, doesn't mean they have all the dates they can handle. They may be discouraged about meeting people just like you might be. See yourself as providing a service to others with this approach and it will not seem so unreal. Making connections is what it's about, and people enjoy doing that, for themselves and for others. Most married people, by the way, love to set up their single friends. So, the scenario above is not unrealistic—as long as you have engaged.

## Dancing

My editor is the best person I know at meeting possible partners. She does it through folk dancing. In most cities and towns, there are frequent dances of all kinds. There are ethnic dances, square dances, round dances, contra dances, and jitterbug dances. I think that the folk dances are the best of all for meeting people because they attract a crowd that likes dancing and flirting. Also the dances have romance built into them. For instance, Contra dancing is made for flirting. And, you will see the same people over and over at certain dances, which will make the first encounter easier (the rule of three).

One thing to be aware of when dating people in a small circle, such as a dance group, club, or association, is that you will have to be very scrupulous about how you handle the dates, intimacy, and endings. This is so you can see the person again and feel fine even if the dating didn't work out. It is great training in integrity to date people in a group that you belong to. Often, misunderstandings develop, and if they are not cleared up, gossip starts that you will have little control over.

My suggestion is to move very slowly, and get intimate with someone from a group that you belong to only after you have decided you can be trusting friends.

---

My editor is the best person I know at meeting possible partners. She does it through folk dancing.

---

## Computer Networks

The latest singles meeting place is the Net (short for Internet). People who subscribe to other networking computer services are finding meeting places there also. You enter into a group discussion, and if you want to go to a separate place to talk with just one individual, you can do that also. The possible drawback is that you may fall in love with the thoughts on the screen, the wit, or the depth, but may have absolutely no chemistry when you meet the person. But this is true for so many meetings in the modern world that you have to think beyond that and remember you are playing a numbers game.

Another problem with computer networks is that some of the people you meet, on-line, will live far away. However, you can be selective about who you follow up with, and also in this situation, follow my advice for personal ads: keep all first encounters brief. In this case, don't spend hours on the computer with someone until you have met in person to see if there is chemistry.

## Distinctive Stores

I was in the Whole Earth Access store looking for a gift for my son when it dawned on me what a great place that would be to meet people. It has a zillion departments (books, electronics, vacuums, kitchen, gardening, hardware, clothing, and furniture) all under one roof. It's different from a department store in that it is more of a sprawl than Macy's with its segmented departments isolated from each other. The overlapping departments make running into people and spotting interesting ones much easier. And think of all the props! "Excuse me, have you ever used one of these before?" "Sorry to bother you, but I wonder if you know anything about this tool?" "Hi, I'm new to this city and wonder if you think this is the best-priced store for this sort of thing?" The opportunities are endless for spontaneous initiations. If you have your engaging lines practiced, you can merge them neatly into almost any department you are in. "Excuse me, would you happen to know if this is a good boot for climbing? . . . You don't climb. Well, I'm new to this area and want to get involved in something new for me, do you have any suggestions? . . . You play volleyball. Where does that happen? Can new people join in? I love to be active and it's hard to get started, any chance of you letting me know about a good volleyball event? I'll give you my number."

What if you spent one hour every weekend in a store such as this one and met two people each trip? Something is bound to happen, and the best thing is, you know that you are attracted to each of these people because you have seen them and spoken with them.

## Special Advertising

You have an alternative to advertising in the personals. A small billboard, a sign on a bus, or some creative ad in media other than the personals section has the advantage of attracting people who would not use the personals. These people might be just what you are looking for. The ad can be tailored to you alone or even to a group that shares the cost and the rewards. Almost assuredly, you will get a huge number of responses, as the movie, *Sleepless in Seattle,* demonstrated. The biggest problem in your search will be how to handle large numbers of potential partners respectfully and efficiently. Another danger to avoid is the idea that you must interview each person as if it were a job placement. That really does not work for finding romance, for all the reasons that are listed at the end of my introduction to this book.

Each person must be treated as if he or she were the only person to be with—this is difficult when you have a mailbag of seventy responses. One tip is to make your ad very specific, with the intention of discouraging unwanted responses, rather than so broad that you get an overwhelming response with no sorting value. For instance, "Hot babe wants to meet gorgeous, rich man around thirty years old. Write . . . " would be a disaster. More helpful might be, "I'm an attractive, smart, financially secure woman who can give a lot and want a man with good relationship skills and willingness to give. Write . . . ". This ad will be easier to deal with because any response that has no energy, smarts, or relationship skills gets thrown in the wastebasket or sent to a co-worker that you are not fond of.

This approach will cost more than the ordinary paper or electronic personals but will yield good results. Of course the ad copy will make a big difference—you would do well to have many people read it and give you feedback before taking the plunge. If you take this approach, you must remember that you are not getting partners or mates with your ad; only possibilities that have to be sorted through. My wife read a newspaper article about four men who put an ad on a billboard and got 800 replies. This technique could be a case of "be careful what you pray for because you might get it."

> This may be a case of "be careful of what you pray for because you might get it."

## Obituaries

This may sound ghoulish at first, but it has its advantages. I read an obituary this morning about a woman, forty-six, described as an active, smart, caring therapist who was involved in numerous projects, and was survived by her teenage son and husband. The idea that I always wanted to try when I was single came back to me—what a great way to find quality people. Here we have a man who has been married long enough to have a teenage son, with a wife who was smart, liberated, and perhaps happy. This man will soon be lonely and available.

Now comes the tough part. When will he be available? How much grieving does he need to go through? If this approach is appealing to your adventuresome spirit, I would recommend two things. The first is that you learn the elements of grief by reading a few books about it so that you know what you are going to be dealing with and can be helpful. And the second thing is that you do not use today's paper for this project, but rather go back a year or two, and search in those papers. Even though I never took the time, or maybe had the nerve, to try this approach, I often thought of it, and still believe it is worth the risk because of the quality of person you may find.

Of course, once your prospect is identified, you still have to be creative and detective-like in going about meeting him or her. I have total confidence in anyone willing to attempt this method to be able to pull off the meeting with great aplomb.

## Making a Project Out of It

This is the key: you have a project to accomplish. If you take an active—I didn't say desperate—approach to encouraging a number of potential mates to come through your life, you will be in a much better position to make the right choice. But, it is a project. And so is marriage or a serious relationship. It always takes attention and effort to have a relationship go well. Why shouldn't it be the same for finding the correct partner?

> You'll be clearing your life of overwork, too many hobbies, lone-ranger pursuits, the cranky need for space, and any other pattern you may have gotten into that will not make room for another person.

I suggested in Chapter 4 that you spend the same amount of time in the search as you would in a relationship. Part of the reason for this is to give enough time and effort to get results. However, the other reason is to make sure that you are making room in your life for a serious relationship, and not just talking about it. You'll be clearing your life of overwork, too many hobbies, lone-ranger pursuits, the cranky need for space, and any other pattern you may have gotten into that will not make room for another person. After all, another person will take time away from something else you are presently doing. Therefore, the best way to check and see if you want to give that time is to put it into the pursuit of a good mate. But don't exhaust yourself either. Have fun throughout the process, gather stories to tell friends of your adventures and risks, and learn about a part of you that is daring and fun. Good hunting!

# Part Three

# Sorting: Is He or She Right for You?

# 6

# Dating Feedback: What You See Is What You Get

How many times have you said, "What broke us up was exactly what I saw on the first date but didn't take it seriously?" How many times have you heard a friend say the same thing? I am convinced that everything in those first few minutes or hours should be taken at face value. In other words, what you see in those first times together is how the person really is. I have been in too many three-month-long relationships that ended for reasons I should have seen on the first date. All of that changed when I started to pay attention to those early warning signs.

> I have been in too many three-month-long relationships that ended for reasons I should have seen on the first date.

Most people date as if they were shopping for clothes. They try people on and see how they fit—mainly on the basis of instant attraction. If they feel uncomfortable with the fit after a few months or years, they end the relationship and go to the next rack for another try-on. A much more useful approach would be to recognize the kind of person you want or don't want right from the start—don't get intimate with someone unless he or she seems like what you are looking for. This is a different approach than most people use today, but it saves a lot of wear and tear on your emotions. I call this sorting.

The single change that will help you date more productively is to stop making excuses for what you see and simply accept whatever it is as feedback. Most of us have at some time seen a potential red flag to a successful relationship during the first lunch or dinner date. Then we go home and kid ourselves into believing that it will change. But this is the small beginning that leads to big trouble.

We ignore feedback for many reasons. Maybe you are strongly attracted to the person for other reasons. Or perhaps you make excuses because you have been lonely, and this is the first person you've met in months who isn't a total nerd. But let's pay attention now. Have you heard yourself making excuses, such as, "He's between jobs right now, and that's why he's in a bad mood." Have you heard a friend say, "She used to be a shopoholic, but she just tore up her charge cards." Or, "He probably interrupted me so much because he was nervous about just meeting." Or, "She doesn't smile because she is worried that I won't like the braces on her teeth." If you look back at the way these relationships turned out, you'll probably see that you were fooling yourself.

## Loretta and Rob

Loretta met Rob by answering an ad in the paper. They talked on the phone and found themselves laughing, cracking jokes, and enjoying the conversation. Afterwards, Loretta felt excited about their plans to meet for lunch in two days. Just maybe there were a few good men out there! In fact, she had such high expectations that she tried to calm herself down by telling herself, "He probably looks like a gorilla." But Loretta was wrong; Bob was quite handsome. When he smiled at her in the lobby of her favorite restaurant, she could feel her face blushing and her voice rising a little. Their first date was even more fun than their first telephone call, and afterwards, she felt like singing and telling all her friends. Her hope had been restored. There were good men!

Six months later, she knew that she couldn't keep seeing him. She told me that this man was really pretty confused and unrealistic about work and life in general. She came to see that he wasn't self-directed enough for her. She was scared that she would wind up taking care of him—somthing she saw her mother do for her father, which she hated. When I asked her if there were any signs of this on their first date, she said he spoke about being confused about his goals and direction. But at the time, she saw it as charming and vulnerable. She ignored her reservations because she found him to be immensely sexy.

## Look Before You Leap: An Introduction to the Concept of Sorting

Most of us have good intuition—and this is especially true on the first date. However, I'm a big believer that when you start having sex, your intuition flies out the window for a few months. This is a good reason to hold back on sex until you are through the sorting stage of dating.

---

> At the time, she saw his lack of direction as charming and vulnerable. She ignored her reservations because she found him to be immensely sexy.

---

**Sorting defined.** Sorting is the stage of dating when you are shopping. It's a stage when you're looking at the qualities of a potential partner and seeing if they fit. It's a time when you're getting to know someone—hopefully with your eyes, ears, and intuition open. This stage, which should last for several dates or however long it takes you to feel comfortable, should take place before *building intimacy*—you finish shopping before you purchase something.

Many people don't separate the two stages of sorting and building intimacy. They build intimacy and see how it feels. Then, when it stops feeling good, they start questioning the relationship. This would be fine if we all had unlimited time and emotional energy for this pursuit. It would also work if we weren't sensitive about being rejected. Most of us, however, do get hurt and begin to doubt ourselves in the process.

A lot of potential pain in dating can be avoided if you sort first, and only after a good selection, begin building intimacy. Think of it as a sequential process in two parts: sorting first, intimacy later. This might be criticized as unromantic, but if you haven't had the results you want up to now, maybe it's time to start being smarter in your choices. Maybe it's time to look before you leap. Going fishing is fun, but you don't have to bring everything home.

I see the sorting process as being smart and being careful. It's like doing research before you buy a car, or getting information about a potential employer before you take a job. The potential for satisfaction or pain in each of these situations is certainly high. And if you've taken the time to get to know someone before climbing in between the sheets, the long-term potential for intimacy will be much greater.

## Intuition Before Intimacy

Attempts at building intimacy—besides jumping into bed—include sharing life stories and problems on the first date. This gives a false sense of intimacy. Deep emotional sharing belongs in the intimacy-building stage because it presumes there is a person who really cares on the other end of the sharing. That isn't always true right away.

The ultimate builder of true intimacy is time. We are often tempted to create "California instant intimacy" when there isn't any foundation for it. Unfortunately, this can wreck the chances of building true intimacy in its own time later on. How many times have you spent a weekend with someone you just met? Then how long has that relationship lasted? California-style relationships that began with a high tide and then lasted happen more often in the movies than in real life.

For most people who want to get off the whirlwind romance train and switch tracks to a relationship that lasts, it's better to slow down. Using intuition on the first few dates and not attempting to get deeply intimate before sorting will give you the best chance of success. You can be personal, of course, but that is different from trying to get intimate on the first date.

## The Wisdom of Taking Your Time

During the sexual revolution of the late sixties and seventies, many people felt that they had to go to bed right away with whomever they were dating. But things are different now. I remember a conversation I overheard back then in a cafe between a man and a woman who were close friends. The woman was telling the man that she wasn't ready to go to bed yet with someone she had just begun to date. Her male friend replied, "Take your time. A good man will wait for you." That was true then, and it's even more true now.

What I'm emphasizing again here is sorting. Wait to be intimate until it feels comfortable and right. If you are seeing a good-looking, funny guy who goes into spasms of laughter to avoid talking about himself, and this doesn't match up with what you want, stop dating him. You'll be better off leaving that beginning as it is and trying elsewhere. If you have begun to date a woman who always interrupts you when you try to talk about yourself, and you're the kind of person who needs a good listener, don't go forward with a relationship. Only go forward if you feel you have a good chance of meeting your primary needs.

> Using intuition on the first few dates and not attempting to get deeply intimate before sorting will give you the best chance of success.

I have counseled many people who are angry at their newfound mate for not living up to their expectations. If certain aspects of the relationship, such as sex, feel really good, it's hard to face the fact that there are too many problems between you to make the romance work. If all you want is casual sex, go ahead and enjoy the chemistry. But if you're looking for a lasting relationship, chemistry alone doesn't work.

## Every Good Relationship Isn't a Marriage Partner

During the time that I was dating, I had to learn two difficult and confusing truths: First, I wasn't going to fall in love with every woman I liked. Then I had to learn that every woman I fell in love with wasn't a marriage partner for me. These were big passages for me into the ways of the world.

Brenda wanted a man who was successful and socially adept. Michael seemed to fit the bill exactly on their first date, which was set up by a friend at work. She did have a strange sensation, however, of being with a brother, not a lover. But all of her friends told her that good relationships should start with friendship, so she decided to give it a try.

After five months of dinners, trips, long talks, and minimal sex, Brenda looked back at her first reaction to Michael as a brother, and realized that's really the way it was. He was a great friend, but she didn't ever feel turned on by him—not at the beginning and not now. She couldn't force the attraction to be there when it was not, so she had to change the nature of the relationship. Five years later, he is still like a brother to her—and to her husband and their two kids.

We often want a relationship badly enough that we think we can will it to work. We make adjustments in our heads about how we can change to fit or how the other person will change if we love them enough. But that rarely happens.

## What You See Is What You Get

American culture is filled with romance and daydreams. Our role models come from Hollywood, and our early archetypes are laced with tales of Cinderella and Prince Charming. But if "happily ever after" has eluded you so far, it might be time to switch philosophies and enter the world of adults—where what you see is what you get.

It's natural to feel on cloud nine when you meet someone special. However, all the qualities and circumstances that you *ascribe* to the other person on that first lunch or coffee date may be wishful thinking. If these qualities aren't there for anyone who isn't wearing romance-colored glasses to see, you may be fooling yourself.

"She thinks I'm wonderful! She's a great listener too. I don't think I've ever met anyone who listens so well. Call me an egomaniac, but it really turns me on." Jeff was ebullient during the second counseling session he had with me. "She's bright and upbeat and just a great woman." Three months later, Jeff had changed his tune. "She doesn't have her own life. I often feel like I'm going out with myself instead of two of us. Sure she's attentive and giving, but who is she? She's got to find a life of her own. She's boring!"

The way we delude ourselves at the outset of a potential romance is certainly understandable. If we feel attracted to someone, we want to make it work. I have often seen clear warning signals on a first encounter that registered somewhere in my brain, only to be quickly forgotten. Three months later, when the relationship wasn't going well, those signals came flooding back into my memory. I realized that I had known the problems right from the beginning and had blinded myself. The person hadn't changed. I had simply wished away the parts I couldn't cope with.

When we want a relationship to make us feel OK, or to make us whole in some way, we are most likely to try and perform magic with

> It's natural to feel on cloud nine when you meet someone special. However, all the qualities and circumstances that you *ascribe* to the other person on that first date may be wishful thinking.

the other person. "He is really 'down' right now, and that's why he never wants to do things that are fun." "She's so beautiful, and I'm sure she must be more sensitive when she's rested." "He's shy, but wait until he gets to know me. He'll be more open then."

The key to successful dating is paying attention to these signals. This means that you continue to keep your eyes open—regardless of how infatuated you are—and not let important information dissolve into those lovely eyes and great smile across the table. Sorting means going through many people to find the right fit. When you know who you are and what type of partner would be good for you, you are in a much better position to listen to feedback about the person.

## Paying Attention to Warning Signals

Let me give you a few examples. If John meets Susie over coffee and notices that she is extremely nervous, he can do a number of things. He can see if she changes the next time they are together; he can ask her about it and use her answer as feedback; or he can realize that she isn't a good match for him because he is also nervous and she is already driving him crazy. He doesn't want someone more nervous than himself.

Like many people, John may be tempted to focus on her "come here, big boy" smile, which is really exciting him, and dismiss the fact that she has nervous mannerisms. If he does this and gets involved with her, he'll put up with her habits for about two months. Then they'll start driving him nuts, making him more nervous, self-conscious, and judgmental. Finally, he'll be angry at her for having these nervous habits—and leave her. It just doesn't seem fair that they both have to go through that.

If Joan meets Geof at a sales conference, is attracted to him, but notices that she feels weird about talking with him about personal things, she also can respond in a number of ways. She can ignore it as the awkwardness of a first encounter. She can wonder about his ability to be personal. Or she can trust her intuition totally and realize that he will not be a good match for her since she is completely at ease and most alive when being personal.

The price of ignoring feedback is the agony of breaking up later. Too often this painful experience takes a toll on each person, leaving them blaming themselves and recovering. I believe it is far better to leave an attractive person as soon as you know it won't work out. It's cleaner that way. If you get feedback that tells you someone is wrong for you in the first hour, you can avoid a lot of pain later on.

Everything potential partners do when you first meet is significant: the way they dress, the way they handle money—whether they pay for your meal, expect you to pay, or offer to split it—how they use eye contact, and what they are willing to talk about. All of this is feedback for you, so pay attention.

If your date's attention drifts to her nails and the contents of her purse when you are talking, that's feedback. If the guy can only talk about business and gets uneasy when you ask about whether he believes in the inner child, that's feedback. If she gives you practical suggestions about how to overcome your shyness on the first date; if he brags about deals and sharp maneuvers more than you want to hear; if there are long, uncomfortable silences, and your date is mystified when you share information about the way you think and feel; that's all feedback.

What do you do with it? You can either act on it right away or file it. If what the person does is clearly a turnoff to you, don't go out with her or him again. If you are more disturbed by it than turned off, you may want to talk about it. Or you may want to see how you feel about it on the second date. But listen to everything. What you have observed is probably some part of the truth about this person. Above all, don't excuse the behavior or rationalize it away as something that you can change.

## The Halfway House Syndrome

You might be thinking right now that this sounds harsh. After all, a person deserves a second chance. You yourself need a second chance from time to time. Let's take a closer look at this idea. Let's say you tell someone you will give him a sales job if he comes to see you right at 9:00 a.m. and convinces you that he would be good at it. The next morning, he arrives eighteen minutes late for the appointment wearing wide checkered pants with a big black belt, scuffed shoes, and a yellow cowboy shirt. Would you ignore what you're observing, namely, a person who is late when it is vital not to be and doesn't know how to dress? Would you give him the job?

---

Everything people do when they first meet you is significant: the way they dress, the way they handle money, how they use eye contact, and what they are willing to talk about. All of this is feedback for you, so pay attention.

---

It's obvious that hiring an applicant with such glaring problems would be inviting trouble later on. If you were running a halfway house, you might take this applicant under your wing and teach him about the way the world works. But are you running a halfway house at work or in your relationship life, or looking for a relationship with someone whose life is working and treats you well?

Is showing up for a date less important than showing up for a job interview? They both seem important to me. They both have to do with a future of sharing problems, responsibilities, and trust. So why not be as strict in judging them both. Have you ever felt as if you're running a halfway house when you are dating? Do you take fix-it jobs for relationships and try to shape them up? If this has been your pattern, ask yourself if you want to marry a person with broken wings.

"But," you may be thinking, "not everyone can make a decision that quickly. Also, some people don't come across at their best until some time has passed." I agree and encourage you to fit my general advice to your own style. If you, for instance, are a person who doesn't put your best foot forward until after a few dates, you'll feel comfortable waiting for the new person in your life to blossom as you do—when you're more comfortable. My advice is not to wait any longer than you would want for yourself. If, on the other hand, you are socially comfortable quickly, you'll want a person who can meet you in that trait. The main point is not to make excuses for the other person that you'll regret later.

## How and Why We Ignore Feedback

I once made a date with a woman for a casual dinner to see if we would like each other. We met through an ad. Throughout the evening, I noticed she would take anything that I said as a lead-in to talk about a similar feeling or experience in her own life. If I said that I was looking forward to my son's graduation, she would immediately talk about when her son graduated. There were never any questions about my son or where he was in school. I began to feel cut off, excluded, and used. So I decided to ask her about it and see what happened. What did I have to lose?

She was shocked that this was a problem and protested that she was only sharing. It was just her way, she explained. I decided that she would always do that, and if I got involved with her, I would always feel cut off. To my credit, that time I heeded my intuition. If such a bad fit is so apparent during the first hour of a date, imagine what would come up after the relationship got past the "being nice" stage?

When we make excuses for qualities we can't deal with, we only cover them up until they come out later as a larger problem. People do this for different reasons. Unconsciously, we may want to have some companionship or physical comfort, but perhaps this isn't the time for a serious involvement. So we start going out with someone, knowing on some level that it won't work out. We date for a number of months and then break up.

There may also be a desperate quality to not heeding the first intuition. Someone may want a relationship very badly and fear that there aren't many chances out there. Then, when someone comes along, they grab on—regardless of future consequences. A lack of belief in yourself can also create a sense of desperation that makes you ignore obvious signs that will cause pain later on.

Another reason for not heeding obvious signs of a mismatch is not wanting to turn someone down. There are people who cannot do the rejecting. When they feel the need to leave a relationship, instead of being direct, they make the relationship so unsatisfactory that the other person will end it. If this is you, it would be useful to get some professional help. There is no need to suffer with this problem for the rest of your life.

Another possibility is that deep within yourself, you are convinced that you can influence your partner to change. You may want a relationship very much and figure that if most of the person seems to fit, the rest could be molded over time. So many couples that I see in my therapy practice are working on getting rid of that myth. They have been trying to make each other change for years, and finally they are in so much pain that they are ready to leave. Marriage partners always have differences that emerge over time. The thing to remember while dating is that it is supposed to start out feeling very mutual and compatible.

## Taking Responsibility from the First Date

What I'm suggesting is that you start taking responsibility for creating a good relationship right from the start. One drawback to knowing this information about listening to your intuition and paying attention to feedback is that if you fail to heed it, you won't be able to blame the other person later on. You'll have to look in the mirror and admit to yourself that you entered the relationship knowing full well that he or she interrupted you and finished your sentences on the first date, but you were so busy drooling over the initial flirtation that you went ahead.

> You may want a relationship very much and figure that if most of the person seems to fit, the rest could be molded over time.

If this or a milder version is your pattern, you may want to check to see if your ambivalence about a serious relationship is keeping you in the three-months-and-then-the-end syndrome. It's a sabotaging technique. You can spend your life falling in love in a qualified way until it becomes unbearable. I'm assuming that you want something more stable.

Once you start listening to your intuition on the first date and heeding it, you won't be in and out of so many relationships. You may go through longer dry spells, but you will probably find the relationship you want in a shorter time.

## Red, Yellow, and Green Lights

Starting a new relationship is never without risks, but there is a very effective system to eliminate most surefire disasters. I call this the red, yellow, and green light system of dating.

A *red light* means your date has one or more qualities that you could not live with. Don't waste your time dating this person if you want to get married. A *yellow light* means the person has some qualities that may not be right for you, but you want to give it more time to see how it goes. Some people are nervous on a first date, and perhaps the behavior that bothers you will go away when he or she feels more comfortable with you. A *green light* means you are excited about your date, and he or she doesn't have any qualities you can see that you couldn't live with.

You use the information just like traffic signals. A green light means go ahead—from your intuition and the feedback you've received, it's safe to go ahead and date this person. A yellow light means proceed with caution. Slow down and take your time—this person has some qualities you should check out before you go ahead. A red light means stop—don't date this person. He or she has some qualities that you wouldn't marry, so don't waste your time.

**Red lights.** Learn to recognize which qualities, personality traits, and circumstances are red lights for you. Maybe your date doesn't take care of himself the way you do. She doesn't stop talking. He is rude. She is too much into her looks and not warm enough. He is only interested in how he looks to others. She doesn't want children and you do. He lives in Alaska, and you don't have any desire to move there. She loves opera, and you're into heavy metal. On top of that, she can't stand being in the country, and you like to spend every Sunday on your parents' farm. He loves his career and works seventy hours a week, and you're the kind of person who needs a lot of time from a partner. She drinks too much. He has a raging temper and can be violent. These are all red lights *if* they don't match what you want. A red light simply means the person isn't a good match for you. Stop! Don't pursue the relationship.

---

A red light means stop—don't date this person. He or she has some qualities that you wouldn't marry, so don't waste your time.

---

**Hint:** I have learned an odd but true rule of thumb. Always believe what people say about themselves if it is negative. If someone tells you, "I have a violent temper," or "I can be a real bitch," it's probably true. But when people talk about their positive qualities, take it with a grain of salt. It might be true, but do some reality testing. If someone says, "I'm really very sensitive and caring," or "I have enormous energy for being honest and sharing in a relationship," believe it after you see it.

People seem to know themselves well when they talk about their failings, but sometimes they fudge or exaggerate when discussing their finer qualities. Just because he says he is in touch with his feelings is no guarantee that the range of his emotions matches yours. Even though she claims she is impeccably honest, her style of honesty may be very different from yours. Trust your own view of their demonstration of these qualities. After all, this is something that is only revealed over time.

I used to believe the positive and minimize the negative. If a date told me that she has a problem knowing where she is going in life, I would minimize it—especially if she was attractive. Then, sure enough, what would start bothering me a number of months later would be that she was clinging onto my strength of direction and had little of her own. Again, I'm advocating paying attention. If you see a major problem right off, don't go ahead. Ignore the chemistry and listen to your intuition. If the feedback is negative, this is a red light.

**Yellow lights.** You notice things that concern you but would not necessarily make you stop seeing the person. Perhaps he wears funny clothes but doesn't seem to know any better. She is in recovery from drugs, and you want to make sure she continues. He hates his job, and you want to see how he handles that. She used to be angry at men, but you aren't feeling that from her right now. She wears too much makeup. His driving makes you nervous. She can't talk about her father without getting furious. He acts like a little boy with his mom. These are all qualities that you should take seriously, but they don't in themselves turn you off completely.

What may turn you off or turn you on is how the other person responds to these concerns. It's a good idea to talk about them early on if they are a yellow light for you. The most important feedback you'll get will come from your date's reaction to your concern. When you bring it up, pay a lot of attention to how he responds and to whether he relates your concern to himself. What if you mention how angry he gets when he talks about his dad? He might say, "Oh, do I?" Now ask yourself, "Do I want to be with someone who hasn't been able to recognize his anger yet?" That may not be important to you, but if it is, take it as feedback. He might also say, "Yeah, I know—you should have heard me a year ago. I've been working through that stuff in therapy." You can then talk about this until your intuition tells you more.

Yellow lights are indicators that you need more information. They will often change to green lights if the other person's awareness and manner of handling them fits well with you. They may also be the tip of an iceberg, hiding reactions, qualities, or lack of qualities that will quickly become red lights.

---

> What may turn you off or turn you on is how the other
> person responds to your concerns.

---

**Green lights.** You feel at ease with this person. You feel comfortable and are not aware of any red or yellow lights. You sense a comradeship between you. Things are easy—they should be easy at first. Enough will come up later in a serious relationship without it having to be hard at first. If you are struggling right at the beginning, look for red or yellow lights.

There is an important exception to the green light not being totally easy. In Chapter 2, I wrote about ambivalence and how a good connection can spark an unconscious fear that may sabotage the relationship. It's possible that a great connection with no red lights or even yellow lights might scare you so much that you'll try and create red lights. This is where it is helpful to know your own intimacy fears so you can catch yourself creating problems when they don't exist. I refer you to Chapters 2, 3, and 10 for more information.

Now that you know the rules, pay attention to green, yellow, and red lights. In this system of dating you look before you leap. It will save you a lot of time and pain later on. Stop at all red lights, check out yellow lights, and go ahead only on green. Then, you'll save your energy for the right relationship.

## What You Are Giving Out as Feedback

I wonder if thinking about what you give out as feedback makes you want to squirm or hide? "I don't want him to see how shy I am." "I've got to hide that I smoke." "I don't want her to know right away that I have children." As if you should be hiding your feedback so your new friend can't get an accurate reading!

Feedback is good. This is what helps us sort through the people we meet, decide who might be a good match for us, and begin to have satisfying relationships. I'm not only talking about serious relationships either. Some great relationships are temporary and declared as such right from the start, but you have to sort through people to choose your match for any kind of a good relationship. If you are not being yourself, you won't learn how the other person responds to you with all your strengths, weaknesses, habits, and insecurities.

So, be brave and honest. Reveal as much of yourself as you can so your new friend can share in the responsibility of making choices. My wife, Linda, and I emphasized in our Meet Your Mate seminar that a relationship has to do with finding a *match*; it's not about good or bad people. A person with red lights for you may be great for someone else. Keeping this in mind as you let someone get to know you is very helpful for both people in the initial stages of dating. It takes the edge off the rejection process, regardless of whose decision it is. It also helps to give you the courage to be yourself, regardless of whether or not the two of you are a match. If it doesn't work here, you'll find it elsewhere.

The beauty of the sorting process is that you get a good feel for whether someone can offer a potentially sucessful relationship right from the beginning—rather than after investing several months in each other. If you're serious about wanting to get married, you really don't want to get involved with someone who isn't a good match, someone who has terrible qualities for you, or someone who will obviously be leaving sooner or later.

> Feedback is good. It's what helps us sort through the people we meet, decide who might be a good match for us, and begin to have satisfying relationships.

## A Practical Strategy for Getting Feedback

A great way to give and get feedback is to share a little at a time about yourself, and see what you get back. For instance, Jim is a warm, personal kind of guy who wants a woman who is similar. So, on the first encounter with a woman who interests him, he would be wise to be warm and talk about a few personal things. Then he can observe if his style of relating is matched by her. If it is, he can share more of himself and see what comes back as feedback.

*Jim:*  Yeah, first dates are awkward. They make me feel a bit insecure.

*June:*  Me too. In fact, I can honestly say that I hate them.

*Jim:*  I think if I didn't want a relationship so much, I probably would be a lot calmer.

*June:*  Sure, but then we wouldn't put out the energy to find the right person.

This exchange is filled with feedback and seems to have ended with a mutual level of being personal. Jim talks about the way he is feeling in a personal way, and June responds in kind with her feelings. Note that she doesn't change the subject or the tone in which they are speaking. After an exchange like this, Jim should feel comfortable and accepted in his desire to talk about feelings. Jim and June have the potential to be a good match in that area.

Now for one that is not so positive. Dan and Lisa meet at a party and feel lots of chemistry. They dance well together, have a similar sense of humor, and after a highly charged political conversation, they exchange phone numbers. To give you some background, Lisa is the kind of person who wants a close relationship where she spends a lot of time with her partner. She wants the relationship to be a priority. After a few dates with Dan, she observes that his life is highly scheduled and that he is not interested in changing his routine in any way whatsoever to accommodate her. This is a serious red flag for her, and despite the potential that she feels about a future with him, she decides not to date him anymore.

In Chapter 11, I discuss the issue of hiding yourself from others in greater detail and give exercises to remedy this problem. You may want to read it next.

## Exercises: A Qualities Index to Help You with Your Sorting

The table in this section provides a list of qualities to help you sort out what is really important for you in a partner. Rating the qualities for yourself and a potential mate will help clarify what kind of a person you want to live with. My list is by no means complete, and may not be in the language that you need, but you can use it as a launching point. Feel free to change the language or add qualities that are important to you.

Once you have gotten clear about which qualities are most important, it will be easier for you to use the red, yellow, and green light system to check out feedback. Then you'll have your eyes open before you enter any new relationship.

**Exercise 1.** In a section entitled "Qualities I Am Looking For," write each quality that is important to you and score it as follows: 5 means extremely important, 1 means not important, and 3 can go either way. The word "compatible" in many categories in the table means a similar style and/or values in these areas. Rate how important that is for you.

| The Crowell-Reaves Partner Qualities Index | | |
| --- | --- | --- |
| *Rate Your Mate* (1-5) | *Qualities* | *Rate Yourself* (1-5) |
| _____ | Physically attractive | _____ |
| _____ | Chemistry with | _____ |
| _____ | Sexually compatible | _____ |
| _____ | Intellectually compatible | _____ |
| _____ | Personal habits compatible | _____ |
| _____ | Values compatible | _____ |
| _____ | Social time compatible | _____ |
| _____ | Leisure activities compatible | _____ |
| _____ | Financially compatible | _____ |
| _____ | Problem-solving style compatible | _____ |

## The Crowell-Reaves Partner Qualities Index

| Rate Your Mate (1-5) | Qualities | Rate Yourself (1-5) |
|---|---|---|
| _____ | Career compatible | _____ |
| _____ | Age compatible | _____ |
| _____ | Upbringing compatible | _____ |
| _____ | Has good friendships | _____ |
| _____ | Independent | _____ |
| _____ | Takes care of me | _____ |
| _____ | Wants to be taken care of | _____ |
| _____ | Passion for life | _____ |
| _____ | Fun in casual activities | _____ |
| _____ | Supportive | _____ |
| _____ | Psychologically aware | _____ |
| _____ | Affectionate | _____ |
| _____ | Physically healthy | _____ |
| _____ | Competent | _____ |
| _____ | Sense of humor | _____ |
| _____ | Puts a lot of energy into relationships | _____ |
| _____ | Puts most energy into things other than relationships | _____ |
| _____ | Politically aware | _____ |
| _____ | Trustworthy | _____ |
| _____ | Relationship available | _____ |
| _____ | Mentally healthy | _____ |
| _____ | Ability to compromise | _____ |

**Exercise 2.** Now pretend that you are looking at yourself as a possible mate. Grade yourself in the same way on the qualities you have copied out. On the opposite side of the list put a number indicating how developed these qualities are in you. Rate yourself from 1 to 5, with 5 meaning very developed, and 1 meaning that the quality is lacking. Then work on developing the qualities you want in a mate that you don't have yourself.

**Exercise 3.** Recall a good relationship from the past and see how that person stacked up to your quality requirements. Do the same with a relationship that didn't work, and take a deeper look at what went wrong. From both of these assessments, what can you learn about your requirements about what works and what doesn't? Write out the qualities that seemed to work for you under "My Favorite Qualities in the Past," and the ones that were impossible to live with under "Qualities I Couldn't Stand in the Past."

**Exercise 4.** Now list your bottom-line qualities. Five will do. For instance, my absolute bottom line was to find a woman who was willing to work out issues. Other qualities high on my list were intelligent, sexual, psychologically aware, and fun. Write your favorites in bold letters under "What I Insist On."

**Exercise 5.** Write a short list of your red flags; in other words, habits or qualities that you are not willing to live with. For instance, a person who talks too much might be on your list, or smokes or uses drugs, or doesn't smoke, or interrupts chronically, or doesn't recognize feelings, or thinks woman should obey men in everything. Whatever your red flags are, list them under "My Absolute No-No's."

However you look at relationships at this point in your life, most people would agree on the need for a good partnership—what I call a good match. You want someone to meet you where you are. The ideas in this chapter are crucial because they affect your dating practices where it counts—at the beginning. The first step is to know more precisely what is important to you and what is unacceptable to you, but then you have to insist on a partner who has those qualities. The funny thing is that you really have to insist with no one other than yourself. After all, you are in charge of who you pick. Hunting is one thing; what you choose to bring home is another.

> The ideas in this chapter are crucial because they affect your dating practices where it counts—at the beginning.

# 7

# I Know It Feels Great, but Does It Feel Safe?

There is a simple intuitive yardstick for evaluating any intimate relation-ship. Ask yourself two questions: "Do I feel safe in this relationship?" and, "Do I feel safe with this person?" From years of observation as a therapist, along with personal experience, I've become convinced that people cannot commit themselves to an intimate relationship unless they feel safe. To help you understand how crucial this is, imagine yourself as the man or the woman in the following scene.

> Why would anyone want to commit himself or herself to a person with whom they felt trapped into a false existence? It would be like volunteering for jail. Yet, the yardstick of asking, "Do I feel safe right now?"—a simple question that can be applied to any relationship—is seldom used.

It was sudden, I had to admit, but it still felt right. The chemistry was overwhelming. We had just met at a dance and didn't want to part, and now we were back at her place.

"Do you want a glass of wine?" she asked.

"Sure," I said, knowing that I didn't really want it, and putting it aside after two sips. I was absorbed with her yielding lips, the way our bodies and hands had become like dancers leading and following. I knew my bravado was masking my shyness about getting our clothes off.

We moved from the living room to the bedroom. Her house was new to me, and I eagerly took in all that the books, art objects, and choices of colors and shapes said about her. It was too much too fast, but instead of thinking about that, my attention was overwhelmed with how wonderful her skin felt. I was relieved when she opened a drawer and pulled out a few different condoms. One discussion we didn't have to have! I wondered what turned her on. Were there things that she was shy about? Did she really like me?

"Just do what you like and hope she likes it," my mind coached.

## The Invisible Barrier: How Not Feeling Safe and Not Knowing It Affects Us

Yes, this is the kind of scene that men and women fantasize about. Yes, these waking dreams sometimes happen in real life. And yes, safe sex and romance are still possible in the nineties. But if you were the man *or* the woman, would you have felt safe in this situation?

The dictionary tells us that the word "safe" comes from the Latin word for health and is related to the Greek word for whole. The definition is "freed from harm or risk; secure from threat of danger, harm, or loss." Being "freed from harm" and "secure from threat" can exist on many different levels: physical, emotional, financial, and so on. All of us have our own particular desires for safety and our own unique warning signs when those needs are not met.

With this definition in mind, what level of safety would you seek in the romantic scenario just described? On the most basic level, would you feel physically safe? Especially if you were a woman in a man's home? On another level, would you feel safe enough to talk about a concern you had, such as how late it was, or when you were going to leave, or whether he minded that you were having your period? On a sexual level, could you completely surrender to the experience? Would you feel safe enough to relax and enjoy it? And on an emotional level, would you worry about whether you were going to see this person again?

I certainly couldn't feel safe on any of those levels during a first, spontaneous, and "blind" encounter. Regardless of what was going on and regardless of how high my passion barometer was reading, I would definitely be spending some portion of my energy, even if unconsciously, worrying and being careful. I would never feel safe enough to give myself totally to the experience or to the other person. My guess is that most people would respond similarly.

It's this undeniable need for safety—on an emotional level—that can create problems in relationships. I remember my therapist saying, "You won't be able to commit yourself to any woman with whom you don't feel safe enough to be yourself." His words fell into me like an axe splitting wood, creating pops and splinters. Suddenly, I was able to understand this basic truth about myself. A truth that seems so obvious now.

Why would anyone want to commit himself or herself to a person with whom they felt trapped into a false existence? It would be like volunteering for jail. Yet, the yardstick of asking, "Do I feel safe right now?"—a simple question that can be applied to any relationship—is seldom used.

## Intuition as a Barometer of Safety

We all have our own ways of feeling "freed from harm" or "secure from threat of danger, harm, or loss." The key is to trust our intuition when we sense danger. It's a very personal thing. I feel intuitively safe, for example, with someone who enjoys it when I'm a bit outrageous. But I sense danger if I'm with a person who loves going into a lot of detailed, factual information and wants my strict attention. For me these things are real areas of concern, but someone else might have an entirely different set of preferences.

Our preferences and the way we live our lives on a day-to-day basis—whether our lifestyle is fast-paced or slow moving, energetic or meandering, artistic or practical—may seem like trivial standards on which to evaluate another person, but they become crucial when a relationship develops into intimacy. If we enter a commitment, these are the things we have to live with every day. And we want to feel safely vulnerable with the person we love.

In a relationship, we are "tied" in many ways to another person. We become affected by their lifestyle, their habits, their crises, their virtues, and their moods. One of the main ingredients of a strong relationship is spending a great deal of time with a partner. A fundamental concern is that the time be positive rather than negative. We want it to be fulfilling, rather than a drain on our time and emotions. And we don't want to feel that the things that are important to us will be squeezed out of our lives if we commit ourselves to this relationship. We also don't want to be criticized and judged for our differences.

If the person we are with expects something that we perceive as harmful, we won't feel safe. Or if our partner threatens to take away something that we feel is important, we'll sense a danger to ourselves. For example, if my partner insists on my listening to long, detailed, factual stories, I'll go nuts. That's a real threat of harm for me. On the other hand, if she hates to talk about emotions, she'll feel threatened by my wanting that. As another example, if a man loves to play basketball, he won't feel safe with a woman who wants him to stay at home every night. If you examine your own life, you'll know what your personal issues are. Then you can use these areas as part of your safety barometer.

## The Wisdom of Being Vulnerable

Intuition can also tell you when it's OK to be vulnerable with someone. Watch especially for nonverbal feedback when you tell stories about yourself. Are you getting real acceptance or merely a show of it? In many dysfunctional relationships, people open up to another person too quickly, without any in-depth knowledge of who they are opening up to. The way to correct for this is to move more slowly.

---

One of the main ingredients of a relationship is spending a great deal of time with a partner. A fundamental concern is that the time be positive rather than negative.

---

I suggest that you test the waters slowly, by gingerly putting out some information about yourself or your lifestyle, and then paying close attention to how your date responds. For me it's easy enough to talk about a feeling I'm having and then carefully listen to what I get back. If I get feelings coming back, we are communicating. If she changes the subject, offers a quick solution instead of listening to my feelings, or tries to make me feel silly for feeling what I do, I know this isn't safe. It is also possible to ask your new date to simply listen to your feelings without any problem solving, letting him or her know that you value that kind of listening. Then see what comes back and check if you feel safe.

Let's look at the word "vulnerable." It comes from the Latin word for wounded. It means being capable of, or open to, being attacked or wounded. Why apply this concept to relationships? Because true intimacy requires that you be yourself freely, letting your strengths *and* weaknesses show. The only way you can truly be loved as you are is to be vulnerable. But in the process you risk being wounded. In this light, it becomes clear why you can't commit yourself to intimacy unless you feel safe.

Being vulnerable is not the same as being sensitive, although these terms are often confused. In a psychological context, "being sensitive" often is used to denote a condition of feeling hurt often. You may be vulnerable in sharing that you are a sensitive person. You may also be vulnerable when you ask for what you want, or when you talk about your fears or about the feelings that you are having. I have found in my work with both singles and couples that the most together people are the ones who can be vulnerable when the situation calls for it. Relationships call for this. When you are going through a difficult time, you want to be able to talk about it to the person you are closest too. On the other hand, in most work situations it is not as appropriate to be so open with your feelings.

In relationships, when you are vulnerable, you take the risk of being intimate. You take the risk of letting another person inside. It takes more strength to be vulnerable than to go around with a lot of barriers that keep everyone away from you.

## How We Ignore Our Intuitive Wisdom

When I was dating Clara a few years before my present marriage, I saw something revealing about her during the first ten minutes of our first date. As we were driving to a picnic with some friends, she was obsessed with her makeup and brushed aside my attempts to start a conversation. Right away, the little voice inside me that tells me important things began nudging me. My intuition knew that her attention to looking good over being personal on our first date was a warning sign. I didn't listen and we both paid the price a month later.

The voice of intuition is usually loud and clear concerning issues of safety and vulnerability. Many people know in the first few minutes of meeting a person whether a relationship has a chance to work—or at least within the first few dates. Maybe your date isn't comfortable when you share information about the way you see the world. Maybe you have core philosophies that are radically different. Three months later, when the relationship fails, it is usually for the reason that you detected and then ignored early on.

When we ignore our intuitive wisdom and fail to use the safety barometer for a new relationship, we are sabotaging our efforts to achieve true intimacy later on. Just as in the opening scenario of this chapter, if we don't feel safe, we cannot be relaxed and vulnerable. Without the freedom to be ourselves, the physical, emotional, and spiritual benefits of a relationship will not materialize.

If we let it, our intuition will tune us into the whole picture of a relationship. Our inner wisdom will let us know if we feel safe or not—if we listen. Our intuition may demand that we keep our distance, even if we don't completely know why. But we can pretend not to hear. Maybe it's been a long time since we've had a relationship. We may want the relationship so badly that we don't want any contrary advice. Still, our intuition is always there warning us. It's up to us to take advantage of its wisdom.

> The voice of intuition is usually loud and clear around issues of safety and vulnerability.

Daniel spent two years alone after his breakup with Joan, but now he felt more than ready to have a new woman in his life. Meeting Tina on the train seemed like a gift from God. They got involved and became intimate quickly. Even talking about safe sex was easy with her. In fact, talking with her about anything was easy. They spent every weekend together for two months, along with one or two evenings in the middle of the week.

Trouble started when Daniel, feeling securely in love, announced that he was going skydiving the coming weekend. Would she like to come and watch? Her vehement reaction astonished him. She knew about his skydiving. Why then was she so upset and threatening to leave him if he went? After a few hours of emotionally charged discussion, he learned that Tina thought all that was in the past. How could he lead such a dangerous lifestyle and be gone so much during their weekend time if he loved her?

Daniel then had a shattering realization: this same issue was what drove the wedge between him and Joan, the woman before Tina. Now that he thought about it, Tina and Joan were much alike. They were both warm and personal, but without an active life of their own. He got quickly involved with Joan just like with Tina, and it was at a time when he was feeling needy and alone. Both of these women were a balm for his inner life, but he thoroughly enjoyed his outer life also. Like most people, Daniel needed both.

The warnings were there at the beginning, but Daniel ignored his intuition. The red flags were waving, but he was lonely. He didn't make an issue about Tina's conflicting needs because he wanted what she offered so much.

## Feeling Safe vs. Protecting Yourself

It will be helpful at this point to make a distinction between the idea of feeling safe in a relationship and the idea of protecting yourself. Feeling safe includes skills such as going at your own pace, listening to feedback from the other person, and paying attention to your intuition. Protecting yourself involves barriers to keep other people away, especially when people seem to be attacking you. In an effort to feel safe, you may protect yourself by not letting anyone get too close. This protects but it also isolates. Learning how to feel safe takes care of yourself and does it by staying in the relationship—a skill that we don't learn as children because, usually, our only option for feeling safe was to flee to our rooms, into silence, or to a friend's house.

---

> Feeling safe includes skills such as going at your own pace, listening to feedback from the other person, and paying attention to your intuition. Protecting yourself involves barriers to keep other people away, especially when people seem to be attacking you. This protects but it also isolates.

---

Pam was date-raped in college, and feels strongly about being able to protect herself. She has taken classes in self-defense and continues to be on guard against that ever happening again. At the same time, she desires a loving relationship. Two years ago she came to me with questions about the difference between taking care of herself and protecting herself. From whom was she protecting herself? All men? All men don't rape or even insist. If she takes care of herself, she can protect herself from a potential rapist and yet let in a potential great partner.

In therapy, Pam learned to be especially keen on listening for respect on first dates. She became attuned to nuances of put-on respect versus true respect. She learned to trust her ability to feel safe, both in terms of situations and timing. Recognizing that the world holds both dangerous and kind people was a hard-won therapy victory, but it empowered her.

If Pam was only protecting herself, she would have seen the world as containing only dangerous men. She would have compulsively protected herself from all men and never have been able to let anyone in. By focusing on taking care of her own safety, she made conscious decisions that allowed for safety and relationship.

## Staying Safe in the Nineties

In the sexual and emotional climate of the nineties, it's realistic to admit that there is a possibility of danger when we get close to another person. With all of our personal histories and the stories of all our friends, we know that relationships can be dangerous—either physically or emotionally. The point is to develop the skills you need to keep yourself as safe as possible, and to develop your intuition to hear the signals of your inner wisdom regarding safety or danger.

My suggestions are as follows: Use the questions in the exercises of this chapter to constantly monitor your safety comfort zone. Learn to broaden your view of safety from physical to emotional and relational. Always trust your intuition, both at the beginning of a relationship and after you become more involved. It's also important to remember that after two people sleep together, intuition flies out the window for a period of time. Also, remember to use the red, yellow, and green light concept developed in Chapter 6.

Everyone has his or her own way of knowing whether there's a green light inside, a flashing yellow light, or a red signal of warning. If there's a green light, go ahead and see what happens. If there's a yellow light, check out areas of concern before you go ahead full force, and give the relationship more time. If there's a serious signal of danger, get out.

Absolute safety is impossible in a relationship, but the risks can be minimized. The point of this chapter is to awaken your consciousness to your right and need to be in relationships that feel safe so that you can enjoy the rewards of commitment.

## Letting the Walls Come Down

Protecting yourself can be misunderstood in a number of ways. When people say things like, "I'm just protecting myself by not letting you know all about me," they may be putting up a barrier of deception. If someone says, "I need to protect myself, and therefore I'm not going to talk to my boss," they may be locking themselves into a very negative situation. In this sense, to protect means to cover or shield from injury, but it puts walls up at the same time. Thus, protecting yourself shields you from experiencing both success and harm; whereas, feeling safe is feeling secure in the face of harm.

Protecting yourself is often reactionary and rigid. When people are overprotective, they can easily mistake normal tasks of relating for threat or harm, thereby preventing themselves from interacting and growing. If a partner makes a request for a change, it can be seen as a threat rather than an opportunity to have a better relationship. Overprotection can keep you emotionally paralyzed. It can also weaken your social skills by shielding you from having to use them. Too much protection can build thick walls that keep everyone away from you—even someone who could ultimately make you very happy.

As a case in point, Jake left a marriage in which he felt abused five years ago. At first he dated casually and made it clear that he was not open to commitment. Then he spent a few years being lonely. With the coaxing of some friends, he went on a camping trip and met a woman who was very different from his ex-wife. She was loving, caring, fun to be with, and appreciated him more than any woman he had ever met. However, Jake rejected her after a few months because he was terrified of making another mistake.

In short, protecting yourself can be a stunting experience; whereas, trying to be safe is an interactive and growth-producing process. Protecting yourself with a vengeance is usually a defense mechanism; whereas, taking care of your safety is informed and conscious. It opens your life to new possibilities because it tells you when the walls *can* come down.

## True Confessions

It's curious how the word "safe" and the male ego clash! A few months ago, I overheard a conversation between two men in a gym. It was about a situation in which one of the men felt vulnerable. Even two sentences of what I overheard is very revealing:

"Feeling safe is a matter of feeling in control of yourself."

"Take charge of yourself, and you won't have to worry about that."

The part of men that resists being weak hates the word "safe"— unless we're making a situation safe for someone else. I can use myself as a good example. For years, I was a risk-taker and downright scornful of any idea about protecting myself or feeling safe with a woman. I'd heard women talk about not feeling safe and was grateful that this wasn't a problem of mine.

Imagine my surprise a few years ago when my therapist pointed out that I was ignoring my own need for emotional safety in my relationships. At the time I was determined to make a relationship work out. I was sick of my string of three-month relationships, and determined that my next relationship was going to be it, come what may! However, my therapist earned his money by getting through my male denial and helping me understand that I could not possibly relax and feel loved if I didn't feel safe.

Maybe I'm a late bloomer, but after I caught a glimpse of the truth, a lot fell into place for me. My need for emotional safety seemed so obvious that I felt foolish to have put up such a fight. Ignoring my need for safety was preventing me from moving forward with this relationship—or any relationship!

I believe that men are prone to resisting the importance of knowing whether something feels safe—especially when it comes to emotions. Men are taught to "handle things" rather than to feel their emotions. Women are taught to nurture and "be good," even at their own expense at times. In my relationships I had never asked myself whether I felt safe. It had never occurred to me that I needed to take care of myself so carefully.

## Taking Good Care of Ourselves

Taking good care of ourselves is an entirely conscious and nurturing decision. Most men have a hard time recognizing the need to nurture themselves. We grow up in a world of "big boys don't cry," and "don't just sit there feeling sorry for yourself, get up and do something." The reaction, to this is to perform and to take care of other "weaker" people. Our defense against being called "sissy" and "crybaby" is to deny that we hurt or have fears. Therefore, why would *we* need to take care of being safe? It's a big shift from that mentality to knowing that we need to have our own loving and caring parent inside ourselves. A big shift but a rewarding one!

> Ignoring my need for safety was preventing me from moving forward with this relationship—or any relationship!

Although many men have a generic blindness to safety issues, women are not exempt from the need for safety glasses. Despite the fact that they respect their own need for safety in some areas, many women are reckless when it comes to relationships. Like men, women can be so desirous of the caring and security promised by a relationship that they shut down their safety mechanisms and their intuition. They may not acknowledge their fears. They may listen to only a single part of the experience—like the sex, the shared intelligence, the financial security, or the excitement of common interests. They may pay lip service to their safety concerns by hoping to change the unwanted or threatening qualities in their partner later.

I believe that people who don't take care of their safety are acting out of misguided trust. They would like to believe the best about others. They may also have an inflated trust in their ability to change what they don't like in their partners.

Many men and women believe that a magical force is operating to make everything turn out OK, if they just trust in it. In reality, trust and safety are qualities that are worked for and earned. Often this "magical thinking" masks a deep sense of unworthiness. People who feel this way believe that they wouldn't be worth loving if someone really got to know them, so they don't see themselves as deserving of this special concern about safety. In reality, however, relationships don't work over time unless you take care of yourself.

## Exercises to Start Feeling Safe

"Do I feel safe in this relationship?"

"Do I feel safe with this woman or man?"

It's time to start asking yourself these crucial questions about every person you date. Then you can start to watch things change for yourself.

**Exercise 1.** Here are more questions to start you thinking:

- How much can you trust the other person to do what he or she says?

- Can you be relaxed about your lifestyle in the relationship?

- Can you talk about what is important to you, or do you feel that you get no genuine response on those topics?

- Is something expected of you that doesn't feel right?

- How do you feel in the relationship—uneasy, guarded, relaxed, spontaneous?

- Are you aware of having to be careful a lot? Do you fear repercussions from your partner?

- Can you be yourself with this person?

Write these questions or this page number in your notebook under "Ways of Checking for Safety" and conclude it with, "I promise to ask myself these questions about any new relationship I wish to continue."

**Exercise 2.** Go over all of your relationships with co-workers, neighbors, friends, relatives, and romantic partners. Ask yourself which relationships feel safe and which don't. See if there are any patterns. Are you different in any way with the people you feel safe with? When I ask myself this question, I find that I feel safest with my best friends because I'm relaxed and myself with them without any acting, without any reservations, without covering up any part of myself—including my vulnerabilities. I feel appreciated by them just for being myself. Write in your book, under "How I Feel Safe and Unsafe," your findings from the patterns you notice.

**Exercise 3.** List in your notebook, under "Important Things Not to Give Up," things about yourself that you wish to keep and not give up to a relationship. These things could be physical pursuits, study, reading, laughing, self-exploration, travel, career improvement, friends, visits to parents, and so forth. This list will remind you of what you hold vital now when you are between relationships and thinking for yourself. Use this list to see how safely a new relationship honors you and your desires. Therefore, as an example, if you are clearly a career person, you need to be in a relationship that honors that; if you love physical sports, you need a person who respects and appreciates that need.

## Putting It All Together

Asking yourself if a relationship feels safe to you can change your life in some very positive ways. The idea is simple, but the effects on your behavior can be profound.

As an example, a woman friend told me about meeting a man who seemed wonderful during their first encounters. One night, they went to a party with a small crowd from work. Toward the end of the evening, he seemed to change from the outgoing, alert guy she knew to a quiet, morose, leering stranger. She felt uncomfortable immediately and didn't know how to handle the situation. Then she decided to ask him about his drinking. He refused to discuss the issue and said he simply got quiet at times. She struggled with whether she believed him or not, and wondered if he even knew he had a problem. She decided to trust her intuition and keep an eye out in the future for other signs that made her uncomfortable. In the end, she had to leave because she couldn't feel safe with his level of self-knowledge or honesty about his drinking.

The issue of safety can also come up later in a relationship. One of my clients, Adela, had been in a relationship for several years and was troubled by her inability to commit to marriage. I introduced her to the process of using the safety yardstick. When she allowed herself the right to feel safe, she realized that she didn't. We explored why this was so, and she discovered that her partner was constantly asking her to change things about herself. He wanted her to lose weight. He pressured her to get a promotion at work, even though she was very happy with the position she had. And he wanted her to take aerobics classes three times a week, even though she told him that wasn't the way she wanted to use her precious and scarce free time. As a result, she didn't really feel accepted by him because of his desire for her to change.

Adela was confused by this because she wanted some of the changes as much as he did. However, when she applied the safety yardstick and trusted her intuition, she understood why she was holding back. His emphasis on her changing made her insecure about his love for her as she was. Eventually, she told him why she didn't feel accepted. He understood the point and realized that he loved her and didn't need her to change. He also realized that he was getting too involved in her growth and that he had plenty of his own issues to deal with. This was a dream ending for a tough discussion!

If a relationship doesn't feel safe, the problem is not always with the other person. Very often the problem is inside ourselves. Perhaps we are hiding out and so focused on being accepted that we are not putting any of our own personality out there. If we avoid the question of safety, we can get ourselves into situations that aren't right for us. When we don't ask ourselves how safe we are feeling, we deprive ourselves of the use of our intuitive powers, which often pick up problems long before our intellect can piece things together.

I remember my first date with a woman I'll call Margot. We talked for hours about her problems. I occasionally attempted to change the subject, but it would invariably get back to her problems. However, there was a lot of sexual chemistry between us, so we continued to see each other.

> If a relationship doesn't feel safe, the problem is not always with the other person. Very often the problem is inside ourselves.

Margot's constant talking about her problems was less troublesome to me when we spent most of our time together seeing movies and swing dancing. But after we had spent a couple of months going "out," we naturally began to have more evenings "in." At that point, the earlier source of discomfort for me came back dramatically. I found myself trying to avoid unstructured time that could be filled with talking. I began finding reasons for being unavailable. Finally, I realized what was happening and tried to talk with her about it. That was a disaster, since this was no small item that she could just switch off. We went through a few more weeks of blaming each other for the problems we were having, and in the end, we both got hurt.

If I had been aware at that time of my need for safety, we probably could have avoided a lot of pain. What would have happened if, in the beginning—say, after the first date or two—I had reflected on whether I felt safe? I might not have known exactly why, but if I had trusted my intuition, I would have had to admit that I didn't feel safe or comfortable. At that point—long before we were involved enough to hurt each other—I could have explored whether the issue that troubled me could be changed. Alternatively, I could have decided to get out of the relationship because of my inner feeling that it wasn't right for me.

## Proceeding with Safety

You can use the safety concept in many ways. The first checkpoint is right at the beginning of a relationship. After a few dates, check in with yourself and see if you feel safe. See if there are any red flags that point to trouble later on. Another crucial time to apply the safety test is when the issue of commitment comes up. If you can't commit to a seemingly good union, ask yourself what is holding you back. Pay attention to any reservations that come up, regardless of whether they are large or small. Depending on what you learn, you may need to ask the other person to make some changes or to make some of your own.

If you begin to use your intuition to determine the safety of a romantic relationship, you'll learn how to sort through people who aren't right for you, and go forward with relationships that have potential. You wouldn't walk into a burning house or enter a business deal that seemed foolhardy. Why should you enter an intimate relationship that seems dangerous? Trust yourself and act on the answer you get.

This method is also useful with friends and business partners. Remember, intuition can grasp variables far more complex than those formulated by the conscious mind. Not trusting it for yes and no types of decisions like safety robs you of a valuable resource. But if you want to find a partner who will be right for you over time, it's time to start listening to your inner wisdom now.

**Hint:** One method of checking for safety in a new or old relationship is to talk about not feeling safe and see what comes back to you. If you get, "Oh come on, you're making too much of that" or, "Don't be crazy . . . " (as Woody Allen is always saying in his movies), you probably won't feel safe bringing up these vulnerable feelings. I'm not saying that your partner should necessarily agree with how you see things, but he or she should care about your not feeling safe.

## The Advantages of Using the Safety Yardstick

Asking the question "Does this feel safe?" is the best way I know to allow intuition to work for healthy and intimate relationships. There are many benefits. You can find out what keeps you from feeling safe and rectify it. You can learn by experience to identify a relationship that allows you to feel safe—and use that knowledge to change any relationship patterns that have been keeping true intimacy out of your life. If a relationship isn't right for you, you can decide to end it. This opens you and the other person to new possibilities. By admitting that the relationship isn't safe, you may allow your partner to admit the same thing. It's much more productive to ask yourself the "safety question" than to deny your need for safety and lose the potential that full commitment can bring to your life.

# 8

# Relaxing into Love

My back had a spasm and I was lying in bed, on some soothing heat, not wanting to move a muscle. After a chat with my son, I asked him to do a few favors for me. At that moment I realized how relieved I was that I could ask him to help me so I wouldn't have to move. It dawned on me that the relief I felt when he said yes was similar to the new feeling of being able to ask for help in relationships.

It's taken some time, but I have finally learned to let the other person share the responsibility for the relationship, instead of thinking that I have to do it all. If you find that you are working hard to make a new relationship work, it may be a sign that you are not being met by the other person. Because of problem areas in their upbringing, many people

> I have finally learned to let the other person share the responsibility for the relationship, instead of thinking that I have to do it all.

are in the habit of doing all the work in relationships. If you relate to this idea, you in particular will find much assistance in what follows.

## The Myth of Making It Work

Mindi used to work hard at all her relationships. She somehow got it into her head that she had to have the relationship all figured out from the beginning so no one would get hurt. She was the one who had to be sensitive to all the issues and see how she and he were going to navigate through them. She also did the planning for both of them.

From the very first date, Mindi gave herself the responsibility of trying to figure out what he would like her to do. Would she be moving too fast if she . . . ? You may, at this point be identifying with this situation and the strain it puts on you. You could be asking, "Will he like me if I'm strong?" "Is it OK to be assertive sexually?" "Does he like me to dress up more, or does he like makeup?" "Can I ask her to make love, or will she feel rushed?"

If you want to be in a relationship that works, it's better to stop trying so hard and think about "being met" by a partner. By that, I mean being with someone who meets you on an equal level in talents, relationship skills, and abilities; someone whose life is working and wants to share it with you. Instead of a fix-it job, look for someone who will share the responsibilities side-by-side with you.

You know you are being met when the relationship proceeds smoothly and easily. This includes both of you dealing with the problems that arise. The opposite of this is a relationship in which one person is working hard at making it work or trying to change the partner, while the other is happy with the way it is. How do you know when you're being met? When you feel relaxed and comfortable. Believe it or not, this is actually possible.

In the how-can-I-make-it-better crowd, there is a myth that one partner is responsible for the health and permanence of the relationship. You are the one who can save both partners from hurt if you try hard enough. You are the one who should know what the issues are for the health of the union. You should be willing to do whatever is necessary to get the issues resolved. This is certainly not being relaxed. Nor is it going to lead to being met.

Mindi's exhaustion and relationship fatigue began to outweigh her need to take charge and make it all work. She then began to drop the myth of working at it so hard and began to learn about being met. You may be at that same place. Read on.

## Why Some of Us Work So Hard at Relationships

The strain that some of us put on ourselves to do it all comes from our roles as children. Most of you in the how-can-I-make-it-better crowd were the helpers, the confidants, the junior therapists in your families. You were called upon to be responsible for others, to listen to parental problems, or much worse, to be substitute mates to one of your parents. This didn't always include sex, but it could have. Think about your role, especially with your parents. What was expected of you? What were your fears for the family and hopes of remedying the problems?

Sharon remembers hearing her parents yelling and screaming at each other a lot. She can remember sitting against the door to her bedroom, wishing that they would stop. She even remembers getting in between her mom and dad when they were fighting to force them to pay attention to her and stop yelling at each other.

Dori remembers how she would wait up for her father, who worked evenings at a newspaper, and fix him soup and ham sandwiches. Her mother was a lounge singer and would come home even later. Her grandmother lived with them, but she always went to sleep early. This arrangement put Dori in the role of spouse with her father.

---

We were called upon to be responsible for others, to listen to parental problems, or much worse, to be substitute mates to one of our parents.

---

David was an only child and remembers long talks over meals alone with his mother while she and his father went through their separation. His mother's tears are what he remembers the most. He can still feel how he wanted to do something to help but also how he liked his dad. In those days he walked around numb with confusion.

Joyce was sexually molested by her father from the time she was twelve until she was fifteen years old. She senses that her compulsion to take so much responsibility in relationships stems from her fear and shame of her mother and teachers discovering this secret. Furthermore, never knowing what kind of a mood her alcoholic father was going to be in kept her ever vigilant.

Camille remembers a time typical for many women, when her father, who had been her pal and trusted authority, pushed her off his lap without any explanation. He stopped stroking her hair and holding her close to him. He probably was aware of Camille's maturing and felt a sexual stirring mix with his love for her. He panicked and held her off to protect himself. She, however, is now hypervigilant when she is out with a man. She feels responsible for the man's sexual arousal on dates. She is also so confused about her own sexual desires that she rarely thinks about her own sexual preferences.

## Taking Charge: Children Who Grow Up Too Soon

Many men remember taking care of their mothers the best they could after a desertion by the father. Likewise, many women remember being a substitute wife to their fathers or a substitute mother to their siblings. These experiences of carrying burdens too great for children's shoulders can have a nasty way of being continued in later life, especially in relationships.

There are usually two factors at work. The first is that children in dysfunctional families are burdened with taking care of one of their parents long before their own growing-up process is finished. In a healthier environment, children are expected to do only what a child is capable of, giving them the experience of accomplishment and a sense of competence. However, when children are expected to take charge at too early an age, they don't have the skills to succeed at being adults. As a result, they are deprived of feeling the achievement normal to their level of growth—and all the self-esteem that it brings. They are continual failures—never able to truly give to the parent what the parent wants since that can really only come from another adult. However, since the child received approval, or at least less abuse, when he or she tried to live up to being the little adult, this pattern continues into adult relationships as the only known way to behave.

The second dysfunctional factor is a control issue: by taking charge the child also takes some control. If, for example, a little boy was abandoned by his father through divorce or death, he will feel some responsibility for it. He may think he was bad or too much trouble, and that's why Daddy left. To compensate, so this doesn't also happen with Mommy, he will often become her substitute little "husband." To live up to the role he'll be the organizer, the wise confidant, or the soothing friend—all this to make sure she won't be unhappy and leave him like Daddy did. As an adult, this same boy-man will take charge, with the hope that this will keep his lover around.

Hypervigilance grows out of this childhood dilemma. In later life, that child will need to take charge in order to control the anxiety that the normal uncertainties of human relationships create. An imposed sense of responsibility too early gave the child-now-man the myth that he can and must take charge of the direction of the relationship. If you would like to read more on this subject, Dr. Patricia Love's *The Emotional Incest Syndrome* covers it very well.

> In a healthier environment, a child would be expected to do only what a child is capable of.

What almost always gets lost in this morass is the ability to take care of yourself. You are the vigilant one who looks out for others' needs so that you can take care of them and not be abandoned. This caretaking is not altruistically motivated. It is motivated by the fear of being left or not approved of in the relationship. It's important to remember that you may be doing all of this "missionary" work for your own perceived security.

## Joan's Story

Joan explains it this way. She was left behind with her mother and two younger sisters when her father simply didn't come home one evening. Her mother was devastated, panicky, and of no help in explaining it. Joan, the oldest child, helped her mother with the younger girls, taking responsibility for them at school and doing the shopping and dinner preparations. Fortunately, she was an energetic young woman and also stayed busy with friends and school activities, including the volleyball team.

During all this busy growing up—helping her mom, studying, and playing sports—she also spent a great deal of time wondering why her father left. She hadn't seen him and couldn't ask him. The answer that always seemed most plausible to her was that her mother and all three girls weren't good enough to him. This idea haunted her from the night he left until she entered therapy.

When Joan was twenty-two and a junior in college, she met Peter. They fell in love and spent the next year getting to know each other. In her senior year, they talked about a future together as if it were the logical progression. She remembers that she made a conscious decision during that period; she decided that she would be better to him than her mother was to her father.

However, since she grew up in an all female household, she really didn't have any firsthand experience about being good to a man. Improvising, she easily slipped into the role of being responsible for Peter's needs and the relationship's needs. That meant cooking Peter's favorite foods, keeping the apartment especially clean for him, and planning a social life for both of them. She also took on the job of supporting his personal pursuits away from her by going with him and watching games and providing snacks for his poker night. As if this weren't enough, she planned all the details of their weekends away from home.

Peter, who was often teased for being a mama's boy, was at first thrilled to be loved so much by Joan. But there were side effects that weren't so easy to take. Joan was always worried about where he was and when she would see him again. He often felt mothered by her. At times, he felt cut out of planning things for a trip or an evening with friends. Joan always had it all under control, leaving no room for his initiation.

Joan is now thirty-eight and Peter is a distant memory. Although there have been numerous other men in her life, they all have had some little-boy quality about them. Finally, Joan came to me in a state of anger and confusion asking, "What do men really want?"

---

Although there have been numerous other men in her life, they all have had some little-boy quality about them.

---

During our work, she realized how tired and angry she was about taking care of everyone. She also faced the sad truth that this role was the only way she knew to feel accepted and wanted. Slowly, she began to learn a more mature way of taking care of herself. She began to assemble a list of things she liked and ways she would like to be treated. Then she was ready to go out and find someone who would enjoy both giving and receiving. Joan was still willing to give of herself and take care of a man, but only up to a point. She wanted it returned also.

## Being Met: Finding Your Relaxed Mode

Here is one of the secrets of being successful in love: you need to find a balance between giving and receiving. Instead of working so hard, think about being met. Give up the myth that you are the one who has to make it work, and think about being comfortable with your partner, finding your relaxed mode, and relaxing into love.

Joan's decision to learn how to balance giving and receiving was the core of a much healthier social life. Here is another secret: a relationship where the giving is lopsided is usually a relationship in which something is being covered up. It is often a quid pro quo situation. "I'll do all this for you if you ... " The trade-off could be "overlook my addictions," "pretend I am healthy," or "make me feel safe." Joan was willing to trade all of the work for being loved.

At first Joan couldn't believe that a man would be attracted to her if she wasn't willing to do everything for him. However, as she tested different styles of behaving with men, she got some good results. There were men out there, if she screened them properly, who didn't want everything done for them.

When Joan finally got the balance right, dating actually became fun. For the first time in her life, she realized she could be loved for who she was. As she discovered she could receive as well as give, she experienced what it felt like to be met by a partner. This was very different than trying to coax him to love her. She found her relaxed mode instead of feeling like a hamster in a wheel running after some nonexistent goal.

> Give up the myth that you are the one who has to make it work, and think about being comfortable with your partner, finding your relaxed mode, relaxing into love, and being met.

## How to Start Relaxing in a Relationship

Finding how to relax in a relationship is one of the hardest things to achieve. It's a balancing act that usually comes from trial and error. Here are some questions to ask yourself to get started.

- What am I tired of doing in relationships?

- If I didn't do the things I usually do, what do I fear would happen? Would he or she stop liking me? Leave me?

- How would I feel about losing control of how our relationship works?

- What would it feel like if I let the other person worry about how the relationship is working?

- What if I just relax and try to enjoy myself? If, for instance, I am tired of making all the arrangements for getting together with friends, what would happen if I didn't do it? Would anything happen? Would we always then get together with only his or her friends?

- Would it make me anxious to release control of that or any sphere?

Now you need to weigh how tired you are of doing all this planning, worrying, and arranging against your willingness to risk some of the possible consequencess. Try it and see what happens. If you are dating, you can experiment and see what feedback you get. Do the expected calamities happen? The ones you knew would happen if you let up? Do things you didn't expect happen, like greater intimacy and a happier partner? Can you feel any more relaxed and trusting that things will work out without all of your work? Or are you surprised with how much better the relationship is going? Can you allow any positive feedback you get to be a sign of growth, not a reason to berate yourself for the way you have tried to control things in the past?

This last point isn't to be taken lightly. There have been times when I have managed to make a powerful and wanted change only to be confronted with the fact that it was my own anxiety and need to control that was creating the problem in the first place. If I berate myself about this, I deprive myself of the joy of a new discovery by allowing a wave of shame to crash over me and make me feel stupid and bad about how I behaved previously. One antidote to making negative judgments about the past is to continually remind yourself that your past was just right for the past, but not necessarily for the present. You did what you had to do. Now you can get off it, and get on with the present and the future.

Transitions are times when we need to be gentle with ourselves. As they say in the twelve-step programs, "Easy does it." We all do what we can at the time. We keep growing and learning, but we can't judge our past with the insights of today.

## Experimenting with Change

When you want to make a change in your life, try it out little by little. That's one of the basic concepts of this book. If you are dating, it's easier to keep trying new things because you are unknown to each new date. If you don't get it right the first time, that's fine. Think it over and make adjustments as you need them.

If you are already in a relationship and want to experiment with these changes, you can talk to your partner about what you would like to try. (Changing behavior on purpose but not letting your partner know you are trying something new is not exactly fair.) It's useful to ask your partner for comments and reactions about these changes. Talking about it will be a test of courage for you, since you have been so helpful and hardworking out of fear of not being acceptable, and now you want something for yourself. Also, watching your partner's reaction will be instructive for the same reasons.

> When you want to make a change in your life, try it out little by little.

When Mike decided it was time to relax and try and be loved for himself, rather than his caretaking ability, he was hard-pressed to know how to proceed. At the time he was in a five-month relationship with Cathy, who liked him a lot and let him know it. He enjoyed Cathy, their sex life, and their shared interests in folk dancing and ethnic restaurants, but did not want to continue doing so much of the relationship work. He was very much afraid that Cathy would leave him if he didn't provide her with the gifts, the planned evenings, the discussions about their feelings, and his careful Cathy-oriented lovemaking.

It turned out that he was right. When he spoke with Cathy about his desire to make some changes and what he wanted to try, she was very supportive. But when he actually put his ideas into practice, they started having big fights about her "feeling abandoned so that he could grow." She was able to admit that she liked him much better the other way. She enjoyed the attention and caretaking.

After struggling for three more months, they decided to separate. The good news, however, for Mike, is that he is now in a new relationship that has lasted a year. He started immediately to balance giving and receiving—which avoided having to have the "big talk." He also reported to me that being relaxed was everything I had promised him it would be.

## Being Met Instead of Making It Work

You'll find out a lot about your partner when you talk about this concept of doing less. Then, you'll learn even more when you put this new resolve into practice. Mike's story is, thankfully, not typical. Often, the partner is relieved. All that caretaking is also controlling, and being free of it is mixed—you lose something and gain something.

Let what *you* want out of a relationship be your guide. This may take time since you have spent years being guided by what your parents, friends, and partners want; but the rewards will be worth it. Also, your partner's response may surprise you. You may have assumed things about your partner's needs and wants that are not at all accurate.

Still, the trick is to know what you want. That may not be easy for you. During an exercise I use to teach couples how to ask for what they want, I often find one partner unable to be "selfish" enough to make solid requests. Mike, in the vignette above, struggled with learning how he wanted to make love. He realized that he had let Cathy control it and had given no input himself. Other people are similar to Mike. When asked what they want in a relationship, they can only think of pleasing their partner.

On the surface this appears generous and self-sacrificing. It is my experience, however, that not asking for what you want deprives any relationship of equality and joy. It creates a one-sided situation where the partner is missing out on the joy of pleasing his or her lover. If you have this problem of not knowing what you want, I strongly suggest you work hard to overcome this handicap. Two solid people make up the health of a good relationship.

You will succeed at this if you begin to make it a priority. Some painful struggle and stubborn persistence may be required, but it will get easier. In your own private time, keep discovering what you enjoy, what makes you happy, what relaxes you, and what gives you energy, spark, fascination, or joy.

> Getting what you want out of a relationship may take time since you have spent years being guided by what your parents, friends, and partners want, but the rewards will be worth it.

Once you have begun to recognize more and more, little by little, what it is that pleases you, experiment with adding these elements to your relationships. You can experiment with friends and at work, as well as with your dating partners. I suggest you try either doing new things or not doing things you have always done. You can also try asking your partner for new sensual pleasures.

Some people have discovered that foot massages are a delightful gift to receive once they were able to ask for them—others go for the whole massage. Receiving flowers at work can also charge up your feelings for your lover. A sincere and loving card can be a big turn-on early in a relationship and later, too, when things get more secure. A cup of tea in bed on Saturday morning can make you feel cared for. Telling your partner about your favorite foods and letting him or her prepare them your favorite way can be an exciting romantic adventure. Asking for a bath together can open the door to some unexpected pleasures.

Receiving pleasure gracefully from your partner can be a challenge, but it is also a gift to your partner. Everyone likes to feel useful and generous. Think of your grateful reception of something your partner does for you or gives to you as a gift from you. This can help you get over your difficulty with receiving.

Above all, be gentle with yourself. Remember, you have spent years denying what you want in order to give to others. Or you have resented having to do things for others all the time. You may also have a rebellious streak that does the opposite of what's expected or asked. What you do out of rebellion does not necessarily express your true desires. They are reactions to commands or expectations. You have never been free to listen to your own desires and wants. Until now.

This compulsive, giving behavior can also feel very strange to a partner. She can begin to feel that you don't really love her, just fear her. You aren't doing all those wonderful things because she is so special to you, but rather because you feel you have to. This can grow over time into that partner feeling like an oppressor or a witch. This is hardly the feeling you have wanted to create, but your compulsive behavior can produce just that effect.

## A Personal Example

Since I have grown through many of the issues discussed in this chapter, my experience may light the way for you. After a few years of unsuccessful dating, I finally got tired of trying to be in charge all the time. I guess fatigue and a sense of not being cared for got the best of me and made me decide to let go of some of the control that doing so much in a relationship entails. I would pick women, unconsciously of course, who believed in the romance of men taking care of them. They never stated this formally, but upon looking back, I can see that they wanted to have meals paid for on dates, enjoyed my cooking for them, liked my arranging social events for us, and waited for me to initiate conversations that I thought were essential to the relationship. I can also see, now that I have learned to relax and let go, that much of this was provoked by my own fear of not being acceptable unless I provided the "goodies."

This expectation and my compliance with it was often very subtle and wouldn't become an issue until the relationship had progressed for a few months. After the initial getting together and my taking charge of much of the relationship, my own needs to be taken care of came roaring up. I would then back off and wait for her to give back to me. That maneuver looked like abandonment to the woman and wasn't what she had hoped for in picking me. We would both get our feelings hurt and then try and work it out.

I, of course, blamed the woman for not giving enough. I accused her of wanting to be "Daddy's little girl," which didn't do much good for either of us. It was only when I began to know what I wanted, and picked women who had similar desires, that I got closer to my relaxed mode. As I changed to taking less control, the woman could exert more of herself and give me more of what I had wanted all along. Thus, a balance began to emerge in my relationships that had eluded me before.

The hardest thing for me was learning how to receive a genuinely generous woman. Perhaps this was because I had little experience with generosity. I realized that I wasn't truly being generous. By that I mean I wasn't doing things for others freely because I loved them. I was doing them so that they would love me. It's a whole different experience. Even though the actions are the same, the motivation changes the dynamics.

## A Golden Rule for Love

At this important transition in my dating life, I made a rule for myself that helped a lot. I decided I wouldn't spontaneously do anything for a woman that I wasn't happy to do even if it wasn't returned. For example, if I wasn't willing to give her flowers or a card or to clean or repair her car unless I got something back, I wouldn't do it. On the other hand, I also learned to ask her to do things for me if I did certain things for her. This replaced my previous one-sided giving situation, in which I secretly expected her to return the favor and felt sour if she didn't. At first, this seemed very cold and calculating. I have since learned how much more fun it is to feel the balance of give and take. Also, with this approach I

> I decided I wouldn't spontaneously do anything for a woman that I wasn't happy to do even if it wasn't returned.

learned to give more freely, because I wanted to rather than because I was afraid not to.

Tandem bicycles work best when both people are peddling—so do relationships. I teach couples who come to my office that giving and receiving are the currency of a relationship. Both are needed by both people. I have seen hundreds of relationships come into a healing wholeness as both people begin to ask for what they want.

A balance of giving and taking is normal, quite acceptable, and actually freeing for both partners in a relationship. Once established, this process can lead both of you to being truly generous.

Out of this came a realization for me that I wanted to be generous, and I wanted a generous mate. If I was with a woman for a while and I stopped wanting to do things for her, I began to think about what that meant about our relationship. Sometimes it meant that I didn't feel I was getting enough back, and was, once again, doing most of the work. Other times, it meant that the desire to be together was being assaulted by doubts.

Through these experiments and reflections, I began to see myself more accurately. I learned that I liked being in the role of giver; I had a much more difficult time receiving. I asked myself, why would someone want to give to me? And without any expectations of getting something in return? Changes came slowly but steadily. Now I'm able to graciously receive all the wonderful things my wife, Linda, does for me. Not only am I relaxed in a way that I could not have understood five years ago, but I am also more generous. Of course, Linda likes that also.

This is a slow process, and it requires fine tuning. It's impossible to make these changes all at once—or perfectly the first time. Most people can't break down all those layers of learned behavior so quickly. They are intertwined with childhood needs and fears and have to be loosened up and separated one at a time.

## Exercises: A Step-by-Step Approach for Change

**Exercise 1.** Learn to recognize what you like to receive in a relationship. What makes you feel loved and cared about? Also, what are the things you like to do and the way you, in particular, like certain activities to proceed? We all have tastes and preferences. Write a list of these under "What I Enjoy Receiving."

**Exercise 2.** Now imagine getting what you specifically want. For example, you state a preference for a restaurant and he says, "Great! I would love to try that." Does any feeling or thought creep into your head that might show you what you fear from getting your way; for example, are you afraid of not being needed or loved? For instance, if she doesn't need your help in her life, do you believe there is any reason for her to love you? Or do you fear that you will be seen as too needy or demanding? Write this fear or fears under "My Fear in Asking for What I Want."

**Exercise 3.** Next, experiment with asking for some or all of these things. Try and pick people who might enjoy giving you treats, gifts, and pleasure; and see how that feels. Since you are breaking a pattern, it will probably feel mixed. But experience how it feels to receive what you want. Can you enjoy the treat, gift, or pleasure? Are there strong fears that surface? Do you feel a responsibility to return the favor immediately?

**Exercise 4.** Learn from this experiment what feels good and satisfying to you. Use this knowledge to shape your relationships. Write what you learn under "Things I Definitely Want to Continue." Play with this process until you feel relaxed in a relationship. Feeling relaxed is the signal that the relationship is working. Pay attention to this, and treasure that relationship!

**Exercise 5.** By emphasizing this active approach of asking for what you want, it will be much harder to continue doing everything yourself and having so much control over the relationship. Asking for what you want frees you from controlling the relationship by shifting your energy from worrying about whether you are OK to taking care of yourself. Entitle a section "My Experiments" and each time you try this approach, write what you asked for and what happened.

## Taking in Feedback and Letting Go

Now let's do some fine tuning of this concept. At this point, I assume you are trying these concepts with friends and people you are dating. Your dating has become an experiment in change. Your first hurdle will be to stop doing some of the things you usually do in relationships. This could feel very uncomfortable; it may feel like you are being cold and uncaring.

When I first tried this, I felt like a heel. The surprising thing was that the relationship was going very smoothly and enjoyably for both of us. This gave me a solid dose of reality and told me that I had been doing much more than most people expect or want. In fact, my old behavior had been smothering and controlling. My new behavior was roomier and gave breathing space for both of us.

If you think you are the one who has to talk about what's wrong in the relationship, stop. Let things go on for a while and see what the other person does. He or she is half of the equation, you know. If you feel that the burden of making arrangements for dates and entertainment all rests on you, stop. Give your partner enough space to feel the void and act accordingly.

This is easier when you are dating because each new date sees you fresh, without any preconceptions. If you are in an ongoing relationship, you'll need to talk about trying all of this with your partner. Otherwise, you are setting up an unfair test that your partner is probably going to sleep through and flunk.

What if the other person doesn't do anything to fill in the void? You have followed the suggestions above, and he or she just lets it slide? You are now confronted with a choice about the relationship. Do you need help? Have you really talked this out? Or is this person just not the type for your new self? It may be decision time.

---

Give your partner enough space to feel the void and act accordingly.

---

It's always difficult to let go of a relationship. You may be tempted to do more than your share until the other person gets the idea. If there are things you enjoy about the relationship, it won't be easy for you to decide to let go just because your partner doesn't take enough responsibility for it. You may have to develop to a new level of confidence before you act on your convictions.

If it is a new relationship without commitments, ask for what you want and see what happens. Then make a decision based on that and not upon wishful thinking. If the relationship is one you have hope for, you can get help, if you need it, from counseling.

Choices about continuing with new relationships or dropping them will be made easier by your successes. Through experimenting, you may feel the rewarding awareness of the roominess and ease that I got in my early experiments. Once past the discomfort zone, you will enjoy the freedom and relaxation that comes with not expecting all the responsibilities to be yours.

If you have experienced some positive feedback, it will be easier to say good-bye to a person who does not share the responsibility with you. Even so, you'll be tempted to find lots of excuses for that person. You'll want to give him or her more chances. But remember, this is the pattern you're trying to break. If you want to be relaxed in a relationship, you'll have to find someone who also wants *you* to be relaxed.

This reminds me of the situation of new parents who are stressed out. The man comes home from work and wants to relax with his wife. She does also and promises to relax as soon as the dishes are finished and the baby is bathed and in bed. But after she's done all that, she's too tired to talk or make love and he gets angry and sulks. What's wrong with this picture? If he really wants his wife to relax with him, he is going to have to help with those tasks to carve out the time for both of them.

In a relationship, there are always tasks or chores: physical chores like cleaning house, clothes, and cars; financial chores like working, paying bills, shopping, and making calls for information; emotional chores like sharing daily happenings, working out conflicts, initiating tenderness, lovemaking, and talking about feelings. If one person is doing most or all of the work in any area, it's difficult to see how that person can possibly relax. Both people have to be willing to share the load to get the maximum amount of relaxation for both.

Listen for feedback on whether your partner is willing to share the load, but be sure to leave enough space for them to do their share. While you are thinking about this, remember that you probably have a need to control the situation in order to avoid that old anxious feeling of not being enough. That anxiety was created by having more responsibility put on you at an early age than was appropriate. Being asked to take emotional care of one of your parents, to intervene in their fighting, or to take care of siblings accounts for a great deal of these feelings in your adult life.

This need to have the relationship under your wing might make it difficult to really let the other person initiate discussions or activities. Some people are like hawks ready to swoop down when the task, question, or arrangement hasn't been made in the time he or she thought it should be. When you're ready to change this behavior, choose one thing that you usually take responsibility for in relationships and give the other person room to take charge. Then see what happens. See how it feels to you. Observe what the other person does or doesn't do. This is the feedback that you can use to make sorting decisions.

> You might feel anxious at first, and it may seem to take forever for the other person to get around to what you saw needed attention long ago. .

This is a slow process and will require some learning and adjusting on your part. Keep experimenting to see how it feels better for you and the other person when you allow more space into the various tasks of a relationship. You might feel anxious at first, and it may seem to take forever for the other person to get around to what you saw needed attention long ago. Keep watching how it feels to make these changes. In exchange for not having things done exactly as you would do it, you should feel more relaxed and met.

**Exercise.** Under "Ways I Want to Love," make a list of things that you are willing to do for a partner as a pure gift—you expect nothing in return except thanks. This could be a loving card, flowers, loving messages left on a machine during the day, small gifts from time to time, help with your partner's project, or any other small gestures you enjoy giving without measuring the return.

Of course, you would be foolish to do a lot of these and have nothing coming back at all. If you are getting nothing back, that's feedback for you to examine and see if you can live with it—I couldn't. However, the task in this exercise is to separate doing certain loving things from earning love or having control. This list is a reminder to you of what you enjoy giving because it expresses how you like to live with a person.

## Janine and Rafael

A friend of mine named Rafael, who was in my men's group, complained about women being flakes. Rafael was very precise and efficient. He knew a lot about communication and feelings, he held a good job, but he had trouble with relationships. He couldn't find a woman who he felt met him equally.

On a business trip to Portland, Oregon, he met Janine—who was definitely his equal. They started having a great time visiting each other and enjoying the early stages of love. However, Janine quickly tired of Rafael's controlling ways. Fortunately, she was able to peek through his controlling habits and see the good guy that he wanted to be. She also wasn't shy about speaking up.

One Monday, Rafael came to the men's group looking like a cat that has eaten the steak thawing on the counter—guilty but not wanting you to notice. Of course, we noticed. After a brief hesitation, he told us how Janine sat him down and lectured him for an hour about his controlling habits. Rafael was lucky. Not many men or women get to be lectured by somebody who sees their underlying goodness and good intentions. He emerged a changed man.

Because of his fearless ability to look into himself, he made amazingly quick progress in allowing more give and take in the relationship. He began letting other people do things their way; also, he began to ask for hugs from us or time to discuss an issue. I never heard him complain about flakes again. He and Janine got married and moved to Florida. A few Christmas cards have kept me informed of their progress. By this time, he has had his own opportunities to lecture Janine. They are great examples of being met equally.

## It's Worth the Effort

Now that you have seen what an awesome task this shift may be, perhaps you are asking yourself if it's really that important. A quick review of why it is might help.

First, if you have read this far, you probably identify with much of what has been discussed. Maybe you see that your relationships have a pattern that this chapter speaks to. You consistently feel that you have to do most of the work and that you aren't cared for in a way that feels secure to you. You may have been accused of being controlling by enough people that you think there is something to it. Maybe even the words, "being relaxed in a relationship" gives you a special yearning for an elusive feeling you know you desire.

Whatever it is that attracts you to this material is a pattern that is creating problems for you. It may be the reason you are not getting the love you want. If you feel that the efforts you put into relationships are not returned, and you feel that you are not really appreciated in those relationships, doing the work discussd in this chapter will make a huge difference.

There are times and circumstances when it is tolerable to be in relationships that aren't mutually fulfilling; if there are many other friends and family members to give you emotional satisfaction and comfort, for example. However, today it is common to be thrown together with our mate in an isolated cocoon. More than in any other age, we are demanding mutual satisfaction, joy, and relaxation from our relationships.

If you can't be relaxed in a relationship, you can't have any of the other goodies either. Being afraid that you aren't acceptable, that you are going to be abandoned, or that you aren't ever going to be good enough is not a fulfilling way to live. If you make the effort to achieve success in love right now, you will enter a relationship that has a far greater chance of future success, joy, and love.

That seems well worth the effort to me. Good luck!

# 9

# Being a Victim:
# How to Remain Unhappy
# and Blame Everyone Else

The best way I know to avoid improving your life is to see yourself as a victim of outside forces. We've all heard the cliches: "There aren't any good men or women out there." "Let's face it, we are the dregs, and that's all that's left." "This society makes it impossible to meet new people." Lame excuses like these are a very effective way to remain unhappy and unfulfilled, and to avoid making changes for a better life.

You may notice that to see yourself as a victim, you have to find someone or something else to blame. Blaming and being a martyr can become a blissful and painless habit. Of course, you suffer the inevitable angst that results from experiencing the world around you as screwed up. However, this existential pain is more than offset by the bliss of never having to see your own shadows, confront your fear of failure, or do something about your lack of skills. But the worst part is you also don't get what you say you really want in your life.

> Lame excuses like these are a very effective way to remain unhappy and unfulfilled, and to avoid making changes for a better life.

Victim consciousness is a tough state to break out of. Victim's perceive their helplessness as absolute and unchangeable. The resulting blame is logical to them, a matter of fact, not of perception. Like someone in a dark room, the person is blind to his or her victim behavior until the light somehow gets turned on. Meanwhile, the habit of being a martyr prevents them from growing and feeling empowered. No real changes can take place until this faulty perception is removed—and until the person takes responsibility for making the best of the hand he or she has been dealt.

## Recipe for Staying Isolated by Being a Victim

If you want to use blaming and victim consciousness as a way of life, here is how to do it. First, when you feel bad about something, build up a case about how unfair it is. You can build your case around a whole menu of possible problems: You don't make enough money, you don't have friends, you had a bad childhood, your body hurts, you have to live with your parents, your car is always breaking down, your love life stinks.

Next, find someone or something to blame. Parents, society, the government, small-minded people, a friend, men, women, doctors, capitalists, and so on. Now the important part: as you begin to feel the pain of these sad situations in your life, quickly shut that out and shift to blame. Get angry and feel the energy as you blame others for the troubles that have been inflicted on you by unfair treatment or by the stupidity or hatred of someone else.

Now you are ready for the reward—the martyr pose. With that attitude, you can wrap yourself in the mantle of sweet suffering. It's a trustworthy companion. Suffering is constant and uncritical. It doesn't desert you and make you feel alone.

If you are having a hard time feeling the joy of being wronged and helpless, use a "blame sentence" to indict one of the agents of your pain from the vast array of people and institutions available. Blame sentences begin with "If only ... " and "They should have ... ," or "Look what you're doing to me!"

## The Sweet Rewards of Martyrdom

There is a certain pleasure in being a victim and blaming everyone else. It can be like taking drugs. It numbs you from feeling pain and gives many subtle rewards. One of these is drowning out critical self-talk that causes painful memories. A second reward is replacing your pain with a less intrusive numbness and a righteous anger that is more fun to talk about. The ultimate reward is not having to take charge of your life and risk failure.

To be perfectly successful at being a victim, don't ever fall into the trap of thinking that it's your responsibility to understand your problems and your role in solving them. If you start doing that, you'll start feeling tense, panicky, incompetent, or worse. The bliss and denial of being a martyr will evaporate. Then you will have to start over by finding other people or events to blame.

---

With the martyr attitude, you can wrap yourself in the mantle of sweet suffering. It's a trustworthy companion. Suffering is constant and uncritical. It doesn't desert you and make you feel alone.

---

## Why Would Anyone Want to Be this Way?

Since this style of blaming the world for all of your personal problems seems silly when you look at it this way, why do people continue being victims and how does it get started? The easiest way to understand victim behavior is to realize that victims are made, not born. Victims act like victims. You may find yourself baffled or outraged by a woman's refusal to leave a horrendous marriage. She may know that she's clearly being abused, but she is acting like a victim by staying in the situation.

A number of current books and movies are bringing vivid detail to this tragic condition. Amy Tan's *The Kitchen God's Wife* and the movie, *The Cook, the Thief, His Wife, and Her Lover* both present poignant, understandable, and compassionate stories of women who see no way out of horrendous situations. In each of these stories, the women are helpless to extricate themselves from impossible situations until they are shown the way by other people.

We all have some victim consciousness in us. This can either be a part-time or full-time habit. Many of us feel powerful over most of our lives except for one area, like standing up to an aggressive person or to a man or woman that we are attracted to. A drunk on the street who is dressed in rags, has lost his wife and kids, stinks, can't work, and is begging in a half-hearted way for a coin, is an example of full-time victim consciousness. But the person walking by him might be as pathetically passive when it comes to dealing with his teenager or his boss.

Most people are part-time holders of victim consciousness. Victims are made by being abused, assaulted, broken, ridiculed, tormented, or treated in any manner that is painful or destructive and over which the individual has no control.

Maggie was made into a victim by being laughed at by her father. As a child, when she came up with ideas about things she read in the paper, he always made fun of her. At an early age, she started reading, asking questions, and sharing her ideas, but this was not appreciated. She was always a straight-A student, and it is entirely possible that her high school dropout father was threatened by how smart she was. He showed this by constantly putting her ideas down and ridiculing her creativity.

The result was that she could not discuss what she read or argue her ideas with her father. She was victimized in that area of her life. Men could not be trusted to take a woman seriously, intellectually. Although she achieved top honors and was even encouraged by her father to go to college—where she excelled—she chose to attend a women's college.

Now Maggie is having problems with men. She will tell you that they don't respect her opinions. They never let women talk long enough to prove a point. She has given up on marriage because she learned that she could either get married or have an intellectual life, not both. Many of her friends disagree, and some are strong examples of smart, married women who are respected by their husbands. Regardless of any new information she may receive, Maggie is acting like a victim and is living the part of her life that deals with men in victim consciousness. She is using blame of men's childish control over women's minds to keep her from risking a loving relationship.

How else should she act? Maggie might see herself as hardly a victim at all compared to a woman or man who was beaten, sexually abused, or emotionally battered by an alcoholic or mentally ill parent. However, that comparison could block her growth, not allowing her to recognize the extent to which she has been victimized. It will take an outside influence to help Maggie, and people like her, find their way out of acting helpless. That outside influence could be a therapist, a lover, a friend, a support group, or anyone who appears in her life at the right time.

> She is using blame of men's childish control over women's minds to keep her from risking a loving relationship.

How Maggie gets ready for this help, since she is a victim, can come about in different ways. Some call it grace, or in other cases, readiness can be triggered by an event. It often happens when people bottom out and just get sick of living the way they are. Others get ready when they see the effect they are having on people they love.

## Why It's So Difficult to Stop Acting Like a Victim

Why is it so difficult to get rid of this style of living? I ask this question because I have been frustrated more than once as a therapist in trying to help clients out of the state of victimhood. Its tenacity is appalling. I have found that victim consciousness can't always be solved by direct methods. Therefore I have begun to think of it is an addiction, rather than a habit that can be broken with practice.

All addictions stem from feelings of helplessness. We use them to shield ourselves from feelings and experiences that seem too painful to deal with. The addiction becomes our alternative life; it is much less complicated and much less unpredictable than real life and therefore seems manageable. Addictions also give the victim a feeling of being in control, even though this is only an illusion.

Addictions are also compulsive. Giving up an addiction is terrifying. It appears to the addict that there is no life on "the other side." The substance or behavior in question seems vital to survival and the very last thing that he or she would be willing to give up.

It is safe to say that there is a victim consciousness in any addiction. But is there an addiction to being a victim?

This is important. If you find that you identify with these descriptions of victim consciousness and don't want to live your life that way, I want to warn you of something. It may be a much more challenging task to stop victim consciousness than you think. If victimhood is a habit, you can change it with hard work. If it is an addiction, you are in a different ball game. You'll have to prepare yourself as though you were going into battle against a desperate enemy. Life may seem infinitely more frightening than your old habit. Also, you may need help to do it. And most of all, you'll need to know that there is life on the other side—the side of taking responsibility for your actions and their consequences.

Whether victimhood is a habit or an addiction depends on how ingrained and compulsive your need to blame others is. An addiction to victimhood could be a way of shielding yourself against all the feelings that surround failure or inadequacy. Little Johnnie was raised by a demanding father who criticized him constantly. As an adult, he's stuck in a boring job that makes him unhappy. Now, John falls into victim consciousness as a way not to take chances and risk failure. If he breaks out of victim consciousness, he's going to have to confront himself with his shortcomings and his strengths; changing might look impossible, the safety of the past might seem preferable, and he'll have to take some risks that don't carry guarantees. However, he might be able to make his life work in a much more fulfilling way.

Another fear that can be avoided by an addiction to victimhood is the pain of having expectations dashed, making you feel abandoned and worthless. Terry learned early to act independent and tough because her parents were either too drunk or too preoccupied to attend to her. They also got angry whenever she asked for help. Now Terry is a victim in relationships, acting independent and then blaming men for not being there for her.

## Addiction or Neurosis?

There is another problem to deal with before we can come to methods of getting rid of victim consciousness. An addiction to victimhood would best be treated in an ACOA (Adult Children of Alcoholics) or AlAnon group. (Adult Children of Alcoholics groups are a branch of Alcoholics Anonymous that welcome anyone who feels they come from a dysfunctional or abusive family—not just people with a history of family alcoholism.) What if you are not really addicted to victimhood, but it is instead a nasty habit that you can't seem to get rid of? This is commonly called a neurosis. Neuroses are best treated in psychotherapy. Now you have a quandary. If the treatments are different for neurosis and addiction, how do you know which one will work best for you?

You have three choices: (1) you can try on your own to solve the victim habits; (2) you can go to either therapy *or* an AlAnon or ACOA group; or (3) you can combine therapy and one of these twelve-step groups. I suggest you first read this chapter and try to change your behavior on your own. If that isn't enough, use your best judgment to choose the appropriate help. If one approach doesn't work, try another.

The main point is that you may have to try a number of things to leave this neurosis/addiction behind. I know people who have used therapy and have changed. I also know people who have used AlAnon and changed. Unfortunately, I know of others who have used these methods and haven't changed.

If you have other addictions and know about them, the group approach may work for you. If you aren't aware of possessing other addictions, you may want to try therapy first. The gray area is for those of you who don't abuse substances and don't think you are addicted to work, food, sex, gambling, or shopping but have lived with addicted people, either as a child or as an adult.

For people like this, the codependence groups and the ACOA groups may be the best thing. One caveat: these are newly formed groups within the twelve-step programs and may not have the seasoned sponsors who are so helpful in older groups such as AA and AlAnon. Often, people who join these newer programs use therapy along with a twelve-step program. This is what I would recommend if you recognize the patterns I have described and feel the desire to change, but have so far lacked the ability on your own.

---

> You may have to try a number of things to leave this neurosis/addiction behind.

---

I have gone to such great lengths to describe these treatment methods because I feel strongly that people who use blaming as a style of avoiding life and seem like victims to friends and lovers have put their lives on hold. They need help to get a fresh approach to solving their problems and gaining a sense of responsibility and power.

## Signs to Look for—Fear and Control

If you were victimized in some way, you will probably go to extremes to avoid feeling pain, and to protect yourself from feeling the hurt you experienced in your childhood. The interplay of fear and control are primary elements in a victim's behavior. Fear drives you to avoid pain in its many forms, and control is what you use to do it. Actually, most of us have some aspects of this type of behavior somewhere in our lives.

Jake, a thirty-three-year-old computer salesman, was unhappy with his life. He was tired of coming home to an empty house. His job in sales was challenging and brought in good money, but he was ready to start creating a future, with a wife, house, kids, and plans. The trouble was, there just didn't seem to be any great women out there for him.

Jake had dated plenty of women since his early twenties, but it never panned out. He told me the women would always start getting whiny about something. He was "too into his work," "his schedule was unpredictable," "he talked too much," "took them for granted," and so on, and so forth. All his relationship attempts seemed to end the same way—fighting, having hurt feelings, seeing how different they were from one another, and giving up exhausted from all the effort.

At this point in his story, I knew that Jake had victim consciousness. I also suspected his way of dealing with women and asked him, "Did any of these women accuse you of being controlling?"

"Oh God, yes! All the time." He answered with a huge sigh, rolling his eyes upwards and slumping in his chair. It was like a kinesthetic morse code that spelled out "helpless in the face of woman—the mysterious and unmerciful."

Jake couldn't see that he was being controlling until he understood that he had been hurt as a boy by his mother. As a single mom, she had been overworked and unable to fulfill her emotional needs. Like many single parents, she used her son as her emotional support and buddy. Jake spent much youthful energy trying to make her happy, comforting her when she was depressed about work, lonely, or disappointed by yet another man. Jake was too young to be able to perform this role for his mother. He needed her comfort and help, not the other way around.

This form of abuse conditioned Jake to be confused around women on dates. A very natural part of him wanted to be taken care of, listened to, and understood. Another part insisted that unless he took care of the woman, she would leave him. He was afraid of being left, afraid of being a disappointment, afraid of being a failure as a man, and afraid that he would never be able to relax and be loved. Some of these fears were easy for him to identify as the therapy progressed. Others, especially the fear of not being able to relax and be loved, were concepts he laughed off at first.

The work progressed slowly until he understood to what extent he had been used by his mother. At the time she didn't know better, but nevertheless, she put enormous demands on a dependent and vulnerable child. After this realization, it was much easier for Jake to look at his fears on dates. He also became ready to deal with his controlling behavior, which was designed to take care of these fears.

> "Did any of these women accuse you of being controlling?"
> "Oh God, yes! All the time." He answered with a huge sigh, rolling his eyes upwards and slumping in his chair.

Jake began to experiment with new forms of taking care of his recently discovered fears in ways that didn't control his date. For example, he asked real questions instead of setup ones: "Would you like to take a hike?" as opposed to "It's a great day, perfect for a hike, let's go, whadaya say?" He discussed options about dinner plans instead of feeling that he had to read her mind and magically make the right choice. He has even begun to relax and ask his date to take charge of an evening every once in a while. At this time, Jake is enjoying his social life and is optimistic about future plans with a mate.

## Looking in the Mirror

One of the reasons I deal well with this issue as a therapist is that I had to work on overcoming certain pockets of victim consciousness in my own life. When my wife, Linda, is going through a rough period and withdraws into herself, I feel helpless and go into sulking mode. Why am I a victim in this area? I could go after her and say, "Oh come on, you can spend half an hour with me." Instead, I get angry and hurt, go away, and try to take care of myself. I find myself turning off to her and wanting her to hurt from my absence.

Writing this chapter and seeing myself do that all in the same week was a humbling lesson. I am not a passive person, but this one area is a glaring exception. The idea that I can have any input into my wife's desire to withdraw and leave me without her enjoyable contact, is foreign to me. What is my fear? I think I'm going to be abandoned! And I feel so helpless in the face of that impending doom. I immediately try to control the situation by withdrawing and trying to make it not matter. In a way more rigid than I'd like to admit, I look for ways to entertain myself or get away from the source of pain—my wife's own needs and decisions.

Using the same exercises presented in this chapter, I can think back to stories of my childhood at a very young age. One example is the time I was left with my mother's friend while she traveled for two weeks.

When she returned (I'm told), I said I wanted to stay with the other woman. This story comes to mind as I reflect on my sense of helplessness when my wife withdraws. I had no control over my mother's leaving me, and I still feel I have no control over my wife withdrawing from me.

> I find myself turning off to her and wanting her to hurt from my absence.

But I do! She listens to my needs and is able to work out deals to take care of herself and help me. It's my own myth of powerlessness that's the problem. If I can't say to her that I need a little attention, she'll never know it. This is especially true because I try to control my fear by acting cool and removing myself from her. When I do this, she sees that I am cool and feels hurt that her need to withdraw is so passively received. It so easily gets to be a mess.

## Control Issues Up Close

Usually, it's easy to see how another person is controlling. He controls the conversation by doing most of the talking, or she listens ever so briefly to you and then switches to her own experiences or thoughts. She might have a teasing and slightly seductive way of getting you to go along with her plans. He is cleverly able to distract you with flattery, or he kids you when you have a problem you want to discuss with him. She uses rage to make you afraid to disagree with her. He uses threats of getting angry to control you from crossing his desires.

How about our own control issues and maneuvers? They are much more difficult to see. We use controlling behavior to take care of well-hidden fears. If we could know these fears, we probably would take care of them in much more effective ways. But since they are hidden, they require unconscious protection—hence, our control methods. If someone is brave enough to tell us we are controlling, we may agree with them but see it as purely a way of taking care that we are not run over by other people: "I'm only protecting a sense of fairness, not really controlling." Others, however, are controlling because they want their own way, like spoiled brats who think they deserve the world for themselves! How about that for a double standard?

In fact, everyone's attempts at control serve unconscious fears. "I won't be liked if he really gets to know me." "She'll leave me if I tell her that." "If I don't watch out, I'm going to be used." These fears are very hard for us to own. We have resisted them all of our lives and have covered them over with defenses that serve to blunt their sharp pain. It's no wonder that we can't see our own attempts at control, because we would have to see our deep and troubling fears as well. It's much easier to gloss over these controlling behaviors as ways of standing up for women's rights, trying to be a gallant man, trying to be fair, or standing up for yourself in the service of justice.

## How Control Issues Affect Relationships

When lovers get married and set up long-term household, family, and financial plans, they have to get through a stage I call the power struggle. This is nothing more than trying to take care of their fears of intimacy by controlling their partner. Since they each try to win the contest, it becomes a struggle between them with no winners.

While dating, a lot of these issues lie dormant, waiting for the time when a commitment will bring them out. However, even before commitment becomes an issue, your unconscious agenda, using control, is doing its best to protect you from your worst relationship fears. The problem is that it is also keeping you from having a good relationship.

Jake, whose story has already been discussed in this chapter, was controlling his dates so that he didn't have to repeat the confusing and burdensome drama that he and his mother played out earlier. The whole idea of being in a relationship was terrifying to his unconscious with all of its memories of childhood burdens and frustrations. His unconscious was protecting him so much that all the women he dated felt controlled and manipulated. Then, when they left him, he sank into victimhood and declared that it was all impossible.

Turning points come when people can't live with themselves anymore. Janelle came to see me after she heard me speak at a church singles club. She too was at the end of her rope with "men and the dating disasters," as she put it. She couldn't, for the life of her, figure out how anyone ever got married or stayed married. She yearned for a partner, but at thirty-eight, she felt that it would never happen for her.

Consulting with me was her last gasp of hope. Janelle had never been in therapy before and was surprised at how quickly she began to see how she was protecting a little girl inside who was terribly afraid of being seen as a phony. This idea was subtly but firmly implanted in her by her perfectionistic parents. Her reactions to their loving but misguided attempts to teach her to excel at everything was to learn to hide out as much as possible and reveal little about herself. She also used perfectionism herself as a defense against being found out for who she really was, and this came out as criticism of her dates. Since nobody is fond of being criticized, it wasn't hard to see why her relationships weren't going well.

Janelle made gradual, steady changes in revealing herself to people around her. I also had her practice one of my favorite methods for changing her particular problem. She would purposely make silly mistakes, one a day for two weeks. These might include confusing her change at the grocery store, droping something, giving the wrong paper to her secretary, and so on. As she became more comfortable with her own mistakes—especially since she was in charge of them during the exercise—she was less critical with others and began to develop a sense of humor about messing up.

## Strategies for Change—Learning to Take Care of Yourself

Changing from victim consciousness is the process of learning to take care of yourself. Victims were never taught how. Instead, they were shown in various and often horrible ways how helpless they were. It is a constant source of shame to victims that they can't take care of themselves. Often the most healing aspect of their therapy is to learn that they can't be expected to know what no one ever taught them. Since knowing how to take care of yourself is learned in childhood as the result of good parenting, it isn't your fault that you didn't learn how.

> Changing from victim consciousness is the process of learning to take care of yourself. Victims were never taught how.

In all too many family situations, children learn survival skills that frequently are not useful as adults. Some victims learned how to take care of themselves in ways that are not conducive to closeness and therefore don't work well in relationships. These people have learned to survive with anger and rage. They are probably still alive and kicking because they were able to marshall that energy to protect themselves. But that is different from learning to take care of themselves *and* be in a relationship. Escaping, another favorite survival technique for children, doesn't enhance relationships either. All the childhood forms of survival seem to keep people out of relationships.

However, adults can learn new skills when they give up the comfortable but unrewarding stance of blaming. Many people today are opening the door to new ways of relating, and they are learning new skills to take charge of their life and shape it more to their liking. In doing so, they close the door to blaming others for their problems.

**First step.** Like detectives, we'll start from the evidence and work back to the motive. You are going to take an imaginary trip back to your childhood. Sit in a comfortable chair and shake your limbs and hands. Then take some deep breaths into your belly and exhale loudly. Make sounds when you exhale—have fun and be as noisy as you want.

When you feel relaxed, think back to your childhood before the age of nine and find yourself in a situation where you didn't get your way. A situation where you were stopped, crossed, cheated, slighted, or abused in some way. Now observe how you reacted and what you did to get your way.

There may be two parts to your answer. How did you react? And what did you *do* or *not do* about getting your way? Look closely and see if you used passive or active methods of getting your way. Did you withdraw, pout, and hope someone would take pity on you or feel guilty? Did you throw a tantrum? Did you connive and scheme, use arguments, or use some other form of persuasion?

Now, repeat this exercise with two more memories. Explore a memory during your early teens (ten to fifteen) when you didn't get your way. Then explore a memory during your late teens. Ask the same questions and observe how you reacted and tried to get your way.

What you can expect to learn from this exploration of three experiences in your past history is how you reacted when you felt abused, contained, squelched, or left out. Describe your methods under "How I Reacted and Tried to Get My Way." Now, underline any part of what you just wrote that is still true today—you still use these methods when you feel contained, abused, and so on. This will be the way that you try to control other people.

**Second step.** Use the information from the first step to learn what triggers the same feelings of not getting your way in your adult life. When do you feel like reacting the same way now? If you saw that you withdrew and felt sorry for yourself in your imaginary trip back to your early years, ask yourself, when do you feel the same way now? When does your face reveal the same feelings? When do you feel it in your stomach?

I can feel my face fighting back tears at certain times. I also want to withdraw and pout. Try to find similar experiences of feeling little and helpless as an adult. Write them under "What Makes Me Afraid of Not Getting My Way." These could be certain types of people, a certain tone of voice, wanting something and being afraid that asking for it will doom it for sure, or other types of triggers.

This knowledge is not easy to uncover. Our unconscious is hidden because these fears and memories are painful. Working as a detective, look for patterns of how you are re-creating your early protecting methods—the items you underlined in the first step—and try to feel the feelings underneath them like fear, hurt, hopeless resignation, and so on. You are a grown-up now and can deal with the pain. As a child you had no recourse; now you do.

**Third step.** The third step to recovery from the habit of being a victim is learning new ways of taking care of these fears and desires. This is the step that no one ever taught you how to do. At this point, you will need to observe other to get ideas. The rest of this chapter will help you with this.

## The "I Don't Know" Cop-out

Have you ever been around people who say, "I don't know" when you ask them what they want? Do you ever find yourself acting that way? If there ever was a statement that embodied victimhood, this is it. Victims don't know how to express their own feelings or desires.

"How does that make you feel?" "I don't know."

"What do you need?" "I don't know."

"What can I do to help?" "I don't know."

"What would make you feel safer or better?" "I don't know."

I often hear people saying, "I don't know," when I ask them, "Who will know how to make things better for you?" But the idea slowly sinks in that if they don't figure it out, no one else will. They can then choose to stay in the painful but familiar place of being abused, being excluded, or being taken for granted; or they can begin to figure out how to take care of themselves.

I'm not talking about admitting that you don't know something when you don't—admitting ignorance is anything but being a victim. It can be a challenge to figure out something you don't know how to do, but that is the beginning of change.

If you recognize areas of victim consciousness, you were probably raised with a hidden or blatant message not to ask for your desires or wants. Your desires were either never given to you, causing the wanting itself to become painful; or you were actively ridiculed or punished for asking. "Listen to this everyone, Jamie wants us to take him to his Little League game. Lost your legs, kid, or just saving them for the game?" Or, "You want some money for a school binder? I just gave you money; you obviously don't know how to handle money. You can babysit your sister on Saturday and make your own money to learn the value of it."

Does any of this sound familiar? Given the number of family histories that resonate with any of these issues, it's no wonder that the number one method of taking care of ourselves, namely, asking for what we want, has been closed off to many of us at an early age. However, continuing this behavior pattern as an adult will just prolong childhood problems.

---

Our desires were either never given to us, causing the wanting itself to become painful; or we were actively ridiculed or punished for asking.

---

## A Practical Program for Change

What to ask for in order to take care of yourself is the next big question. Here is a useful tool to give you that information.

1. Identify your frustration with the person and note your anger about it.

2. Ask yourself, what is the fear or hurt under this anger? It's always there, but it may be slippery to get hold of.

3. Now ask yourself, what is the childhood memory underneath that hurt or fear? Use the hurt or frightened feeling to search through your childhood until you find a similar feeling. Memories that emerge from this scanning will usually feel exactly right once they are given some space to emerge to full awareness. These memories may not be what you expected when you began the process, but they will make sense on an emotional level; that is, the feeling of hurt and fear will be similar now and in the past memory.

4. Use the hurt, the fear, and the memory that has surfaced to understand what you didn't get in childhood. What you discover will be something you also need now in order to feel better.

Let me give you an example. Lynn was angry at Lou. She was frustrated that he didn't say complimentary things to her during the time they spent together. She also discovered that she was **afraid** of being on the periphery of his life and not important to him. This **hurt** her feelings because she didn't feel special to him. She used these feelings to remember her childhood and found that the **identical feelings** popped into her consciousness when she remembered the way her father would ask her to go with him to his Saturday job. She looked forward to it all Friday night until she fell asleep. But after the day with him, she would always feel confused and bad. She now realized that although he acted as if she was special, he never said loving and positive things to her. Thus, as an adult, she still had these same needs—to be complimented verbally in a positive and loving way.

It is no surprise that this is exactly how she was feeling with Lou. He acted as if she were special, but didn't say the words. Moreover, it was particularly bothersome to her because of her relationship with her father. As a child, she never felt that she could influence her father's behavior and therefore never learned how to take care of herself in this way in her adult life.

Working together, I helped her with one more step—how to make requests that work. She wanted to say, "Lou, I need you to make me feel more special." I helped her learn to say, "Lou, I want you to compliment me on how I look at the end of our date. I want you to tell me that you had a really good time with me if you did, and any other nice thoughts about me that you have." While you are reading this, I want you to notice how much more specific these new requests are. They are doable, and they don't require Lou to read her mind.

Josh, as you may have guessed, wasn't good at being demonstrative. He wanted to be closer but didn't know how. He was happy to be given these directions and in a short time improved his efforts. He also had fun learning how to be more demonstrative. Josh was easy.

### Avoiding Two Common Mistakes

It isn't always that easy. However, your chances will be much better if you avoid the two most common mistakes couples make. The first is to ask for a personality change right after a lot of criticism. **Example 1:** "I feel so hurt and insecure with you; you never think of me. If you love me you'll start paying more attention to my needs." The other common mistake is to make negative requests or demands. **Example 2:** "Leave me alone when I don't want to talk."

Requests are not demands. They are positive, not negative. They refer to a specific behavior rather than a general attitude. For a more effective result, the first example will become: "If you love me, ask what I would like to do on Saturday night and agree to do it half of the time." The second example will become: "When I say I don't want to talk, give me a little space and then ask if there is something bothering me."

Compare these revised versions of the requests with the two examples above. I'm sure you will see how much more workable they are in that they are positive and describe a specific behavior.

### Asking for What You Want in a Way that Works

This might seem simple, but you may find these new skills difficult at first when you try to use them. Try it and see how hard it is for you. Then keep practicing until it becomes more comfortable.

The most demanding thing I ask couples to do in therapy is to make requests in this manner. Many couples find that making negative requests is easier than asking for what they want in a positive and behaviorally specific way. But negative requests make your partner feel like you appreciate their absence more than their presence. Changing a negative request, such as "Leave me alone," into a positive one, demands that you take care of yourself and stay in the relationship. This is a skill no victim has ever learned at home.

Since this is new information for many people working on relationship issues, here is a list of helpful ideas and examples. Begin with, "If you love me and want me to feel that you do, you can . . .

- compliment me on how I'm looking.

- call me when you say you will.

- tell me what you want to do.

- tell me what you love about me.

- say personal things that you are feeling.

- ask for what you want instead of hoping I'll just know.

- let me know if you had a good time with me.

- listen without interrupting until I am finished.

- initiate affectionate hugs and kisses.

- tell me you want to make love to me.

- bring me small gifts from time to time.

- bring me flowers.

- write romantic cards to me.

- say to me, "you are really special to me."

These examples will give you ideas for asking for what you want in order to feel better. You might realize from doing the steps outlined earlier that you need to feel safe or special or loved or cared about or treated with respect. You might also realize that it's important to you not to be taken for granted. All of these needs can be addressed with a request that is positive and specific.

---

Many couples find that making negative requests is easier than asking for what they want in a positive and behaviorally specific way. Changing is a hard process.

---

Yelling, screaming demands, or withdrawing are the favorite ploys of victims to stay isolated and blame others for an unsatisfying life. Making positive, behaviorally specific requests is the exact opposite. You are taking charge of your life and your needs, and it's a great way of making your life work. You can't force another person to take care of you, but you can give them clear requests that they can fulfill to show you that they care.

**Exercise.** List a frustration that you have had recently on a date or with a friend. Write it under "Becoming Good with Requests." Now, follow the steps above and write what it is about the frustration that makes you angry, the hurt or fear under the anger, and a childhood memory that feels similar. Finally, make a couple of positive and behavior-specific requests that would feel better if the same situation were to occur again. If you need help, refer to the examples of each of these steps earlier in the chapter.

Changing from blaming to taking responsibility is a difficult but rewarding challenge. Good luck!

# Part Four

# Sharing Intimacy

# 10

# Intimacy Freak-out: Relationship as Mine Field

Scott and Sue met and quickly fell in love. Both were convinced that they had finally met the right person, feeling content and delighted with their connection. It felt special and they knew it. Without actually talking about it, both Scott and Sue were counting on this relationship for the long term.

Knowing they both felt committed, Sue overcame her fears and entered into a discussion about monogamy. It went as she expected, both calmly and freely agreeing that monogamy was what they wanted. But the next day, out of the blue, they got into a bitter fight over whether to drip-dry the dishes or dry them with a towel. Scott was frightened at his own stubborn refusal to give in to Sue's way of drying dishes. She also was stunned by the energy behind her feelings.

When the adrenaline subsided, they were able to emerge from their stubborn cocoons and share how shaken they were by their first serious fight. What in the world made them both so adamant and quick to attact the other's views? They were both psychologically sharp enough to wonder what bigger issue than drying dishes was causing all the heat. The only thing that stood out was the discussion about being monogamous with each other—which both had enthusiastically agreed they wanted.

What then, was the problem? Did one of them secretly not want to be monogamous and therefore was fighting out of resentment? That's possible but not probable. It's much more likely that they were having an "intimacy freak-out"—a fight, withdrawal, or blown-out-of-proportion problem cooked up by a couple who are unable temporarily to tolerate any more intimacy. Their openly discussed commitment to monogamy was a huge step to getting closer in a serious way, and the ramifications were enormous, especially subconsciously. They couldn't handle any more intimacy, so their systems cooked up a fight to get some distance in order to cool out.

> They were both psychologically sharp enough to wonder what bigger issue than drying dishes was causing all the heat.
> The only thing that stood out was the discussion about being monogamous with each other—which both had enthusiastically agreed they wanted. Intimacy freak-out had hit home.

## Fighting as a Smoke Screen

Fighting can serve a useful purpose of creating some distance without going away or feeling abandoned. It's a way of keeping your partner at arm's length without letting him or her go entirely. In many ways it's safer than withdrawing. But fights are confusing and frightening, especially when they occur for the first time or in repetitive patterns.

Knowing that you can panic even when things are going well is an important new area of self-knowledge. It provides a balance to learning the skills of sorting and choosing partners who are right for you. Mistaking these intimacy freak-outs for incompatibility, or using them as excuses to leave, can keep people without the love they want forever.

Besides this practical purpose, knowing about your intimacy tolerance level is important self-knowledge for developing an intimate relationship that works for you and continues to get closer while respecting your own needs for space and independent nurturing.

## When to Suspect that an Intimacy Freak-out Is in Full Force

When you find yourself having a heated battle over something that seems ridiculous but which neither of you can let go of, you can suspect that the fight is serving another purpose. The fight is reducing the heat or the intensity of closeness between you and your partner because your systems are temporarily overloaded.

A common occurrence for couples who move in together, whether married or not, is that their sexual interest diminishes for the first month or so. I remember this happening to me and how weird it felt. I was very nervous about it at the time. After all, one of the reasons we are attracted to a partner is because of the good sex we share. What was suddenly wrong?

Friends reassured me that this happens to most people, and time restores the desire. I now see that what happened was an intimacy overload. We had moved all of our "stuff" together. This involved making decisions about space on the walls, floors, closets, and cupboards. Her stuff had definitely invaded my freedom to do as I wanted, and her desires had curtailed my selfishness. I was feeling overwhelmed by her, and I didn't want sexual closeness on top of that.

> The fight is reducing the heat or the intensity of closeness between you and your partner because your systems are temporarily overloaded.

We don't hear much about it, but there are side effects to intimacy, just as there are side effects to drugs. Look at penicillin as an example. It's a great drug with wonderful qualities, but it has such powerful side effects that doctors always ask if we are allergic. Intimacy too has powerful side effects. Along with its benefits, it can also get us into enormous trouble. If we are aware only of the goodies of getting close and being loved, we might find ourselves shocked by the hidden demons that emerge at times. The truth is that most people can tolerate only so much intimacy before they have to stop or freak out. Being aware of this is very helpful preventive medicine.

## The Up- and Downside of Intimacy

People tend to focus on the enchantment of love—the flowers and notes, the exciting sex, the warm and cozy aspects of finding and being with someone special. This is what we are promised by television commercials, billboards, and magazine ads. The popular myth is that finding and winning a lover is the real trick. What's important, the advertisements say, is how you look, dress, or smell. Or if the message is more sophisticated, the issue is how considerate or how giving a person you are or, at least, could appear to be with the right product. The implication is that after you win your love, you are home free. Sure, you'll have fights and hard times, but all will be well because you now have a relationship with someone who really loves you.

The shocker is, that's exactly the time and the reason for the allergic symptoms to show up. Intimacy freak-out! Since you are not warned about this side effect, you are taken by surprise and don't understand what is going on. Just yesterday you were loving and considerate, and now you seem like enemies. What went wrong? What happened is that the downside of intimacy made its ugly appearance.

Intimacy's downside is made up of all the unconscious memories of what happened when we as infants had our first lessons about being close to another person. Learning about attachment had two major components—yearning for being loved and our disappointments in not getting all we wanted. The tension between these two elements creates very distressing memories that we defend ourselves against. We block them out of our awareness, toughening ourselves to the pain and the yearning. Many people can't remember large blocks of their childhoods, or remember only happy times with very little detail. We tend to forget the disappointments. And this is where intimacy ambivalence lives.

In working with single people in my practice, this issue comes up often. Let's take Michelle as an example. She has learned to be herself on dates and does well with sorting, listening to feedback, and looking for a person with whom she can feel safe. She is good at saying no to men who aren't right for her. What is plaguing her now is the way she bolts from what appears to be good relationships.

Lately, we have been talking about a pattern that influences her ability to get closer to Raul. Whenever they spend the weekend together, he likes a lot of physical contact—lots of hugging and snuggling on the sofa and in bed. Half way through the weekend, Michelle finds that she gets crabby and is likely to pick a fight over little things that don't seem to matter at other times. Obviously, an intimacy freak-out. After learning about the concept of intimacy freak-out, Michelle now intends to limit the amount of hugging and snuggling to her comfort level. She hopes to find her own tolerance level so that she can enjoy being with Raul more fully.

> In limiting the close time, she hopes to find her own tolerance level so that she can enjoy being with Raul more fully.

As another example, Joel has learned that he needs to say no more often to Margie. She wants to be together more often than he does. He is tired of his habit of giving in to her requests to spend time together only to fight with her over things that seem really stupid.

Spence is really upset that Rhonda isn't going to all of his son's Little League games anymore. Rhonda is my client and has made these decisions based on learning more about her own needs for space. However, Spence is happy that when she is with him, they don't bicker and argue as they used to.

Consciously asking for space can be a valuable contribution to a relationship. It often takes nerve because you have to go against the prevailing thinking that intimacy means togetherness. However, when people respect their own needs, the quality of the time they spend with their partner dramatically improves. By listening to your own needs for time alone, you will be rewarded with a more exciting, positive relationship.

## Understanding the Downside of Intimacy

Stress can be defined with the single word "change"—whether the change is desired or undesired. Life is change and therefore always stressful to some degree. The amount of change going on in your life can be translated into a scale of how much stress is in your life.

If you consider all the changes that beginning a serious relationship brings to your life, you can get a sense of how stressful it is to fall in love. The most obvious changes that occur are the daily physical ones like sharing time, decisions, recreation, and food choices. If you are living together, there are additional decisions about floor space, closets, dishes, cleaning habits, vacations, and sometimes cars, clothes, music, and TV. These changes, because they signify that you are with someone you care about, can create much enjoyment as well as stress.

We tend, however, to focus mostly on the upside of love, and deny or reject there drawbacks. Sharing, we fantasize, means we love each other and we are making a life together. Just what we said we wanted.

What we don't focus on is that underneath these happy benefits, there are often scared and panicky feelings that are just as powerful. This is the hidden stress that a new serious relationship can bring. Because this isn't often discussed in movies or magazines, we might not even consciously know we have these fears. In fact, some of our energy is devoted to staying unaware of them. The feeling of being scared to death is hard to live with.

But our actions betray us. Sulking, blaming, grumpy moods, sharp words, or hidden resentments let us know that something is not going as happily as expected.

> If you consider all the changes that beginning a serious relationship brings to your life, you can get a sense of how stressful it is to fall in love.

Beginning to share our life with a partner puts us back in touch with the yearning to be loved that we had as infants and children. From the first moments of our lives onward, we yearned to be held close, caressed, understood, told we were great, and reassured that what we found interesting was good. We also yearned to be ourselves in a natural way and feel safe with our parents, rather than fit into our parents' mold for us.

When I talk about this picture of early loving parenting, I am touched by how often tears well up in my clients' eyes. Most do not remember their childhood years as being this loving. My clients, instead, remember having to perform to get praise, watching warily to see what kind of mood their mom or dad was in, whether they would be yelled at or hit, held or touched inappropriately, or pushed away. My clients have memories of being scolded for their dreams or desires, being criticized for doing less than the best, being left alone and scared, or sometimes being unprotected from abusive parents, siblings, or their parents' friends. They remember not being taken seriously.

When we are getting close to a potentially good partner, we activate that deeply submerged memory bank that holds our yearning for loving and the pain and fear of childhood disappointments. The stress that is created by sharing space or decisions is compounded by what our memories do with the changes in our life. Even the best part of a new relationship triggers childhood yearnings and deeply buried memories of terror or pain.

## Kim and John

Kim and John started out like a house on fire. After three months of a torrid affair during which they hardly came up for air, they began to look like a real couple to their friends. Kim loved the outdoors and was ecstatic that she had found a man who also loved to leave his white shirts and ties behind and get on a trail or a river. Why then, she wondered, was she feeling so weird when she was at home alone or at work? Was this relationship making a wreck of her? Deep inside, she knew the relationship was good, and she yearned to spend every minute with John. But if it was so good, why was she so out of balance when she was away from him?

Over numerous lunches with me, Kim, a friend of mine and a therapist, spoke about this relationship and finally made sense of it. She knew that with John she had found a partner who met her on many levels. He was as competent, evolved, passionate, and adventure-loving as she felt herself to be. This turned up the volume of her expectations. It also brought back an odd feeling created by having an extremely close relationship with her father—a relationship that was too close and imbalanced to be healthy.

Kim's father leaned on her for emotional and social support. His wife, Kim's mother, was a steady, caring, but unemotional and essentially unpassionate person—a support to all, but a partner to no one. Kim's father found a real partner in his daughter, with whom he had frequent long talks and shared his love of hiking, adventure, and nature.

The problem for Kim was that she always thought she had the greatest relationship in the world with her father until John came along. Suddenly, lots of painful memories began to come back. They were confusing and powerful enough that she reentered therapy for a short time. What emerged was that the closeness with her father was a violation of boundaries. She was put into an adult partner role with him, yet she was not able to fully share that as a grown woman would. She also was incapable of fulfilling the expectations that the extreme and exclusive closeness with him seemed to cry out for.

In her therapy, she was able to reclaim the cast-off memories of being fourteen, and lying awake at night feeling confused and helpless to give what her father needed. Even though he never made any sexual advances or innuendos, there existed an emotional closeness that she was incapable of fulfilling. She felt incompetent and a failure.

Another insight dawned on her that explained a lot about her relationship with her mother, which was never close. Her mother always seemed angry at her, but Kim could never understand why. Suddenly it was clear. Her mother was jealous of her! How could she not be? (For more on this theme, see Patricia Love's book, *The Emotional Incest Syndrome*.)

Besides all of this, Kim remembered feeling strange at school, which was one of the only places that she was away from her father. It was the same kind of strangeness she was now feeling at work. Kim didn't hang out with her schoolmates when they got pizza or went to movies; nor did she participate in school plays or clubs. Her father was her fun and social fulfillment. But it was an uneven match and one that left her feeling confused and frustrated.

> Kim's father found a real partner in his daughter, with whom he had frequent long talks and shared his love of hiking, adventure, and nature.

Until John came into her life, Kim was completely unaware of the negative consequences of her relationship with her father. She is fortunate to have pieced it together sufficiently and hung in there with John so that she can enjoy their relationship—one in which she is truly equal and capable.

When two people start feeling serious about each other and begin to talk about future plans, they frequently trigger intimacy freak-out. Talking about commitment, especially, touches off a sense of being "stuck with" or "hitched together" that reminds us forcefully of our infancy, with its dependency, yearnings, and disappointments.

> When two people start feeling serious about each other and begin to talk about future plans, they frequently trigger intimacy freak-out.

## Three Basic Fears About Intimacy

As first discussed in Chapter 2, there are three basic fears that emerge when you get close and begin to experience dependence on another person. Even before these three fears, the expression, "dependence on another," may cause a reaction in you as you read this. Being dependent makes you vulnerable. If your childhood was painful, you aren't likely to ever want to be dependent again. The trouble is that you can't have closeness without getting mutually dependent.

As long as both people learn to lean on each other, it's a healthy dependency. Intimacy demands this healthy yet balanced dependency, which is mutual but not all-consuming. You can never get all of your needs met by any partner and shouldn't try. But the "falling" in "falling in love" does speak to the experience of losing some of your independent self-sufficiency. Most people have deep fears and reservations about dependency. It makes them feel naked, out of control, and as helpless as a child. That's why "dependent" is such a dirty word in society today.

Let's return to the three basic reasons why you might fear letting yourself learn to depend on anyone—fears that are there for all of us. The big three are (1) fear of abandonment, (2) fear of engulfment or being taken over, and (3) fear of loss of self-esteem. When things are beginning to look serious for a new couple, or at a particularly stressful time for an older relationship, one of these fears will come booming up like a housing development on a hillside. All three fears are a source of anxiety, but usually one in particular stands out as a very real threat to your existence at these crucial times.

It would be hard to overstate the power of these core fears. They come from our childhoods and are reinforced throughout our lives.

### Fear of Abandonment

Let's look at an instance where fear of abandonment causes an intimacy freak-out. Audrey began to see that she was repeating a pattern in her relationships. She said she wanted a long-term, committed relationship but was not turning any of her promising starts into good finishes. She was puzzled because she was meeting men who were bright, who liked adventure and fun as much as she did, and who also shared her values about giving to others less fortunate than herself. The relationships started out great, but when she and the man began to talk about a future, things changed.

After working on this pattern with me, she came to understand what triggered her intimacy freak-out. The closer she got to a man, and the more she liked him and felt met by him, the more she resisted the relationship. What she was resisting was letting go of her independence and learning about healthy dependence. The fearful memories in her unconscious were undermining her desire to continue in a relationship that seemed good. She discovered that her fear of losing this man and his love (being abandoned) was responsible for her ending the relationships. Her unconscious figured if she left first, no one could leave her.

Audrey realized how strong her pain still was when she spoke about being at her father's bedside after his car accident. She watched him slip away into a lingering and slow death. Then, two years after his death, she lost her best friend, who moved to France with her family. That was surprisingly devastating to her. Now in her adult life, whenever she got close enough to a man to consider forming a long-term union, the unconscious fear of being abandoned welled up in her. It created a terror that was so powerful she found "good reasons" to break off the relationship.

## Fear of Engulfment

Scott, who we met in the opening scenario, was afraid of being engulfed. As he was growing up, his mother continually bossed everyone around the house. She was always nagging his dad about his shortcomings and how things should be done. Scott remembers frequently wanting to do a project of his own, but having to argue with his mother about what she thought he should be doing. Most of the time, she won. He especially remembers the haggard look in his father's eyes—giving up out of frustration but deeply resenting it. Scott alternated between feeling sorry for his henpecked father and hating him for being so wimpy.

Scott found that he would explode in an uncharacteristic manner when Sue "made" him agree with her. She was completely unaware of how she was pushing buttons that were lighting up individuality and self-determination fears. Planning a vacation was always good for a fight. Scott could never figure out why he was so stubborn or why there was such a charge to his feelings. Sue insisted she was open to his plans but wanted her own feelings to be taken into consideration. She wasn't trying to control things in the way he perceived. His anger was shocking and frightening to them both.

Learning about intimacy freak-out was a big help in shortening the fights and defusing the charge. Scott kept remembering the same picture of his father being criticized by his mother. He realized how deeply he resented his mother's controlling ways and his father's opting out of fighting for his rights. He had to learn to balance his two parents in his relationship with Sue. He also had to keep telling himself that Sue was not his mother, nor was he his father.

## Fear of Losing Self-Esteem

Lance's story can illustrate how fear of losing self-esteem can create a mine-field environment in a relationship. Lance grew up with a father who constantly put him down. He was criticized for dropping the milk carton, for not sweeping properly, for bringing home less than perfect grades. To complicate things, he had a sister who was brilliant as a toddler and ever after. His father was so forceful a personality that his mother's love and support were overshadowed. Lance grew up thinking that he was a failure and became defensive whenever events seemed to prove it.

These painful memories were stored and released in torrents when Lance grew up and entered relationships. Anything that looked like a put-down or implied that he wasn't measuring up set off an alarm. These incidents became wounds that festered and made him sulk or lose his temper in unpredictable ways.

It's easy to see how this would prevent Lance from feeling safe and relaxed in a new relationship. However, once he began to understand the nature of his fear of losing his fragile self-esteem, he began to take care of himself differently in the relationship. He did that by choosing women differently. He would go out with a woman for a second time only if she was completely nonjudgmental. He also began to learn how to make workable requests, the kind discussed in Chapter 9.

## How Much Intimacy Can You Tolerate?

These three fears and their combinations generate the side effects of intimacy. They are always present and affect us all in different but predictable ways. Often when love feels like war, the explanation is here. They are fears for our survival. Usually they are on the subconscious level, and because they are hidden, have a potent influence on us.

It may seem that their influence is completely negative, but that isn't so. Serious survival is at stake. These fears and the issues attached to them are protecting your unique self from being lost or deeply hurt. You are protecting yourself from being merged and lost in another person or from being abandoned in a manner that would cripple you. Or, you fear losing your carefully nurtured sense of self-esteem.

When you are unacquainted with these fears, they can, like earthquakes, give relationships unpredictable and profound disturbances. However, when you learn to know your fears and their origins, these same fears can become friendly guides helping you see how to take care of yourself. If you don't understand their influence and let them dominate or strangle a relationship, their positive purposes are thwarted. When they are blindly activated, they run rampant, bursting out in behavior that can range from embarrassing to destructive—from hurtful words to impetuous and cruel actions.

The basic lesson to be learned from these three fears of closeness is to value both the desire to draw close in a relationship and the desire to keep some distance. Both are healthy and nurturing.

If Scott and Sue both understand their intimacy freak-out triggers, they can use them to demand respect or space for themselves and give it to each other. Often the person who feels the need for more closeness accuses the one who is trying to get some distance of running away. Scott needs space periodically in order to take care of his fear of being engulfed. As Sue learns to appreciate this, she will see this periodic moving away as taking care of himself as well as taking care of the relationship.

> These three fears and their combinations generate the side effects of intimacy. They are always present and affect us all in different but predictable ways. Often when love feels like war, the explanation is here.

On the other hand, the one who needs space accuses the closeness-seeker of being smothering. At times like these Sue might need some reassurance from Scott that she won't be abandoned. He needs to understand this as something Sue needs and not as a ploy to control him. The situation can then change from something frightening to a way he can show his love.

As difficult as it is to see in the midst of a fight, the health of a relationship lies in both directions of closeness and distance. Our yearnings want the closeness, but our fears want the distance. Being understanding and nonjudgmental of both directions is the key.

## Defusing the Mine Field

How does this knowledge help a couple or an individual? Fighting is a necessary part of any two people working closely together. This is true of any kind of real closeness, romantic or not. Fighting is also scary to almost all of us. But not all fighting is productive. When we learn that the purpose of a fight is often to get some space and not about the way we do the dishes, we have a tremendous advantage.

> As difficult as it is to see in the midst of a fight, the health of a relationship lies in both directions of closeness and distance.

One of the signs that a relationship counselor looks for in a couple is the amount of "self-focus" each person has. That means the ability of each person to look at his or her own contribution to the problem instead of blaming the other for it. In the examples above, each person was helped most by realizing that something deep inside them was the real source of the problem. Both started out believing that the problem was the other person, or maybe relationships in general.

Knowing about intimacy freak-out and the underlying fears that bring it about is a useful tool in looking at relationship difficulties. Awareness of the powerful and hidden influence of the three major fears can be the beginning of self-focus. Talking about how you might be reacting to your own deep fears can also be a wonderful source of closeness in a serious relationship.

When blaming is put aside, real understanding and compassion can emerge. It's like a cease-fire followed by negotiation and compromise. The issues and fears are real, but trying to understand them in each other and ourselves is the only way to get beyond them.

Learning about the hidden triggers of our fears is a lifelong process. Knowing how to recognize that they are around is the principal tool. With that knowledge, you will be reminded always to check what is going on with your own fears before you blame your partner for all the problems. Three excellent books to help you with this are *Getting the Love You Want*, by Harville Hendrix, *The Emotional Incest Syndrome*, by Patricia Love, and *Intimate Partners*, by Maggie Scarf.

Scott and Sue didn't break up following the earthquake of a fight they had after talking about a monogamous commitment. They were stunned and confused, but once they began to understand the idea of intimacy freak-out, their fights took a different turn. Fighting became a means of understanding each other's deep fears about commitment and intimacy. Scott and Sue still have fights, but they are also sensitive to each other's mine fields. Now they feel much safer and more committed than they ever thought possible.

## Exercises to Explore Your Intimacy Needs

**Exercise 1.** Drawing on the examples of this chapter, write down which you are more drawn to protect for yourself, closeness or space. Write this under "My Intimacy Side Effects."

**Exercise 2.** Looking back over your past relationships, how did you go about protecting this closeness or space? By nagging, blaming, fighting and leaving, processing the issues all the time, appearing in dire straits and needing help, hiding out and being unavailable but always having a possible excuse, or another creative but indirect method? Write your ideas in your notebook under the same title given in exercise 1. Now evaluate how well they served you. Did they give you real closeness? Did they give you free time alone? Write the drawbacks to your method under the same title.

**Exercise 3.** If you wanted more closeness in the past and couldn't get it, try to visualize asking for it directly; for example, "I'm aware, John, that I'd like to see you more often, and wonder if that's something you want too?" What are your fears of this direct approach? What might you be afraid to learn about John or yourself? What judgment do you fear might be made against you as a result of this direct approach? Are you afraid, for instance, that you can't be satisfied, and in fact, will drive people away from you if you let them know your desires for closeness? Or are you afraid that John will say he isn't interested in more time together, it's fine the way it is. Then, where will you be with him? Write your fear under "My Fears of Not Addressing My Needs for Closeness."

**Exercise 4.** If, on the other hand, you seem to want more space than the other person wants to give, try visualizing asking for it directly; for example, "I'm finding that I need more time for myself than our current schedule allows—do you feel the need for that too?" What are your fears of this direct approach? Many people will see this direct request for space as abandoning them. Do you fear being seen in that way? Do you have to take care of the other person? Do you hide your requirements for time alone in order to be the caregiver? Write your fears under "My Fears of Not Addressing My Needs for Time Alone."

**Exercise 5.** Time to experiment. In your next relationship, or one you are in currently, try assessing your need for more closeness or more space. Ask directly for what you think would make the relationship better for you. Review the examples in this chapter to help you see more clearly. Very likely, you'll find that if the person who needs more time alone actually gets it, he or she will be more present and close when time together is scheduled. Ask for what you think you need, and be ready to compromise to see what works well for both of you. Nature seems to hook up closeness seekers with those who need time alone. Balance will come with talking and experimenting.

It is essential to redefine intimacy if you think it means closeness. It isn't togetherness. It's the ability to be yourself with each other. In order to do this, closeness and space must be balanced. An accordion makes music when it is pushed together and pulled apart. So do relationships.

# 11

# Being Unapologetically Yourself

Do you have a self that is for public consumption and a self you don't want anyone to know except you? Do you find yourself getting anxious or secretive around certain questions or teasing? Are there issues that you just don't want to discuss with your friends or bring up on a date? Over the years, I have tried to help many clients merge these divided selves into one complete self. One self they are willing to stand behind. A self that is comfortable. A self they enjoy and can relax into without apologies. A self they can be loved for.

While other chapters describe in greater detail the origin of the hidden parts of yourself and the reasons you may hide them, this chapter gives a concrete approach to coming out and expressing yourself more fully. You will explore hidden parts of yourself that are closer to the surface and within your awareness. My focus is to help you take these first steps to becoming whole—one private and public person—in as many ways as possible. It's what I call being unapologetically yourself.

> Over the years, I have tried to help many clients merge these divided selves into one complete self. One self they are willing to stand behind. A self that is comfortable. A self they enjoy and can relax into without apologies. A self they can be loved for.

As you become this freer person, you give yourself the opportunity to be loved for who you are. Does a relationship in which you don't have to hide, where you aren't worried about being found out, and where you are feeling loved with all your good and bad sides sound good to you? Then keep reading.

## The Wisdom of Being Open

Being open is one of the most essential ingredients of a good relationship. When either member of a couple feels the need to hide parts of themselves, it seriously conflicts with having a comfortable relationship. It's a losing situation for both parties.

It takes much more energy to hide parts of yourself than to be open. The partner who is hiding is stressed by the effort it takes to conceal him or herself, and the other person is confused by weird or conflicting signals. Of course, more often both people have hidden selves that they are afraid to reveal. But this doesn't help either of them. Taking this issue a step further, imagine what happens in conflicts, when hidden agendas are influencing things but not coming out into the open to allow clear communication or solutions. There's not enough information on the table for a workable solution.

Imagine a man who wears tight jeans and open shirts, makes funny and suggestive comments, but is really quite afraid of getting sexual and can't admit it. He dates a woman who is charmed by his overtly sexual manner and is secretly lusty. The messages are confused. Within a short time, fights erupt and wounded feelings smolder. She wants to ask him questions about the mixed messages coming her way, but she doesn't ask and he doesn't volunteer. Their fights and bantering are dancing around a public image and a secret self that are greatly in conflict. The arguments that result seem heady and not grounded. Both of their stomachs are tense with anxiety. Their dates are unpredictable, and conversation often seems forced. Do any of these feelings sound familiar?

Many single people are so interested in making a good first impression that preparing for a date with a new person can sometimes begin with a checklist of ways *not* to be. They are primed and ready with the latest list of dos and don'ts from self-help books and magazines. Then they go out the door feeling like a kid entering a sports contest after being pumped up by the coach.

On the other hand, a couple trying to be themselves, without hiding, can relax and feel safe in the knowledge that there aren't any traps they might fall into. When problems come up, they can focus on what is being said and try to figure out what the underlying feelings are without fear of being "found out." Yes, this approach to dating is much more open, and it's infinitely safer and more comfortable. Feeling *safe* and *comfortable* are the two most important elements in the environment of feeling loved for who you are.

In the long run, being unapologetically yourself is much easier than wearing a mask or trying a technique that doesn't fit. If you use this natural approach when dating, you will find that you are happier and more comfortable. Yes, you have rough edges, but being aware of them and not spending so much energy defending yourself against admitting them creates more rewards for everyone.

---

Many single people are so interested in making a good first impression that preparing for a date with a new person can sometimes begin with a checklist of ways *not* to be.

---

There is an inner joy and peace that comes with being yourself in a relationship. It comes from accepting yourself as you are, rather than trying to receive approval from your lover, who on some level you are also trying to fool. Imagine having someone in your life who *knows* you are disorganized and binge on chocolate periodically, and still wants you. When you have no secrets and are loved as you are, it feels wonderful!

However, knowing this and even embracing it as a goal doesn't make your reluctance to be totally yourself go away. As you already know, you have been practicing your defenses for a long time. It will understandably take a while to let them retire. You will also have some fear and anxiety to push through.

## Why We Pretend to Be Different than We Are

At some point in our lives, most of us have been trained to present ourselves in public as different than we are. We want to seem better or, at least, different because we are afraid we won't look as good as we want. We build up a public or false self that depends on an image. If the image falls, we fear we will fall with it. We are frightened that we will no longer be liked or we will be laughed at. Thus, we try to protect ourselves with the false self we present to the public.

As I will explain in Chapter 12, a split develops within you at an early age. The split is a reaction—a way of protecting yourself from feeling any more rejection, ridicule, or neglect. It is a self-taught strategy to get some form of stroking or attention. As a child, it serves a useful purpose of allowing you to grow up as sane and well as you are. But now, as adults, childhood defenses and strategies for attention are likely to get in the way. For example, as a child, Jim needed to focus on his mother's moods in order to avoid getting yelled at. As an adult, he has to stop being so driven by the moods of others in order to achieve his own balance in a healthy relationship.

People who can't admit to their faults, mistakes, or bad habits have a handicap. They can be easily intimidated or pushed into angry, defensive reactions. The worker yelling, "I am *not* being defensive!" at his foreman is the classic example. He's completely vulnerable.

In relationships, people who can't admit their faults and weaknesses can't relax either. They must be hypervigilant. People like this feel a survival-level need to cover themselves all the time. Many of my clients have used the expression, "checking out the weather," to describe how they grew up and interacted in their home. Even now, how they act is determined by the "weather" of others in the same way that the decision to wear a coat is determined by the temperature and possibility of rain. This habit is learned and refined by living with unpredictable, ill, alcoholic, or self-absorbed parents who were usually critical and often flew into attacks or rages without apparent cause.

## The Wisdom of Admitting that You're Human

During the early stages of dating, many people get caught in pretenses. These range from hiding elements about themselves—such as fears, bad habits, desires, or opinions—to fudging or exaggerating stories to look better. The ten people who came to a lecture you gave miraculously turn into "around fifteen." Bad habits like smoking, leaving clothes on the floor, eating too much or poorly, and not exercising are hidden in the first few months of dating. Above all, your hidden feelings and desires can't be revealed lest you appear too needy or self-centered, or even worse—stupid, lazy, crazy, or bad.

> People who can't admit to their faults, mistakes, or bad
> habits have a handicap. They can be easily intimidated or
> pushed into angry, defensive reactions.

If Sam were to admit he likes praise, he's afraid Julie will see him as weak and not be attracted to him. Likewise, Julie wants to hide her frightening love of chocolate from Sam because she's afraid he'll see her as a potential blimp. So they, like many of us, will hide these desires.

To get around this, you, along with Sam and Julie, might try and get the other person to say what he or she wants, desperately hoping it's what *you* want. You ask, "Are you hungry yet?" when you are feeling completely famished. Or you try and get what you want without having to admit to it by asking them what they want first. If the answer isn't as you'd like, you then argue about why they don't really want that. The entire convoluted interaction could go like this:

Sam is starting to feel hungry as he and Julie are driving up the coast to visit Julie's best friend. He asks, "Are you hungry yet?"

Julie answers that she is, but doesn't want Sam to know that she is looking forward to having lunch and is ravenously hungry. She doesn't want to appear gross, so she adds, "But I can wait."

Sam, who skipped breakfast and is starved, doesn't want to seem needy and unmanly, so he says, "OK."

They are at that moment driving past the last little town with a deli or cafe for the next hour of the journey. In twenty minutes both of them are smoldering with a mixture of hunger and annoyance at the other person. "Why didn't you want to stop for lunch back there?" Julie asks.

"You didn't want to stop, not me!" Sam slings back.

"Me? I said I was hungry."

"You wanted to wait!"

"I didn't say I wanted to wait. I said I was willing to wait," she says with a rising tone of anger and accusation.

"Well, why don't you say what you mean. I would have stopped," Sam retorts, his voice rising with a hurt-boy quiver mixed with impatience.

Does this sound familiar? Even if they had stopped earlier, they still would have hidden parts of themselves. For example, if the waiter had offered Julie a rich, moist piece of chocolate cake, she probably would not have taken it. In fact, she probably would have refused it with as much feigned indifference as possible. Of course, two days before, at lunch with a female co-worker, she had ordered chocolate mousse and laughed it off as a just reward after the grueling morning she had.

While we're on the subject, Sam will be complaining a few days hence to his buddy about the scene and about how women can't come out and say what they want. Both of them will agree that women speak in weird ways that leave everything fuzzy, and Sam will never reflect on *his* inability to say what he wants in a clear manner.

## Be Yourself Right from the First Date

Recently, at a gym, I overheard a conversation between two contestants for stud-of-the-month who were working out at the weight machine. One of them was obviously starting to like a woman named Anita. He seemed to be quite fond of her, but he sighed, "If she ever found out who I really am, she would dump me so fast."

This is, unfortunately, typical American dating behavior. In fact, early dates are the most fertile spawning ground for fudging, exaggerating, and pretending. Most people keep secrets out of fear that they won't be accepted if found out. You may have health conditions like allergies, herpes, chronic fatigue, depression, or previous operations. Or maybe you are recovering from addicitons to drugs, alcohol, eating, gambling, or work. But did you ever think that if someone is going to love you for a lifetime, he or she is going to have to live with these things?

Some people hide their desires for certain types of recreation or sports until much later in the relationship when a commitment is being formed. She loves skydiving but doesn't want to confess until he is hooked on her. He loves going away every weekend in winter to ski but doesn't reveal it right away. She is highly sexed, but right now she's playing that down. He loves symphony concerts and goes to the opera every Thursday night. She enjoys deep psychological talks and long hikes. He is committed to low-calorie eating. She has an intense craving for chocolate. He goes to church on Sundays. She has been meditating for the past ten years. All of this is being concealed at first out of fear of rejection.

At this point, you're probably thinking that there is a much better way to act *right from the beginning*—and there is. The better way is being yourself. People hide who they are out of fear of not being acceptable, and often much of this hiding is unconscious. There are also plenty of secrets people hide as a conscious choice because of their belief system. You might believe that no one would want to date a recovering alcoholic except another member of AA. Or you might be convinced that herpes is so terrible that you must firmly hook your new romantic partner before revealing this secret. The potential for backfiring with this strategy is very high. "Why didn't you tell me this in the beginning?" is not an idle or defensive question!

You'll reap big rewards if you gradually change your behavior—slowly, bit by bit—to expose your secrets. When you allow others to see you without pretense, you'll feel relaxed, confident, and loved for who you are. This is not to say that timing is not important. Clearly, you should wait until you are in the intimacy-building stage—after the sorting stage—before sharing some of these things.

> He loves going away every weekend in winter to ski but doesn't reveal it right away. She is highly sexed, but right now she's playing that down.

## More True Confessions

When I began dating after my divorce, my public self was the nice, sensitive man. At the same time, my private self was frequently hurt and angry at those who didn't appreciate me. I covered the hurt I felt with a caustic or mildly attacking manner. Sound familiar? This way I could deny that I was hurt while using just the right word to make the offender feel put down. It was hard for me to take criticism because I was already critical of myself. I dared not reveal my inner turmoil and fear of not being seen as competent. I wasn't aware of all of this at the time, but even what I knew, I kept hidden.

My childhood experiences had pushed me to feel that I could never be "enough." I was my mother's confidant and the "little man" after my father died. These roles made me feel that I should perform at a higher, more mature level than my age allowed. I was also supposed to be "good" most of the time.

As an adult it was difficult for me to admit my shortcomings or insensitive actions. I had to be seen as supercompetent and totally together. It was hard to ask for my needs in a vulnerable manner. I wanted to hide how needy I felt, and succeeded in that so well that I almost believed it myself. If people broke through that facade, I was sure they would lose respect and not approve of me.

I continued living in this defensive way into my forties. It made working with me hard on others. (It still isn't a piece of cake.) And you can imagine that issues in relationships were not resolved in the cleanest ways. I was defensive in certain areas but very open in others. This confused people and gave me ammunition when I was told I was not being open. "Me, not open? Look at what I told you about . . ."

Finally, I reached a point where I was sick of it. I knew that I was defensive and took criticism poorly. While I did have a strong self-image, it was driven and carefully defended rather than understanding and compassionate. My self-image was more of steel than flesh—built on too much competence- and approval-seeking.

At first I didn't know what to do. I remember asking a friend to practice with me by insulting me in all the ways that would push my buttons, so I could develop a thicker skin. That worked a little but didn't go to the heart of it.

In a men's group, I spoke about this issue and asked for help. At this time, I was in my formal training in counseling. I was aware of some of my childhood issues, but that wasn't doing it either. So the men did role-playing with me. What worked best at that point was one of them saying, "Why do you have to defend yourself? Why don't you come back with something like, 'you really got me with that one.' Or make a gesture of scoring one for them?"

This was a revolutionary insight for me. I didn't have to defend myself? But then everyone would know my failures. However, I quickly experienced the genius behind this approach and began to develop it as a strategy for being more open. As a therapist, I even developed a course in Verbal Aikido to keep from feeling defensive. The heart of this technique is the realization that we don't have to defend ourselves all the time. (If this course strikes a chord for you, I have it on tape. Send $10 to me at 643 Green Ridge Drive, #3, Daly City, CA 94014.)

One woman put it so aptly in my Verbal Aikido course. She had come to the course hoping to find a way of defending herself against attacks while remaining above them. However, she couldn't understand what she was supposed to do. The aikido approach seemed weird to her, and the idea of just admitting to the criticism in the practice session was beyond her sense of reality. I came over to help and asked her to go through the sample attack she had written earlier from her memory of a real incident. When I told her how to respond, she looked horrified and said, "Oh, you mean . . . admit it?"

Yes, admit it! Admitting anything takes the defensiveness out of it. It lets you be yourself. When you aren't hiding anything, you aren't afraid of having to apologize for yourself. Learning the aikido approach isn't simple, but it is closely connected to learning how to be unapologetically yourself. You'll find that your life works better when you honestly say what you are feeling and what you want without apology.

> This was a revolutionary insight for me. I didn't have to
> defend myself? But then everyone would know my failures.

One word of caution—being unapologetically yourself doesn't give you permission to be a real bastard and not apologize for it. That would be using this approach as a cover. I'm talking about owning your real self—the one with wonderful qualities *and rough edges*; being willing to be seen for who you are without hiding, exaggerating, or omitting. You could spend a long time in therapy to discover your early wounds and defenses. In time, you would realize why you hide your real self, and that time would not be wasted. However, I believe that you can also increase your self-esteem by changing your behavior and pushing yourself to new levels of revelation.

## Success Stories

Jeff, a client in his late twenties, was dating and quite intent on finding the right woman. However, he was having a hard time breaking off from women who didn't seem right. That's a hard thing for most people to do, and he wanted to learn how to do it in a way that would allow him to be himself and increase his comfort. After we discussed the concept of unapologetically being himself, he practiced new ways of saying things that were difficult but honestly the way he felt. For example, "I've decided not to call you again because we don't seem to be a good match." Or, "I realize that this seems to be a relationship you want, but it isn't working for me."

This new way of behaving required that he believe he had the right to decide these things on his own terms. Jeff had to learn that certain decisions are unilateral by nature and can only be made by one of the parties. He didn't want to hurt women and in the past would have just disappeared. Then he had to hide out and feel guilty and awkward if he saw the woman at a dance or a party. We discussed how his old approach of disappearing was actually harder on the woman than his new one. It left her wondering, questioning what happened, and never able to finish that particular romantic chapter.

Jeff pushed himself to try this approach with the woman that he had been seeing for a short while. The relationship wasn't feeling right. Much to his surprise, he got good feedback from her. He came in to see me after telling her that the relationship didn't seem like a good match to him and he wanted to stop seeing her. He confessed to me that his hands were clammy, his voice almost broke, and he had to pause once—but he did it. She was relieved. She also felt the relationship was strained and agreed that it might be better to end it. After the conversation, she told him that she felt he had treated her with a lot of respect and wished him well in his search.

Jeff tried more experiments in being open in areas where he had been holding back. Each time it seemed to work. Being himself began to feel better and better to him, and to his surprise, it felt better to the women he dated as well. All of this made him less "apologetic" about his desires and requirements in a relationship.

That is precisely how the process works in building self-esteem. You get in touch with what you are really feeling or wanting, and say it as if it were your right. At first, you do this as an experiment and pay attention to the feedback you get. The positive feedback then reinforces your new openness and the belief that you have a right to be yourself. This, in turn, propels you to continue the process of discovering yourself and experimenting in revealing that self.

For Jeff, this process became more complex as he became better at it. In one case, he told a woman he had been seeing for quite a while that he really liked her, but he wasn't feeling the kind of love that would indicate a long-term commitment. He told her he felt stupid about not knowing this sooner and had fought the urge to sabotage their good times so that she might have been forced to end the relationship before he did. Making his brave and honest statement averted the strange feelings that could have resulted from a less direct and honest approach. The benefit that he gained was self-respect and the ability to run into this woman around town without wanting to hide.

How would this apply to other situations? Here are some examples:

"I'm really exhausted this evening, Emma. It has nothing to do with you, but I would rather call it a night and go home."

"Elliot, I like spending time with you, and I definitely want to get to know you, but I want more time to get to know each other before we get physical."

"You know, Evelyn, I get tired of making decisions. I wonder if you would decide what to do on Friday, and we'll do that."

"Jeremiah, you're a nice man, but it doesn't feel to me like we're a good match for romance."

"Phyllis, would you mind driving tonight? I've been driving all day and I'm tired."

"I'm really attracted to you Pete, but I'm not feeling that we are getting any closer. Do you feel that also?"

Or even: "Cathy, I'm feeling terrible about this because I really like you a lot, but it's been clear to me that I want a serious relationship with a person who is open to having children."

Or even more daring: "I want to be clear with you, Josh. I'm not ready for a serious commitment right now. I see our going out as only temporary, you know, to have a good time, but nothing really serious."

## Secret Habits

Besides fears of saying what you want, you may also have fears of fessing up to your bad habits. At the beginning of a new dating relationship, many people hide their habits, interests, or any circumstances about which they are not completely comfortable. You may be embarrassed to admit you can't quit smoking, or you may even enjoy it. While you are keeping this secret, it is keeping you apologetic about yourself. You're convinced that you're not OK and that you alone have shameful habits or desires. Others—you allow yourself to believe—don't have similar embarrassing habits or pursuits.

This is poisoning you. You can't come out into the light of day with your secret because if you do, you're convinced you'll be seen for the worthless person that a part of you thinks you are. So you hide the habit, feel bad, or pretend that you feel fine. Then you justify your secrecy with the rationale that other people can't know about it because they just don't understand.

I find that letting habits and interests out in a natural way is a real relief. You neither advertise nor hide them. When they come out, they can be discussed if either person desires that. Emma found an opportunity in the conversation and took advantage of it. "Oh believe me, I understand struggle. I've been working to cut out my sugar craving for three years now."

I spent a few years on the steering committee of a herpes self-help group. Also at that time, I was preaching the gospel of not keeping secrets. My point was that everyone has some bad habits or drawbacks, and herpes is simply one of these. So what? Put it out there, and it will allow the other person to express their hidden, dark secrets. If the other person can't handle it, at least you'll know before you get further involved. Se-

---

I find that letting habits and interests out in a natural way is a real relief. You neither advertise nor hide them.

crets can make you feel like you alone have things to be ashamed of. It's a bad illusion to perpetuate.

How does keeping secrets affect a relationship? The stress of hiding is obvious. Sneaking habits creates a duplicitous feeling in one or both partners. It also sets up a barrier to a close, safe, and vulnerable relationship. Hiding makes only certain areas of the interchange safe. Part of who you are is open, while another part is in shadow. Or else, all of a sudden, you show up with a bad habit, pretend that it was always there, and insist that the other person has no right to have any say about it.

This drives a wedge between any two people. Moreover, the habit might have been accepted or worked out if it had been brought out into the open as a topic for discussion. But now it has become your own carefully guarded and defended territory where you feel both hostile and rejected. You're so sure you will be rejected that you act as if you already are. This, in turn, does a lot to create the rejection you have feared all along.

If each person does this over the first year of a relationship, it's easy to see where the trust and nurturing that they yearn for is going to go. Right out the window. When the relationship ends, each will blame the other for being judgmental and withholding.

## Tell the Whole Truth as Soon as You Can

All along, the problem is that people judge themselves. They are apologetic about themselves but don't own up to their faults. Deep down they feel they are bad and/or unacceptable. They hide parts of themselves so they won't be found out. Then, when they can't hide certain habits or circumstances any longer, they project their own rejection of their "weaknesses" onto their partner and get hurt or angry about it.

This is what happened to Judy when she started seeing a man who worked on another floor of her building. Judy was thirty-five and hated the fact that she couldn't quit smoking. She felt even worse with the onslaught of prohibitions about smoking in public places and restaurants. She determined to try again to quit smoking and, meanwhile, not to let Doug know that she was doing it.

They began to see each other after work a few evenings a week and then once each weekend. Gradually, this evolved into the entire weekend. The relationship was feeling right to both of them and getting better. Judy couldn't give up smoking as planned but could hide it fairly easily until they began spending the weekend together. She tried to smoke on Friday and store it up, but she feared her breath would smell and had to stop at noon. Then the wait until Monday was just too long.

Judy didn't know how to deal with her problem because she had hidden it so long. She was sure Doug wouldn't want to go out with a smoker. She decided to tell him over the phone. She couldn't make herself do it in person, as her lunch buddy at work kept telling her to do. She called him at work and began with, "Doug, you aren't going to like this, and I wouldn't blame you if you didn't want to see me." He was stunned to hear this opening, then angry about the deception, and then confused about Judy as a person—at her lack of self-acceptance and fear, which had caused her to handle this issue the way she did over the last few months.

She came to see me after this incident. The last I heard, the jury was still out on their relationship. She was convinced that she needed to do something differently. I am convinced that she needs to tell the truth from now on. Completely. And as early as she can. Judy certainly isn't alone in this dilemma. It could be chocolate craving, herpes, drinking, food binging, work or travel schedules, computer addiction, the need for alone time, sexual quirks, shopping sprees, credit card debts, driving records, jail time, recovery histories, HIV status, divorce, or separation stories. These are all areas that require honesty to create an honest relationship.

## Develop the Habit of Accepting Yourself

Let me repeat here that being unapologetically yourself does not mean being a bastard. I am drawing a distinction between being uncaring, self-centered, and not giving a hoot about anyone else, versus being sincere in your efforts to be responsible and honest in the relationship while attempting to overcome your own fear of not being accepted. This does not mean trying to develop a callous disregard for other people's feelings and rights.

As an example, I'm a bossy person. I've worked on softening my personality for thirty years. I've made some gains, but I'm still bossy. Following these principles, I now admit to being bossy. I saw a poster in a women's cafe that said, "pushy bitches of the world unite." That humorous approach helped me. I figured if it could be cute to be a pushy bitch, why not a pushy bastard? I recently got the following feedback from a friend working on a project with me, "At least you know you're pushy, Al. It helps." Before, in my hide-all-rough-edges days, my bossy quirks had contaminated my working relationships. Now it's something that I can bring up by way of a disclaimer: "I have this bossy side, don't let it get in the way. I'm really pretty democratic deep down." This approach allows others to ask me to back off a little or, best of all, tease me about it.

Here I am admitting these awful things about myself in print, and I feel fine! I've worked as hard as could be expected to soften my rough edges and only got so far. Now that I admit to having them, I get much better responses from others. This allows my relationships an ease that the earlier protecting and hiding mechanisms did not allow.

What has made the difference? My acceptance of myself with feet of clay. I am much more comfortable with myself because I'm not hiding out and feeling bad or scared that I'll be found out. I'm more relaxed and therefore even better at not being bossy. It all came full circle. By pushing myself to say that I can be a bossy person, I learned to accept my bossiness. It no longer controls me, and I have a more relaxed position from which to watch it. I now even apologize for it. But I don't apologize for being me.

## Anxiety as a Signal of Growth

All of this talk about admitting things may sound obvious and simple, but try admitting your own dark secrets, bad habits, embarrassing feelings, or desires. You will soon be in touch with your inner voices and fears that try to keep you undiscovered, and you'll probably feel anxious.

Anxiety has a terrible reputation. It certainly isn't the feeling you want to have around for dinner. But this frightening force actually can be a friend if you are trying to push beyond your confinements and give yourself new options and more conscious choices. When you feel anxiety, you are growing by breaking new ground. Knowing this fact can be a real help when you are trying to make a change in your life.

---

> Anxiety can be a friend if you are trying to push beyond your confinements and give yourself new options and more conscious choices. When you feel anxiety, you are growing by breaking new ground

---

If you say you are changing some pattern or habit and it's easy and natural for you, you probably aren't changing. It's only when you're feeling anxious that new paths are being forged. In this way, the feeling of anxiety can become a friend. With it you are aware of change; without it, you are still following your old patterns. After you push through the desired new behavior, get feedback, and begin to feel good about it, your anxiety disappears.

## Exercise: Putting It All Together

Being unapologetically yourself is a huge change in behavior. However, the end result is as striking as a new body after a diet and exercise regimen. You will feel freer, more energetic, and more relaxed in relations with others. The transition is the hard part. Try these steps to begin doing this program:

1. Think of a few areas of your life in which you think you are hiding things. For example, your intimate relationships. Certainly at work you wouldn't want to be as disclosing.

2. Now think of what you really feel in the situation and what you would like to say about those feelings. For example, "I would like you to plan a date for us this weekend." Or, "I'm really exhausted and just can't go out as we planned." "I wish we touched each other more." "I like you a lot, but I don't feel like getting together as often as you do." "We've been seeing each other for a few months now, and I don't know how you feel about me."

3. Explore what you think it would be like if you said these things. As you do this, and afterwards, listen to your fears and your anxiety. Frame the words that you would like to use if you felt free to be yourself. Also, remember that a real change in behavior is accompanied by anxiety, even in this imaginary exercise.

4. Now role-play with a close friend. Practice doing or saying the things you have thought of. Then get your friend's feedback. This is essential because what may sound callous, cruel, or pushy to you may sound just right to objective ears. Even if your friend thinks you should tone down the statement, it will help you feel better about saying what you want.

5. Go out and try it. Dating is a perfect opportunity because people you have just started seeing don't have any preconceived ideas of who you are. You can try new approaches easily.

6. Take in the feedback for future reference. The feedback I urge you to listen to is twofold: how you feel about disclosing your true feelings, and the reaction of the other person. You will find very often that you get positive responses from something that you feel is going to be terrible.

Maybe you have a health condition, habit, or history that you like to keep secret. You might experiment with telling people about it in a role-playing situation with a friend. Find out if your secret issue has some beneficial side effect that others might not recognize. For instance, in the herpes group, many of us felt that we put more thought and caring into a relationship because of having to deal with herpes. That's a plus that comes out of a negative.

You can also practice talking about your hidden issues in front of a mirror. Even a few sentences may be enough. Again, find the value in it for you. For instance, being a recovering bossy person is scary to admit, but it's a whole lot better than being an unaware bossy person. What have you gained by your recovery process? Stress that when you talk about this part of yourself.

A recovery history can have the same positive traits as overcoming health problems. These issues may still be embarrassing and are certainly not appropriate to share with everyone. However, it is important for you to claim whatever the issue is as part of you, both the positive and the negative sides. The key is to put it out there with the pluses and minuses, not apologetically.

## What if It Doesn't Work?

What if you do all that I have suggested and you get rejected? Your biggest fear, right? The theme of this book is to find a way to be loved for who you are so you can be your best self in a loving and accepting atmosphere. If you have an illness, habit, quirk, history, or anything else that the other person cannot accept, why do you want to put yourself in that relationship? Clearly, it isn't right for you. You may want to look again at the section on rejection at the end of Chapter 4.

When you apologize for yourself, you deny the other person the opportunity of taking you seriously. Think of someone you know who is always apologizing for herself or himself. What is your reaction when they do this? Do you hold them in high esteem? This is an issue of respect, not an issue about caring. If you want respect, you have to be who you honestly are. Ask for what you want honestly. Decline to do things you honestly don't want to do.

Work on one issue at a time. As you master letting go of hiding one aspect of yourself and accepting it as a part of you, you can go on to another. The good feelings that you get from this process should spur you

---

Being honest about the whole you, warts and all, allows you to begin feeling comfortable in the relationship. It lets you know whether the person out there has long-term potential.

on to more and more self-acceptance. Remember that the more you accept yourself, the more acceptance you will get from others. This process stretches you into self-acceptance the same way a cast forces bones to heal correctly.

When you are not hiding parts of yourself but allowing them to be seen as though there were nothing that you were ashamed of, you look more confident. This, in turn, gradually helps you begin to adopt that vision of yourself. Remember that being ashamed of yourself is a very different matter than having quirks and habits. As you will see as you begin to move into relationships that work for you, having quirks and habits is OK. It's something you share with everyone else on this planet.

## Earning Your Self-Respect

You may find yourself frightened by this approach—if left to be the real but hidden you, you might turn into a monster. It's like letting the demons out of the box. If there is no restraint, what are the limits? Something that is crucial to keep in mind whenever you work on change, self-acceptance, or healing your inner self is that *you have to earn your own respect*. If you don't respect what you are doing, you will feel guilty. This is appropriate—this kind of guilt is healthy and is present to tell you that you are not living up to your own values.

It often helps to look at the friends around you. Do you respect them? If not, maybe you are like them. Perhaps it's time to clean up your act. And what are friends that you respect saying about you? That should tell you a lot. You can then decide if you need to work on yourself, appreciate yourself more, or come out and own who you are in a more honest and relaxed manner.

This isn't as easy as it sounds because you have internal critics from earlier days telling you that all kinds of things are wrong with you. The point I'm making is that if you stop hiding and keeping secrets, you will begin the journey to full acceptance of yourself. It will open the door to being accepted as you are.

Many people know they aren't perfect and have tried for years to smooth their rough edges. Don't they have the right to live as best they

> If you don't respect what you are doing, you will feel guilty. This is appropriate—this kind of guilt is healthy and is present to tell you that you are not living up to your own values.

can in a public and unapologetic way? We all have rough edges. Too often we think that getting rid of the rough edges is what self-improvement is all about. Not usually! More often it is about self-acceptance and compassion. People who have come to terms in a compassionate manner with themselves will be more compassionate with others, too.

It's healthy to admit that you aren't perfect. It's healthy to admit that even though you have bad habits, you still love yourself. The quickest way to rid yourself of self-condemnation is to rid yourself of secrets. Others can accept you fully only when you are fully present.

## The Impress/Express Shift

Here is another internal guide for this process. When you are saying something or doing something around others, ask yourself if you are doing it to *impress* others or to *express* you. The former is not enjoyable, the latter is. Impressing is a full-time job and never lets up. Expressing yourself, on the other hand, is a source of joy.

I wasn't free enough to write this book until I stopped feeling I had to impress people with my competence and insight. I can only write knowing that it expresses the journey I've been on, which has had lots of mistakes and wrong turns. I now know that just being myself and sharing who I have become and where I've been can be valuable. And it's a great joy to me to no longer apologize for it.

When you catch yourself feeling anxious about something within you, which you wouldn't want others to know, that is the time to be unapologetically yourself. You may be surprised by the self-acceptance that begins to creep in with the disclosure—along with the acceptance and love that comes from the people you most care about.

## Exercises for Being Unapologetically Yourself

Becoming unapologetically yourself is a step-by-step journey that takes place over time. It's a learn-as-you-go experience. Don't expect miracles overnight, but you can anticipate a journey of self-awareness, self-acceptance, and self-love.

**Exercise 1.** Make a list of the things you try to hide about yourself: habits, desires, thoughts, medical problems, decisions, and so on. Write them under "My Secret Self." These are things or qualities you do not want people to know about.

**Exercise 2.** Take the area from the above list that seems to pervade your life the most and devise some small admissions to try on friends (who more than likely already know them). Let these admissions come out casually in conversation—just to let them know that you know these things about yourself and are admitting them. "Ha, ha, ha, you are so funny Ms. Clean. I can be controlling with the best of them. We all know that." Or, "I'm a smoker. I smoke half a pack a day and really enjoy it. I'm considerate about it around other people and have no intentions at present of giving it up." Or, "Oh, come on, we all make mistakes. Don't feel bad about spilling your wine. If I felt bad about all the things I forget I would go nuts and take everyone with me."

As you remove one thing from the list made in exercise 1, cross it out and go to another one until the list is almost or completely crossed out.

**Exercise 3.**  Now, look at your methods of getting to know new people to see where you can be more yourself. It might be in making decisions about what you do or don't want to do. This could include food, time, sex, opinions, or decisions. Write this list also under "My Secret Self." Examine what is difficult on dates. What are you afraid of asking for or admitting? What do you feel that you have to do even if you don't want to? Pay the bill, offer to pay the bill, pick her up across town and drive her home, make out, put on a tie, hold hands, make a move, talk constantly? Pick one of these areas and try being more yourself by not doing it or doing something you want to do. Then check the feedback from inside yourself and from your date or new friend. Did they think it was too much, terrible, or rude? Does it make you more comfortable or remove hidden resentments?

Keep escalating these areas until you feel you are being yourself most of the time. Note: you might find that you are becoming more and more aware of what you want and like as you do these exercises.

## The Rewards of Being Yourself

It's hard to look at parts of yourself you don't like. It's even harder to think about them, and admitting them is even worse. Why would you want to go through all this? Do you really want to air your dirty laundry in public?

The answer is one of the central themes of this book: if you want to be in a relaxed and loving relationship, you have to start by learning how to accept and love yourself. I know of no better way of making real changes in this direction than the method I am teaching here. The rewards multiply over time. They begin with attracting the most suitable mate into your life and continue into the relationship itself by diminishing defensiveness, enhancing self-knowledge, honesty, compassion, and respect for others' feelings.

All of those amazing rewards can be yours for making the effort to push through your anxiety and embarrassment and bring your most honest self on dates with you. The ultimate reward is a loving relationship that lasts for a lifetime.

# 12

# Respecting Each Others' Feelings

Your feelings may rule you. Other people's feelings may scare you. Since each of you comes from a different culture, it isn't surprising. By that I mean you come from different families with defined rules, habits, myths, and opinions. One very influential aspect of your family's imprint on you is how you learn to handle feelings—stuff them, shout them, rationalize them, or deny them. The method your family uses seems natural and normal to you until you run into another culture in a person you love.

Nature seems to steer a shouter of feelings to a stuffer of feelings. These two get along fine at first because their styles are interesting and exciting—something like vacationing in a foreign country and enjoying the differences. But soon these two people begin to try and solve problems together, and their disparate ways of handling feelings become as much of a block as foreign languages and customs can be.

Since skills at understanding and expressing feelings are essential for equal relationships, this chapter will provide an overview of the nature of feelings, what they teach us, and why we should respect them in ourselves, partners, friends, parents, and children.

---

Feelings serve us like the instruments in a satellite. They are guides. However, unlike the satellite, which is mechanical, our guidance system also reveals problems of a more soulful nature that reflect our human complexity.

---

## Unraveling the Mystery of Feelings

Feelings serve us like the instruments in a satellite. They are guides. However, unlike the satellite, which is mechanical, our guidance system also reveals problems of a more soulful nature. At different times we feel fulfilled, hopeless, angry, jealous, anxious, joyous, worried, and scared. Everything and its opposite.

Feelings are messengers—insistent ones at that. They want to be heard, and if they aren't, they persist and often change into physical symptoms to grab our attention. We're lucky they are so stubbornly dedicated because they bring us vital information. Nevertheless, we often heed the annoying beep of our seat belt warnings more promptly than we listen to the warnings of our feelings.

Gail's date serves as an excellent example. Gail feels a gnawing sense of dread about going out with Ricardo. She may dismiss this feeling as unimportant, or even invalidate it by telling herself not to get so uptight—it's just a date. However, Gail's sense of dread has something real to tell her. Something will happen on the date that will click with the uncomfortable feeling, and remind her that somewhere in her psyche, she knew that something about this date wasn't right for her. Ricardo might have said something on the phone that triggered her warning system to blink a caution light. It could be as simple as his mentioning that he would feel more comfortable going dutch on their lunch meeting. She may have had bad experiences connected with not being taken care of, and this was what the dread was telling her.

Or it could be more complex—his voice triggered memories of a man in college who raped her on a date. Something is going on for Gail, or her feelings wouldn't be warning her. If she is in the habit of ignoring her feelings, they'll be as useless as a satellite transmission to a sleeping ground control crew.

But if it's as simple as that, why would people ignore these messages? It seems simple enough that if we listen to the guidance system we have, we'll be better off. The answer propels us back to childhood—the origin of our feelings.

## Feelings Begin in Childhood and Repeat All Through Life

We are born with certain basic feelings that begin as messages about our physical needs. The infant hungers and is disgusted with certain foods, turning away with scrunched-up nose and lips, an expression that will soon be associated with another kind of disgust. Also, this infant is startled by surprises and smiles when full and warm—more expressions that will grow into fuller meanings as the infant becomes a child. As you can see, the purely physical messages gradually develop into more sophisticated messages about the complex needs or satisfactions of the human species. They give us information of a more spiritual or soulful nature. We hunger for acceptance, are disgusted with certain behaviors, grow afraid of losing our self-esteem, and smile with the satisfaction of success. What we experience emotionally when young is how we feel that emotion all through life. Once experienced, it is repeated when a similar situation generates the same message. If we smiled and felt happy when we were held safely in our father's arms, we will smile and be happy at feeling safely held in later life. Conversely, if loud voices terrified us as infants because they always announced the beginning of yelling and fighting, we will fear loud voices all through life.

> What we experience emotionally when young is how we feel that emotion all through life. Once experienced, it is repeated when a similar situation generates the same message.

Western culture's legacy to parenting up to the mid twentieth century is one of purposefully disregarding or attempting to squash children's emotions ("for their own good"). This was especially true if the children's feelings conflicted with the values of the adults around them. Therefore, one answer to the question about why we aren't more conversant with our feelings is that we have been taught to ignore them, fear them, or hide them by parents who knew no better.

Besides being trained to suspect your feelings, you have another force that controls your emotional awareness: your defenses. You are probably more familiar than you want to be with "getting defensive." You know the experience of feeling hot or flushed and not knowing what to say. We've all been in situations where we wanted to run away or blast the person who made the remark that produced such an instant and powerful reaction. But you may not know what your defenses are and why you have them.

## Defenses Rescue Children

Since emotions are a child's natural warning system, what happens if they are disregarded by the caregiver? If a child is crying, and this display of feelings is ignored or punished, what does the infant do? This is where defenses come in.

Little Eddie is hit by his mother and father when he cries for a long time or wants more than they want to give him. His crying is an expression of his feeling afraid and hurt. But Eddie's feelings aren't heard as cries for help. In fact, they are seen as a cause to abuse him. Eddie's body shifts to another system of taking care of himself; it produces defenses to shut out the pain and abuse so that he can continue to grow. Thus, while he is growing up, Eddie is being numbed to the hurt by his defense of denial (he stops being aware of the abuse), or by rationalization (my parents love me and do this so I'll be good), or by projection (that bad dog needs to be punished, not me), or by an amnesia reaction (I'm so lucky that my parents really loved me). If the abuse is severe, it can result in multiple personalities, with each personality remembering only selective parts of the experience.

Eddie's defenses serve him as a shield. If he didn't have them, his pain and confusion would stunt his physical growth and development. Therefore, his defenses could rightfully be credited for keeping Eddie alive. However, defenses take their job so seriously that they continue to protect Eddie as he gets older and even after he leaves home. They protect him from these same painful feelings as long as they can. In fact, they keep him from experiencing any reminders of the pain he experienced. A conscious observer can see this when Eddie gets defensive over certain statements.

Now Eddie is twenty-eight and in a relationship; however, he is closed off to certain feelings. His whole system resists anything that reminds him of his childhood pain. For instance, even though you can't catch him crying, you will notice that he can't ask for help or any pleasure that might create "trouble" for others. Also, he still can't stand any criticism or innuendo that implies he is bad from his partner. To ward off reminders of his early pain, he uses defenses to block the impact of any perceived accusations about his failings. For instance, he uses blaming and rationalizing. He tells Cheryl that the problem is not his but hers; if she would be calmer about what she asks for, he would respond better. He tells her how stressed out he is, and that her timing of her discussions is lousy. That's the only reason he can't always be reasonable in talking about their problems. Eddie is not aware that any of these avoiding defenses, blind spots, and handicaps to self-knowledge exist in him.

---

Little Eddie's defenses serve as a shield. If he didn't have them, his pain and confusion would stunt his growth and development. Therefore, his defenses could rightfully be credited for keeping Eddie alive.

---

## Defenses Are Friends and Foes

Like Eddie, we too have hurt feelings buried in our psyches that are valiantly locked off by our defenses. The answer, therefore, to why we don't always listen to the messages of our feelings is that the warning system that God or nature has provided for us has been badly damaged. It has been carelessly mangled by caregivers who, deprived of a good owner's manual, could not understand what a vital role feelings play in our system.

It isn't easy to remedy this situation because the fall-back system of your defenses is now firmly entrenched. While defenses were once your friends, helping you continue to physically grow and develop, they now become foes by hindering your inner awareness and self-knowledge. They protect you as if you were still a child even though you are an adult. One might hope that they would ease up their control as you grow older. But, instead, they bar you from that early pain for as long as possible—even if they're ruining your adult life in the process.

Everyday, therapists see examples of how powerfully and stubbornly defenses persist. Take a man who lashes out at his wife and says that she deserves it. When asked if he remembers being treated that way himself as a child, he answers that his parents were good to him and only hit him when he "needed" it. This same man, after months in therapy, begins to recognize that he was afraid of his parents, felt unfairly treated by them, and eventually allows himself to feel the pain of the helpless little boy dominated by strict, punishing parents. By this process he learns to accept his own feelings, which enables him to treat his wife more kindly and be loved for it in the process.

Another client comes to therapy out of desperation. Her life is a mess both at work and romantically. She keeps picking men who want to be taken care of. She had a caring and warm home, she says. Her mother was ill during much of her childhood, but still treated her well. She didn't even mind doing all the chores and making dinner for the family, because it was her way of contributing and helping her mom. Only after six months of being listened to and validated in my office, does this same woman feel the confusion and loss that she experienced—but quickly and dutifully hid—when she lost her school chums and became a thirteen-year-old housewife. Gradually these clients convinced their defenses that it would be OK to feel their pain again, and they began the healing process that would free them from the tyranny of feared and hidden feelings.

A relationship has a special way of bringing out your defensiveness. This is because the ambivalent forces about being close—yearning for the goodies, while at the same time being scared to death of abandonment or engulfment—re-create the essence of the childhood experience. This powerful combination stimulates both the soft and warm childhood memories and the dark and scary ones. When they are triggered, they are acted out—just like in the childhood years.

---

A relationship has a special way of bringing out your defensiveness.

---

When a partner, friend, or parent does something that doesn't satisfy your yearning to feel special, your defenses come to your aid and shield you from this pain and the pain of all your abandonment in earlier life. If you used denial as a child, you will use it in your current situation. If withdrawing was your way to escape, it will still serve you that way now. If raging and blaming was the way you shielded yourself from the pain of an abusive, drunk parent, raging and blaming will still be your defense of choice.

When two people come into my office together to discuss relationship issues, I know that I am going to see their early years acted out in front of me. Their problems with each other will always have a connection back to their own childhoods. I can see the man's face change into a boy's when his wife reports that her problems with him are that he doesn't understand her and puts her down with patronizing comments. His defenses rise, and he lashes back that he can never do anything right for her. He says that she is a bottomless pit of needs. My work is to help them both see that these judgments come more from their childhood conditioning than from their partner's actions. This is a daunting task for me since they are convinced that their partner, sitting across from them, is deliberately trying to crush their spirit.

## The Six Most Common Defenses

Here is a sketch of the most common defenses your unconscious is likely to use. Like all habits, defenses run in families. The first, and favorites of many families, are the blocking defenses of denial and repression. When your ego uses **denial**, it simply rearranges facts in some mysterious way so that you become unaware that something happened or is happening. The classic case is the family that doesn't recognize that Mother is an alcoholic. This is like having an elephant in the living room but no one is talking about it.

**Repression** pushes the troublesome feeling or memory out of awareness. Your ego represses data by not letting it come to your conscious mind. You might, for instance, not recognize as abuse the fact that you were threatened with beatings during your childhood. Then, during therapy or some other triggering event, it clicks in your mind that you were abused as a child in a way that explains a lot of your current behavior. Somehow, the repression is lifted and the event is seen more accurately.

**Projection** is the defense that attributes others actions or feelings that are difficult to accept or that you are blind to in yourself. In this way the other person becomes a movie screen that is playing a movie about you. However, it is a movie about you that you don't like, and therefore, projection makes it seem like it is about the other person. This goes on all the time in relationships. If you are afraid of being scatterbrained, you might find yourself criticizing your partner's constant carelessness. This defense allows you to avoid the pain of accepting something about yourself that is unwanted or feared.

Three more common defenses do their work by distracting you from early childhood memories. **Intellectualization** lets you stay away from feelings by talking about them or using logical and rational words rather than feeling words. You can talk about painful issues, analyze them, even understand that you have them, but not really experience them. Jay might say he gets angry like anyone else. He will tell you how he was criticized by his father during his childhood, but by intellectualizing, he will be unable to admit being angry with you. Or he won't be able to feel the pain and the tears for the confused, little Jay who was treated so harshly when all he wanted was to be patted on the head.

**Addictions** also avoid feelings by keeping you distracted and numbed. You are distracted from experiencing your pain or feelings by giving yourself over to the addiction. This is often called self-medication. Like taking a drug, an addiction numbs you to the pain of shame or sadness. It keeps the edge off.

Opposite of intellectualizing, but just as effective, is **emotionalizing**. With this defense, you are constantly overwhelmed by your feelings. You can avoid deeper feelings by controlling which feelings emerge and how deeply you experience them. Nancy gets teary whenever she starts talking about her divorce. And no one would be able to say she doesn't feel. But in reality, her defense of emotionalizing is guarding her from feeling the really hard stuff like guilt, shame, failure, and hopelessness.

Many other highly sophisticated defenses block us from feeling by blurring memories, editing material, or substituting one thing for another in our minds. Two examples are rationalization ("Let him cry, he has to learn about the cruelty of life") and idealization ("My parents were tough on me, but it was good for me").

The defenses I have discussed above are among the most common that you can discover if you observe your patterns. Of course, you can't observe the defense itself, or it wouldn't be working. You will have to use detective work and indirect methods to discover how you defend.

---

> Opposite to intellectualizing, but just as effective, is emotionalizing. With this defense, you are constantly overwhelmed by your feelings.

---

## Exercises to Learn About Your Defenses

Before you can regain the full use of your warning system of feelings, you must first learn about your defenses. They are the gates, slammed shut, protecting you from the invasion of your feelings. But how can you learn about your defenses when, if you knew them, they wouldn't be doing their job very well? This makes the task more challenging, to say the least.

Like a detective, you will have to work from observable facts to conclusions. Remember that defenses defend you against feeling an emotion. This single fact will keep you on track. If you feel defensive, what feeling are you being shielded from?

**Exercise 1.** Your friends know your defenses just as you know theirs. Ask someone you trust how you get defensive and whether they observe a pattern. If you are comfortable doing that, write in your notebook under "My Defenses" the ones they claim you use. Then you will have accomplished the first step—knowing which defenses you use. If you aren't comfortable asking others, you'll have to think about each defense listed above and guess at your own. Look at your family members; they will probably be using similar styles of avoiding feelings.

**Exercise 2.** Look for patterns in your life. What problems keep repeating themselves? Problems with money, with love relationships, with bosses, or with teachers? Write down the area (or areas) you think reoccur. Now within those areas, for example, bosses and relationships, what is the pattern that seems to trip you up? For instance, if you find yourself starting relationships with depressed people, and then breaking up because you can't stand his or her low energy or constant complaints, you can be fairly certain that depression is a feeling that touches you somehow. The defense of *projection* is doing this. It projects onto others something that you do not want to deal with in yourself.

"The finger pointing at your partner is really pointing at you," is a wise saying; it underscores how projection is used in relationships. You can use this knowledge to your advantage in your search. For instance, if the depression example applies to you, imagine letting yourself feel depressed and ask yourself how that would be. You may feel resistance from deep inside that indicates your fear of depression—which is really a form of helplessness. You might never want to feel helpless again. That would be a concrete sign that you felt helpless at one time and your defenses sealed this experience over to protect you from feeling it again.

---

> "The finger pointing at your partner is really pointing at you," is a wise saying; it underscores how projection is used in relationships.

---

Examine all your disruptive patterns by "trying on" different feelings and waiting for your inner voice of resistance or fear to indicate when you score a direct hit. Record your initial findings and hunches for confirmation with further reflection.

**Exercise 3.** Is there a pattern to what makes you feel emotional? For instance, at the movies, what brings tears to your eyes? What actions in others around you, or in things you read, affect your eyes or your heart? I get teary in movies when someone is truly understood or appreciated for who they are, whether it's an adult or a child. I've noticed this reaction for a long time and now know that I felt misunderstood as a child. In my adult life, whenever my actions are misinterpreted to be selfish or hurtful, I get defensive. From this, I remembered how hard I tried as a child to be good and helpful. Start paying attention to your own similar emotional experiences, and look for repetitive triggers. Write down the pattern and what you think it means for you.

**Exercise 4.** Are there certain traits in people or kinds of people that you can't stand? Make a list of the people you can't stand and write down their annoying qualities under "Traits I Hate." This is usually a sign of something in you. Finding it in other people first and then figuring out why it bothers you so much is another example of the detective work required. I can't stand opinionated people who speak as if they had a direct link with the font of truth. Now why does that bother me so much? It doesn't seem to carry the same punch with other people. They brush it off, but with me, this trait becomes a call to arms. This indicates projection. If I can find someone more opinionated than myself, I don't have to feel bad about being opinionated. My unconscious can tell me I'm not so bad compared to them. Write out your findings about the traits you discover. Then reflect on what it may mean you wish to avoid in your own personality.

**Exercise 5.** You may have noticed that a theme is emerging in these exercises. Anything that carries special force or extra energy in your life almost certainly has roots in your childhood. Therapists listen for the energy flow in their clients' stories and reports. The trained ear can detect what is from childhood and what is current and more neutral. You can also learn to become sensitive to this defensive hallmark. If you feel strongly about something, or have a dramatic reaction to it, most likely this will be one of these childhood reactions. Learn to sense the difference between rational disagreement and emotional reactivity. The latter will have a certain feel to it. It will involve more of your body than your brain. You might feel warm or flushed. You'll also notice that others don't share your strong reaction.

Becoming skillfull in identifying your defenses is well worth the monitoring it takes. Once acquired, you will have a window into self-knowledge that is almost foolproof. You will be able to monitor when you are caught in a reaction from childhood that is defensive and doesn't call for the level of emotion you are giving it. You will then be able to slow down and use what you learn from this chapter about feelings to figure out what the message is for you in the situation. Write under the title, "My Reactivity," any suspicions you now have about yourself. As you acquire this observation skill, add more and more of what you uncover to your list.

## The Split Within Us

Most people who are dating want to be as truthful and real as possible, and seek the same quality in another. This seems, at first glance, to be a relatively simple matter—not hiding the warts and all that. However, it is much more of a quest than you might think. Being authentic means being totally yourself, and I am about to explain how part of yourself is hidden from your conscious mind.

Children, commonly at two years of age, begin developing a sense of self. They start discovering what they like or dislike, what they are naturally drawn to or uninterested in, whether they are mental, physical, dreamy, curious, or another way of being. At this age, children need parental validation to develop a strong sense of themselves. However, parents also have to handle their own fears. They might be concerned for little Michael's safety when he climbs on trees, fences, and rocks. Or they may be worried that he is going to be so physically active that he'll never be able to get an education, or that he daydreams instead of going out to play. Or, perhaps he is playing with his genitals all the time and confronting their moral and sexual values. Whether it is something like this or just getting in their way too much, the full and rich development of the child is usually a collision course with the parents' values, needs, or concerns.

The accidents that occur on this collision course are our early wounds. They are the many ways that we learn that we are not OK. Most of us grow up feeling we are bad, lazy, stupid, or crazy. Children read their parents' faces for signs of acceptance and receive grunts and groans of approval or disapproval. They are smiled at, yelled at, or withdrawn from as they display their developing personality. All these forms of expression matter greatly; children are experts at reading faces. Being yelled at hurts; so does being withdrawn from. But, at such a young age, what can the child do about it?

This is when the split occurs in most of our lives. Little Patty learns that her questions about how things work make her father grumpy. She also learns that doing little favors for him makes him smile. Therefore, to avoid his grumpiness and to get his smiles, she learns to intuit what he

> Children, commonly at two years of age, begin developing a
> sense of self. They start discovering whether they are mental,
> physical, dreamy, curious, or another way of being. At this
> age, children need parental validation to develop a strong
> sense of themselves.

needs and does it for him. But this isn't really her true self. Her true self is inquisitive and intellectual, but that didn't go over very well in her family. So she developed a split in herself to compensate.

Now, Patricia is divorced from her second husband and is really angry at men for holding her down. She meets men who seem to love her, and then when the relationship turns serious, they try to hold her back. She feels suffocated by them. She's convinced that men just want bimbos. She's resolved to use the smarts that God gave her and not let any man hold her down.

The problem for Patricia is that she hasn't yet united her split parts. Until she allows herself to feel how painful it was to have her intellectual nature scorned, and lets herself get angry at her father's control of her personality, she won't be able to empower herself with a man. She will helplessly swing between being a doting, giving female and a woman angry that men won't give her the respect her intellect deserves. She won't be able to pursue her mental development without an internal struggle, which she will avoid feeling by projecting it onto her partner.

The early wound to your personality development is the root of your defensive hot buttons. Patricia, for example, will be sensitive as an adult to any remarks that make her feel criticized for being too smart, above people, having her head in the clouds, or being too theoretical and not practical. She'll bristle and defend herself when comments are addressed to her by well-meaning friends if they touch on this sensitive area. Her past is still running her life.

## Exercises to Discover Your Split

Looking for your hot buttons is the single most helpful thing you can do to begin to free yourself from your early childhood split. As with the exercises for discovering your defenses, here too, you can search for patterns and interview friends.

**Exercise 1.** Start by asking your friends what they know about how to push your buttons. Write in your notebook under "My Split" what you learn about how your buttons are pushed.

**Exercise 2.** Go on a fact-finding mission into your family at the time you were two. What was happening that would affect the way your parents behaved toward you? You can ask relatives, parents, older siblings, or look at pictures of that period to learn what was going on that might have influenced your childhood.

For instance, my natural father died when I was two. Obviously, this greatly affected my mother, forcing her to support herself and her four children, and to be the sole parent responsible for our future. Your father may have been out of work or making a career change by working all day and going to school at night. Some people have learned that their mother was depressed for three years after their birth, or that their father spent nights away from the family while traveling on business. At those times, the children enjoyed their "little family" with mother all to themselves, but felt displaced when father returned.

Asking your parents, aunts, uncles, or grandparents will certainly yield rich returns. They will have their own view of what happened, which may agree with yours, your parents, or may be sufficiently different to give you a new look at an old memory. You may get new information that could give you a new vein to mine in the mother lode of insight about a critical part of your personality.

A bit of theory will help you with this. When you were an infant or small child, completely dependent on your caregivers, you believed what they said about you. If, therefore, they told you that you were stupid, lazy, bad, or crazy—literally, or with other expressions or gestures—you believed them. They were your gods and had to be honored and trusted. So, you grew up with these "truths" forming your convictions about how you behaved and what qualities you possessed or lacked. Only when you became old enough to search out a larger sampling of feedback, could you disassociate from your parents' view of yourself and begin to view yourself differently.

If you are stupid, how come you learn new job assignments so easily? If you are lazy, how come you get feedback from your friends about your generous support? If you are crazy, how come so many people seek you out to talk over personal problems? And, if you are bad, how come you have so many friends who respect you? The larger world is a much

---

The larger world is a much better mirror to determine your identity than your early childhood conditioning from possibly very stressed-out or imbalanced parents.

better mirror to determine your identity than your early childhood conditioning from possibly very stressed-out or imbalanced parents.

However, it isn't all that simple. You don't change your sense of self so easily. In fact, your early imprinted sense of self stubbornly, and often despite contradictory evidence, persists well beyond childhood and young adulthood. Your defenses are at it again. Because being called stupid was a source of pain in your youth, you began to create an alternate personality to compensate. You wanted to earn your parents' approval. Patricia, in the example above, ignored by her father when she showed intelligence and smiled upon when waiting on him, learned to get approval by being generous. But then, she never learned how smart she was because she became the generous, thoughtful friend, chum, and lover.

You can see how discovering your split-off parts, as they are technically called, is a big job. Patricia has to find a way of rediscovering her intelligence and balancing it with her generous persona. As she resists doing favors and always accepting dates with her friends in order to spend more time with her intellectual development, she'll feel selfish and bad. She'll need a kind person in her life to help her make the transition.

**Exercise 3.** Distill what you have learned in exercises 1 and 2 into the words that push your buttons. They usually are variations of bad, lazy, stupid, or crazy. Once you have identified them, you can begin to test their validity in the real world. You'll notice that every time you return to family gatherings, you will get a fresh dose of the old family view of you. This might be a helpful place to start your search. What do you fear being called at family gatherings? What do you dread being judged as? Write the word or words that really get you steamed.

**Exercise 4.** Once alerted to the expressions you fear, search the way you live your life for your persona, or the way that you have compensated. "Persona" means the face you put on for others, the self you portray to the world. For example, Jack's father was threatened by his son's intelligence and began to make fun of him, calling him smart alec and know-it-all. Jack, flinching in pain at this, began to hide his intelligence and took up the role of family clown, which won smiles and laughter from his father. Jack, therefore, split off his bright intelligence and took on the persona of the clown.

**Exercise 5.** Now, put your discoveries about yourself out into the world for testing. The same Jack, from exercise 4, discovered that he didn't believe he was particularly bright because of the way his father used to mock him for it. He took my advice, and went out in the world to get a better reality check. After earning a Ph.D., he finally had to concede that he was not stupid and could probably do whatever he wanted intellectually. This is the path you need to take to reclaim your lost self, if it was ridiculed or scolded away at childhood.

You'll find that there are parts of you—emotions, desire for love, intelligence, curiosity, desire for more in life, love of poetry—that you have always been hesitant about showing. These are the pay dirt of this search. Now start exposing these parts of yourself to a larger reality check—like your work, friends, clients, or partners. Watch for the feedback. Does the world hold the same opinion as your family? Or are you getting strokes for your talents everywhere except from your family? Write these things out in your notebook and call them "Split-off Parts to be Reclaimed."

## Sitting with Your Feelings

The surest way to self-knowledge is through your feelings. They are your guides to knowing how you are doing. Now that you also know that defenses blind you from feeling all your feelings, you can begin to work with both your feelings and your defenses. You can allow your feelings to emerge and broadcast their message. You can also locate some of your hidden feelings by identifying when your defenses are working overtime. Learning to "sit with your feelings" must become an activity that you embrace rather than fear.

> The surest way to self-knowledge is through your feelings. They are your guides to knowing how you are doing.

When you experience shame, anxiety, sadness, fear, and self-doubt, your immediate reaction may be to run. Like a hand yanked back from a burning log, your body—with the help of your defenses—will want to yank you away from painful feelings. This will stunt your growth and keep you a child emotionally. However, the process of learning to sit with your feelings will help you reach beyond fearful flight, into the self-knowledge that feelings can bring.

This growth came for me by slowing down when feelings pricked at me painfully. Since I was already good at identifying my feelings and their message, I rushed to a solution. If I felt fear, I checked to see what was happening and what I needed to do. In rushing, I missed a lot of deeper self-growth, and remained stuck at a level of life management that, while good, wasn't as rich, liberating, and joyful as I now feel. I gradually changed from getting a quick idea of what was going on, to forming an in-depth and compassionate relationship with my inner guides. It was as different as greeting a friend in the supermarket with a quick "Hello, how ya doin'," to sitting down with him over a cup of coffee and really catching up with each other.

What changed? I allowed myself to be depressed without frantically trying to get over it. I allowed myself to experience loss and sadness. I suffered with confusion and feeling incompetent without defending myself or brushing these feelings off as misdirected intruders. I let the feelings of being a failure and being bad sit with me for a while and tell me what they wanted me to hear.

During this period of my life, I became hospitable to all the feelings of my psyche. When I felt like hiding and moping, I resisted the urge to get active and drive those "downers" away. When I was hurt by comments toward my ideas at a meeting, I went home and braved how bad it felt to be criticized. My feelings knew they could come and stay a while and be heard. I learned the meaning of the expression, "There are no bad feelings." Before, I specialized in anger, hurt, and excitement. Now, I have learned to welcome the full orchestra of my feelings.

When I let fear enter my abode and converse with me, I learned about the value of being safe in a relationship, rather than putting myself into heroic and foolhardy situations that always blew up and left me feeling stupid or used. When I allowed depression in for a chat, I learned about my own needs to be approved of and to be successful. When I didn't banish my sadness so quickly, I came to understand the need to ask for help and to rejoice in being cared for. This open and integrated hospitality didn't come all at once or even in a year. It came in fits and starts. I was like a card that opened at a fold; each time I opened a little more easily. Gradually, the crease was more like a hinge. Slowly, I had created a new habit that remains the way I treat my feelings. However, now the process is easier and more natural.

The end result at this point in my life is that I can live with the fact that I am, at times, depressed, and at times, sad and lonely. I am also, at times, angry, hurt, and afraid. But much of the time, I am joyful, fulfilled,

---

The end result at this point in my life is that I can live with the fact that I am, at times, depressed, and at times, sad and lonely. I am also, at times, angry, hurt, and afraid. But much of the time, I am joyful, fulfilled, and at peace. Like most people I can be a jerk and a prince.

and at peace. Like most people I can be a jerk and a prince. I accept my drawbacks as part of the human condition, and I allow my feelings—both the easy and difficult ones—to help me find my way.

## Making Feelings Your Friends

When you enter psychotherapy, the goal of the work is to get to know yourself better and to manage your life in a more fulfilling way. Much of this is accomplished by the therapist helping you get back in touch with your feelings and work through the early influence of your childhood. This is done by helping you feel past your defenses in order to reexperience early pain, fears, trauma, and yearnings.

The therapist usually works with your patterns and the early feelings that lie behind them. In this way, you are helped to use your feelings as indicators of what's going on and what is needed, thereby slowly changing threatening feelings into necessary guides for taking care of yourself. This process will change your defenses—especially projection and blaming—into signals of discomfort, directing you to look more deeply into yourself.

Since this is a self-help book, I offer the opportunity of achieving these same goals by working on yourself using exercises in place of a therapist. This works well for many people, but be advised that it is not a quick process. However, the exercises in this chapter are a superb method of learning to sit with your feelings and gain all the benefits described above. The process of therapy I have just discussed is the same process that anyone must go through individually. Therefore, these exercises will lead you step-by-step to accomplish the same goals.

It is a process that builds over time, with one success leading to another. Learning about the message of one feeling will free up others. Those will then lead to new experiences, and accordingly, new feelings will arrive. Often you will find that you must let some time elapse before you can discover new feelings. Gradually, you will become good at listening and learning from these inner guides. Then you will begin to feel more in control of your reactions and better at taking care of your needs.

Out of that, a greater sense of wholeness will emerge. An integration of all parts of yourself will break through into a more relaxed and comfortable manner of being with yourself and with others. It will take time—sometimes years—to realize the full benefits. However, the process itself is rewarding, as each success leads to a greater sense of self-knowledge.

Remember that the early pain, which created the feelings that seem like such threats, happened when you were little and vulnerable. You were totally dependent, and not able to defend yourself. But now you are more developed, experienced, and just plain bigger. You can handle your feelings now. It's time to ask your defenses to let go a little and give you another chance at working out whatever pain there may be.

The change for me has been as major as moving from the city to the country. Whereas before, I ran from the first hint of the feelings I had judged as "weak"—like hurt, sad, depressed, or bad—I now invite them to teach me about my progress, difficulties, areas I need help with, and avenues to explore to feel more alive.

## Exercises to Sit with Your Feelings

In trying these exercises, remember to be compassionate with yourself. Use them more for observing what's happening than trying to change things. Many people want to analyze why they have certain feelings. This keeps them in the defense of intellectualizing. Just observe and feel the feeling. In this way, the feeling itself will tell you what you need to know and do. That's what they're for.

Think of the satellite. Its instruments relay information. Ground control then uses this information to set direction and make corrections. In the same way, you need to first learn how to listen fully to the messages of your feelings. This will take practice and often may be unsettling. However, only practice will put you in a position of being able to listen respectfully. Once you have accomplished that, you can learn the ground control skills about what to do with the knowledge.

One last caution about the possible need for individual counseling for this work. If it seems like an enormous stretch for you to do these exercises, be kind to yourself and seek help from a therapist to make the process easier and more productive. It will be the best gift you ever gave yourself.

**Exercise 1.** Breathing connects the mind to the body where your feelings are. Breathing down into your stomach and exhaling out of your mouth helps you establish this connection. Now that you know this, you may become aware that you normally breathe shallowly, into your chest. Even the thought of deep breathing may make you aware of how that would connect you to your feelings. It may even be scary to think about it.

When you are relaxed, try this breathing to see how it feels. As you breathe, observe what you are feeling. You don't have to do anything about the feeling until you understand its complete message. As you ponder the meaning and "try on" different messages in your mind, your body will give you cues about your accuracy. When you figure out the true message, your body will feel more relieved. When you get used to this process, you can use it with feelings that you know will be harder to handle. Again, the point here is to learn to just feel. Let the feeling just be, without trying to do anything.

**Exercise 2.** Your body often will be the first clue about a feeling that isn't being heard. Try to locate the sensation in your body. It may be in your stomach or neck, shoulders or head. Focus on the sensation and breathe as above. Try to let the physical feeling become an emotional feeling. You might put words to the physical reality, such as: "This gives me a pain in the stomach. I'm sick to my stomach of . . . " Or, "What a pain in the neck _____ is." Or, "Oh, my back, I can't carry _____ anymore," and so on. Your body will signal an accurate statement.

**Exercise 3.** Keep a daily journal of your feelings. It's like talking to a friend who won't judge you, analyze you, or try to solve your problems for you. The journal simply and quietly receives your feelings. The end of the day is a good time for this. Sit down and go over the day in your mind, recording the different feelings you experienced. This exercise is one of the most powerful in this entire book because it will help you stay aware of your feelings. It will also help you grow in finding ways to label them and allowing them to become part of your life.

**Exercise 4.** Learn to use *focusing*, a tool for safe feeling exploration. Focusing helps your feelings to teach you about what is going on inside. With this tool you can learn to feel safe listening to any feeling. You will also learn that your feelings have messages for your good. This process has been developed by Eugene Gendlin in his book, *Focusing*. I have drawn this particular exercise from Dawn George's three-hour tape series, "Focusing: Unlocking Your Body Wisdom." See "Further Reading" at the end of the book for ordering information.

There are safety precautions built into the exercise for a good reason. By doing this exercise, you will be opening yourself to material you have spent your life avoiding. Respect the seriousness of these feelings.

The best way to experience this exercise is to have a friend read it to you step-by-step as you feel it. A second choice is to tape record the steps that appear in italics and play it for yourself, using the pause button after each step.

1. ***Clearing a space.*** *Relax and let go of everything else in your life during this time you have allotted. Do some deep, relaxing breathing. When you feel removed from your daily cares and worries, ask yourself, "Is there anything in my life right now that is keeping me from feeling really good?" When you reach one clear answer to the question, put it aside and ask the question again.*

Most likely some answer will come to you from this question. When you know what it is, remember it and then clear your mind so that you can ask the question again and get other answers. The purpose of this first step is to make a list of the issues bothering you. You will then choose the most pressing one. If you already know what you will be focusing on, you can start with it instead of building a list of issues. However, if you are only aware that something is bothering you but aren't sure exactly what it is, the list would be a better idea. Ask yourself the question in step 1 until you feel you have covered what may be the problems facing you at this time.

2. **Choosing one.** *Trust your body sense to choose one of these issues on which to focus. Which issue on your list carries a charge or seems to be calling out for attention?*

    *When you know what issue you want to proceed with, use your body's awareness to check to see if it is OK to focus on this issue. You can do this by monitoring whether you are experiencing too much fear to proceed. If so, mentally place this issue at a distance—outside of the room, the house, or the neighborhood. If it is still too scary, put it in an old mine shaft and see if that imagined distance allows your body to feel comfortable enough to proceed. Or perhaps you can't deal with it right now at all. That's fine. Put that issue off and try another one in a similar manner. When you are comfortable with an issue, proceed to the next step.*

3. **Being with the feeling.** *Now allow the issue to become a feeling. If you feel it primarily in your body, allow the physical pain to change into emotional pain. You can help this by allowing an image of the feeling to emerge. See if some shape or figure arises in your consciousness. It will come in some form. If an image doesn't come, perhaps a sound, a smell, or even a physical awareness other than the pain you started with will emerge. For most people, an image will emerge.*

    *Try and be with the feeling and the image in a friendly, compassionate way. You are an observer. You are present to learn from the feeling and nothing more. You are safe and can observe without fear. The feeling can teach you and heal you.*

    *Then allow the "more than" or a story around the feeling to emerge. Is there a story from childhood that is being triggered? If not, is there a story from more recent years? Let yourself go into it as if you were a leaf being taken by a current of a river. This is the "felt sense." This is sitting with your feelings.*

    *If at any time it becomes too scary, honor that by mentally putting the feeling at a distance from you (down a tunnel, across a pond, or at the other end of a football field). This allows you to continue observing, but at a safe distance.*

4. **Sensing all the layers of the feeling.** *Now that you are comfortable and have prepared the way, allow all of the feeling to emerge. Ask, "What's the worst of all of this?" or, "What is the crux?" or, "What is it about this whole thing that feels so bad?" Or you can use the image that emerged to ask what it has to teach you. For example, if the feeling became a volcano, ask, "What is so volcanic or hot or jagged about all of this?" Just calmly observe the answers coming to you.*

5. **Resonating.** *Now check in again with your body in order to see if you are resonating with this. That means that your body may feel relief. Or you may actually experience a shift in your body, such as a physical awareness of settling or changing, maybe letting go of tension. Or perhaps, a lighter feeling may emerge as the whole sense of the feeling and story come together for you. Whatever the sensation, it feels right to you.*

   *If you experience a tightening in your body, focus on that. Let it change into a feeling and an image. Sit with it and see if a story from childhood emerges. As a story emerges, bring this new material to the body resonating part. If you are aware of more sensations coming up, you can go through the same steps again. Or you can come back to it at a later time. Your feelings will wait for you to be ready. Be easy on yourself, and don't do more than feels comfortable.*

6. **Appreciating.** *Before you end the exercise, take time to breathe and relax with this whole experience as a way of saying good-bye. Take time to appreciate the wisdom of your body and your feelings. If you are feeling pleased, smile and enjoy this new experience that you have had with your feelings. Leave, knowing you will come back to this space whenever you want this inner comfort and wisdom.*

Learning to do this focusing exercise—uniting your body, feelings, imagination, and awareness—is learning to sit with your feelings. It is a transforming experience. In learning this skill, you move away from avoiding feelings and toward befriending them as counselors.

## Ten Ways Making Friends with Your Feelings Helps in Relationships

While dating and sorting:

1. Your intuition will be sharper because you will be more at home with your feelings rather than avoiding many of them. Therefore, you will not be blind to obvious feedback about your date of unconscious feelings of loneliness, fear of rejection, or other "negative" feelings that often interfere with your intuitive sense.

2. You will be able to observe how you feel treated rather than being overly concerned about how you are treating him or her.

While building intimacy in a relationship:

3. The tendency to blame your partner will be reduced in you because you are more at home with your feelings. Therefore, you are more adept at knowing when you are uncomfortable, anxious, or unhappy. These feelings are often projected onto partners by blaming them for something in order to distract you from the unwanted feeling.

4. Your communication will be real and effective because you can hear your own feelings, and respect those of your partner, without so easily getting defensive and attacking.

5. You will be more centered when your partner blames you because you are not at the mercy of your buttons. You will be able to listen with some distance, not letting the blame push your buttons. In this way, you will allow your partner room to look at his or her own issues without having to deal with counterattacks and hurt feelings. You will become a healing environment for your partner.

6. When you are feeling unhappy or anxious in the relationship, you'll be able to discuss the feeling and understand what is creating the problem.

7. When your partner is feeling difficult feelings and wants to talk about them, you'll be able to listen and not be threatened by them because you know that feelings are important counselors.

8. When you are upset or angry, you'll be able to figure out the cause instead of mindlessly taking it out on your partner or children. The upset and anger may be coming from work or other people. Maybe it's about your health, your job success, your personal worth and fulfillment, or your parents.

9. When something is bothering you and you have figured out that it is something you don't like about the relationship, you'll be

able to talk about it, expecting to be heard, rather than avoiding it or being apologetic about it.

10. You can give praise and compliments because you feel less competitive with your partner and more at ease with your childhood feelings of not being enough. You also can receive compliments and praise—by far the more difficult task—because you are not internally putting yourself down. You really do believe you are deserving.

It seems that no matter how we view our problems, learning more about our feelings is the solution. Good luck on your journey.

# 13

# When It Starts Falling Apart: Staying Open to Understanding

An anxious couple walking into my office one hot afternoon in October were discouraged and in trouble. They came seeking advice about salvaging their young and, at one time, glorious relationship. They had been dating for a year but didn't know what to do now.

"We're here because we don't know if we should give up or try and save what we had." Bryan began with a little-boy, desperate look on his face. "We've had a great, solid relationship for a year, but for the last few months, it's been going downhill fast—we're fighting all the time and don't seem to be able to stop."

"Do you feel the same way, Paula?" I asked.

"Yes, it's terrible," Paula responded. "Bryan and I felt perfect for each other until the last month or two . . ."

"Two or three, I would say," Bryan broke in.

> "We're here because we don't know if we should give up or try and save what we had." Bryan began with a little-boy, desperate look on his face. "We've had a great, solid relationship for a year, but for the last few months, it's been going downhill fast—we're fighting all the time and don't seem to be able to stop."

"Whatever," Paula continued on a roll. "We're totally stuck now, and I'm not willing to just let this relationship slip away. I want to at least understand what we're doing. We're doing it wrong! That's obvious! But we can't figure out how to get the relationship back."

"What was the early relationship like?" I asked.

"Great sex, great talks, lots in common, and no criticism or fighting," Bryan quickly shot back.

"And much more respect and caring," Paula joined in. "We were there for each other; *we* were priority number one! We also didn't cancel dates or squeeze time together into little time slots."

This opening scene was beginning to be familiar. In my psychotherapy practice that specializes in couples, I have begun to see more and more unmarried couples. They come in to figure out either how to regain the good feelings they once had, or how to end it and get on with their lives. You may one day find yourself in this dilemma, or perhaps you already know how it feels.

## Early Fears and Panic

At this point in a session, I start explaining the concept of intimacy freakout—the hidden monster behind the scenes of even the best relationships. I also explain its basis in the concept of ambivalence about being connected to another person. I use the word "connected" because it conveys the positive partnership quality that so many people yearn for—along with the frightening, stuck together or trapped quality that so many lovers panic about. I let the couple know that all people experience a yearning for the joys of feeling connected to a partner, along with the fear of being either smothered or abandoned when they surrender and become vulnerable.

The media bombards us daily with the yearning side of this ambivalence. We know about it. We are inundated with commercials that exploit our yearning for security and warmth—the ultimate American dream of relationships. We're very familiar with that part of the bonding process.

However, the fear part—whether it's the fear of being connected only to be abandoned, or the fear of being invaded and smothered—is not publicly discussed. It doesn't sell products! Therefore, most people are caught unaware when these fears suddenly surface and create alarming distrust in the very person that, only recently, offered warm acceptance.

I explained to Bryan and Paula that their surprising and disappointing fights were most likely the result of these hidden forces. This made them at least feel normal, even though it didn't do anything to remedy their situation.

## The Defense Cycle of Yearning and Dependence

The swing between the forces of yearning and depending triggers our mind to go into a defensive stance. We yearn for a secure bond, all the time hoping for perfect safety and love. But life is not this safe and secure. We all were failed in childhood in many ways, many of which made us stronger—but not without pain and disappointment.

Feeling dependent on anyone for all that we yearn for triggers memories of those early years, with its limitless desires but helpless dependency. As adults, every time we allow ourselves to feel dependent—deliciously enjoying sex with our partner and wanting it to happen often is a dependency—we tap into unconscious memories of those early years of helplessness and frustration or pain. Infants are dependent for everything. There are bound to be times when we were let down by caring parents. However, most of us were also hurt by demeaning and punishing behavior from our confused and poorly equipped parents. The memories of the helplessness of having to depend on parents is usually not pleasant. So much so that most of us can't remember it very well. But once in a relationship that matters—one that strikes our yearning buttons—these memories are triggered, and we get scared.

When it seems that our yearning for love and acceptance could be fulfilled in this new and wonderful person, our memory of the past activates unconscious forces. In their own misguided way, these forces go into hyperdrive to take care of our fragile souls that don't like being abandoned, shamed, or smothered out of existence. This is the fear side of our ambivalence, and it is there to keep us from feeling too dependent and thereby getting hurt.

## Growing Beyond the Power Struggle

Paula and Bryan were taking this all in with trancelike, blank faces. I went on to explain that this shocking transition stage is a necessary part of growing in commitment and can't be avoided if they want a close and equal union. It's often called the power struggle stage because it is an attempt to control life so we can have just what we want from our partner, forever. This control doesn't go over very well with our partner, who then retaliates in kind. You can see how bewildering and frightening all this is because, first of all, it is really subtle, and second, it's such a drastic switch from the sweet and passionate romance everyone hopes will last forever.

Nowhere in our educational system are we prepared for negotiating this event in our lives. Tools are required to help us repair broken emotional trust, fabricate understanding with someone who is making us feel terrible, and weld agreements with someone who can make us feel like we are the most special person in the world—or the worst. These tools are not handed out at the singles bar, the dating service, or the marriage license window.

At the juncture between the romantic stage and the power struggle stage, couples face a number of choices. The first one is to quit and go find another person to have a romance with. This works well when you are younger and are exploring the various types of people in the world of relationships. However, the older you get, the less satisfying this choice becomes.

The second choice is to learn to live parallel lives. With this choice, the goal is to keep the strife and flack to a minimum, and savor the calmer joys of the relationship. Couples do this by avoiding the areas that bring conflict. After a while, people become good at it. They can avoid emotional topics and yet entertain themselves and raise children in a way that resembles polite traveling companions. This method works well for people who don't need high levels of intimacy.

However, the choice of parallel lives doesn't work well for people who want closeness, warmth, and a lot of passion. People who want a deeper and more satisfying commitment have a third choice, which is to work through the power struggle and improve their skills as practitioners of love. This requires growing into conscious lovers who make choices about their behavior, rather than knee-jerk fighters who are constantly guarding their turf and pride.

> Nowhere in our educational system are we prepared for negotiating this event in our lives. Tools are required to help us repair broken emotional trust.

Relating to your lover in a conscious way is learned behavior, which takes hard work and a stubborn commitment. I am continually inspired by working with people of all backgrounds and levels of education who wish to embrace this demanding apprenticeship to Eros. Bryan and Paula were ready for option three. They were beyond the experimental time in their lives and had tasted how good the love could be between them. As a result, they were willing to do what was necessary to get a good relationship back.

## Staying Tuned to Yourself: Why Self-Focus Is So Important

Bryan was thirty-two and had been married once before. It was a youthful, hurried marriage with no children. He remembers being thrilled to get into the marriage, and then sadly eager to get out of it. He had since been single for five years, which was like a resting period before he was willing to jump into the fray again and try his skill at the "game without rules" as he called romance.

When he met Paula, she felt like the right person at the right time. After seven or eight very happy months together, he was getting settled into the idea of making a life with her. However, as soon as they started talking about making a commitment, their relationship began falling apart. Along with that, he was struggling with his real estate job in a bad market. Much to his dismay, he was finding Paula to be demanding and critical of almost everything he did "for his own self-interests," as she called his work. At this point, Bryan was feeling trapped and blamed. He could also feel the heavy pull of his old pattern tugging on him to run from this connection, which was beginning to feel like a prison.

Paula, who was twenty-eight and had never been married before because she had been "too absorbed in her law career to have time for it," was also totally upset by the sudden turn in their relationship. She, of course, had an entirely different slant on it. According to her, Bryan was afraid of commitment—like all the men she knew—and was trying to find an excuse to leave her. Why else, she argued, was he so unavailable just when they started talking seriously about making a life together? A life that had seemed to both of them unbelievably good. Now, he was calling to cancel dates and was backing off from spending nights together.

It's clear, from this brief statement about their "cases" against each other, that Bryan and Paula were spending their thoughts and problem-solving skills on how to get the other person to change back to being the good partner they had been at the beginning of their relationship. This is the control that I spoke about earlier when describing the power struggle.

Most people who come to my office are hoping that I can straighten out their spouse or sweetheart. The *other person* is always the problem. This is a very natural tendency, which unfortunately does little except keep the cycle of blame going.

Our task now was to shift their focus from partner-blaming, to self-focusing. The concept of self-focus is a real stretch for people who are convinced that they haven't changed at all. They know the problem is completely with their partner. Many people who come to couples therapy are totally blind to their own shifts in feeling and behavior. But the shifts of their partner are as shocking and frightening as seeing a character in a play change from a nice quiet fellow at work to an enraged wife-beater. When each person is blind to their own behavior and hyperalert to their partner's shifts, blaming and attempting to correct their partner seems to be the major preoccupation. In fact, it's the number one couples' fighting style.

> It's clear, from this brief statement about their "cases" against each other, that Bryan and Paula were spending their thoughts and problem-solving skills on how to get the other person to change back to being the good partner they had been at the beginning of their relationship.

I should know. I was humbled at the beginning of my own marriage to realize that although I knew all of this theoretically, it was almost impossible to see my own changes directly. It was something like trying to hem my own pants. If I looked down to see if they were even, my body contortions threw off the proper hang. The only way to get a correct view was by standing normally and looking in a mirror. In the same way, when my marriage reached the power struggle stage, I could only see my own fears and the changes in my behavior that they created reflected in my wife's comments and feedback. Until I could give her feedback an honest hearing, I was deaf to what I most needed to hear at that time.

This is why the shift to self-focus is so crucial. Without it, nothing can move the two lawyerlike combatants out of being stuck in the issues of their power struggle. Only when Paula and Bryan change from protecting themselves and their turf to attempting to understand the other person's feelings and problems will they find the partner they once had.

The key to making any relationship work is to shift to self-focus. Stop blaming the other person and look in the mirror. Not because it's a clever gimmick invented by psychologists, but because it's the truth and it works.

The real source of difficulties in relationships is the changes in behavior that *both* people are making—and the reactions to them by each other. Usually, the reactions alone are the tinder that sparks the fights. "He's withdrawing and doesn't even give me much notice when he cancels." "She criticizes everything I do now." Yes, but why? Lovers hardly ever are skilled enough to explore the real source of their shifts in feeling and behavior: their fears, worries, panics, and shames.

When they accuse the other of clinging or withdrawing, it's almost always done as blaming and threatening. The internal thinking goes something like, "He used to be such a good person, but now he's turned into a monster. I wonder which is real?" "She is so screwed up, I wonder just how screwed up?" "He is commitment-phobic, I just knew I shouldn't have gotten involved." "He is getting so tight about money." "She is demanding more and more, what will it take to satisfy her."

Focusing on these fears and doubts going on within yourself, which are motivating your actions, is called self-focus. It gives partners the understanding to get beyond the power struggle stage. When both people can do this, good things begin to happen. It turns enemies into partners for a long-term relationship. Having said that, I also have to say, it is nearly impossible without certain tools to restrain our defenses.

## Protecting Yourself Will Destroy You and Your Partner

Our natural response to a threat is to protect ourselves. And in reacting naturally in this way to the perceived threats of our partner controlling or abandoning us, we crush, smother, or chill the relationship out of existence. It's a curious phenomenon, but it's true. The majority of relationships controlled by this dynamic feel like war zones instead of safe havens.

The expression, "protecting yourself," means doing what is necessary so that you aren't seen as wrong in any way. It's doing whatever weird or contorted thing you can so you don't seem like a failure. The common knee-jerk reaction when someone is blamed or criticized is to protect. In my office practice I see hundreds of examples of this. "He just can't talk to me about how he feels about his work," she says. To which he responds with only a nanosecond of time lapse, "Who would want to talk to someone as negative as you?"

Or the man in another couple says, "She's really a great mother and businesswoman. I can understand how she doesn't have any time left for me." She responds with, "And what do you call last weekend's trip to the mountains?" Another couple: "You're not present for me; you're always reading or watching TV!" The response: "When you have something more interesting than the latest list of my failures to talk about, I can be persuaded to turn the TV off." It goes on and on. Reaction to reaction to reaction without a break to stop defending and listen.

> The majority of relationships controlled by this dynamic feel like war zones instead of safe havens.

I blame this cycle of perpetual defending on the inability of people to do anything more constructive. It's a lack of knowledge and skills. One thing I want to make very clear is that there's a big difference between knee-jerk, self-protecting statements and actions that are meant to take care of yourself. Self-protection is always defensive, while taking care of yourself is positive and constructive.

Partners who constantly protect themselves live their relationship in a war zone by always being defensive. Most couples hate this, but they don't know how to change it. There exists an alternative. It is learning to understand each other. Partners take care of themselves best when they learn how to make the relationship safe for each other; when they work at understanding themselves and their partner. There are ways that you, like many others befor you, can learn these techniques and change the war zone of your relationship into a safe haven. You can choose between being like two lawyers battling in a courtroom or two business partners struggling together to resolve a design flaw in their new product. For a more in-depth and example-rich explanation of this concept of protection versus understanding, I recommend the book, *Do I Have To Give Up Me To Be Loved By You?* by Jordan Paul and Margaret Paul.

## The Alternative: Practical Tools for Success

If people were taught from an early age how to resolve conflicts with people they love, we wouldn't see so much bitterness and painful confusion in relationships today. But we are not taught these skills in school (with the hopeful exception of conflict resolution training in some elementary schools) or in our homes. Most people, therefore, struggle to contain nasty conflicts the best they can, or they learn to live with rages and withdrawals as if that were the best they could expect.

---

Partners who constantly protect themselves live their relationship in a war zone by always being defensive. Most couples hate this, but they don't know how to change it.

---

When Bryan and Paula decided to heal their relationship instead of abandoning it, they were open to learning new ways of relating. That was when I told them I would teach them an important communication skill that would allow them to hold different viewpoints and not be made to feel crazy or wrong for having them. They liked the idea.

This skill is called a dialogue, and it is mainly carried out by the listener. It has three parts that the listener performs to enable the speaker to feel understood:

- Mirroring
- Validating
- Empathizing

The speaker can say whatever he or she wants with one exception: he or she must confine the amount said to a single "thought chunk." That is a reasonable amount of verbiage to express one idea at a time.

The key here is speaking in quantities that are small enough for the listener to handle. If a speaker goes on and on, the listener can only remember the last few sentences, thereby losing the entire first part of the communication. This creates lots of problems: inefficient discussions, hurt feelings that aren't addressed, and ideas that are expressed but never responded to. If the speaker tries to deliver smaller thought chunks instead, and the listener concentrates on listening with these simple rules in mind, the quality of communication is much more full. It feels strange at first, but over time, the quality of communication that is achieved is very satisfying.

## Mirroring in Practice

Bryan was ready to go first. I asked him to be the speaker and tell me what problems he was experiencing. Then I told Paula that the first task of this three-part skill was to "mirror" what he said—to act as a tape recorder and say back what she heard. I asked her to try not to allow herself to get defensive or correct what he was saying. Simply mirror back what Bryan said as if that were her only concern. When she finished, she would ask if she heard him correctly.

Bryan took a deep breath and started speaking. "My main problem is that I can't do what I think I have to do for my business and give Paula everything that she wants from me. She starts getting critical and telling me that I'm afraid of commitment and am running away and really hurting her after she's already fallen in love with me and let her guard down."

Paula began as I had instructed her. "What I heard you say was that you can't get your work done as you want to and also satisfy me, and then I get critical . . . " She looked at me and said, "This is really hard. I don't agree with this!"

"It isn't about agreeing or disagreeing, only about listening and working on understanding what he is saying. You'll have your turn as a speaker in a moment." I gave this instruction for the hundredth time in my practice. At the beginning of this exercise, most clients feel this same bind. The concept of simply working at hearing the other person—instead of agreeing or disagreeing—is a tough new skill for many people. It requires a behavioral shift.

Paula was ready to continue. "OK, I get critical and blame you for running away and being afraid of making a commitment right after I have let my guard down and fallen in love with you. Did I hear you correctly?"

Bryan gave her high marks for accuracy and a small smile softened his face. It was now her turn.

"My problem is that Bryan has gotten very busy and doesn't give me the same respect or importance as he used to. He often cancels dates, and I feel low on his list of priorities. And I do feel like all this happened after I let myself fall in love and get vulnerable. But I'm not critical or blaming, just disappointed and hurt."

## Validating Your Partner's Experience and Feelings

When Bryan mirrored that to her satisfaction, we went on to the next two parts of this skill: validation and empathy. I have a theory that relationships are set up to make at least one person crazy. We humans like being right and hate not having what we say taken as the truth. Therefore, we tend to handle a difference between us by trying to gain authority for our position by making the holder of the other position crazy or wrong. We do this by saying things like: "You're too emotional! That's why you can't see it." Or, "You stay in your head so much, you can't understand feelings," "You work too much," or, "You're such an airhead."

These common attacks and judgments are used to make the other person crazy or wrong—and therefore not worthy of being taken seriously. Then we can have our way. Like all grand schemes, this doesn't always work out the way we planned. When treated this way, our partner begins a campaign of his or her own, which turns into a smoldering, long-term battle.

Validating your partner's viewpoint is the antidote to this struggle. It is a switch to a new and unfamiliar mode, and may be difficult at first. I stress to my clients that viewpoint is what we are talking about here— and not truth. If two people were to witness a car collision, one from behind and the other from in front of the accident, they would both have different viewpoints. When testifying about the occurrence, it is very likely that they would disagree.

> I stress to my clients that viewpoint is what we are talking about here—and not truth.

It's much the same with relationships. We come to relationships with different points of view about many things. We are male or female, we come from different family backgrounds and cultures, and we have had many different life experiences. Basic differences such as poverty, affluence, education, illness, or health shape the way we see things. The two members of a couple always come to the relationship with a different life experience. To create a long-term relationship that is vital and fulfilling, this has to be worked out.

When two people are locked into a disagreement, they confuse facts with points of view. It's just like the situation with the car collision seen from in front and from behind. If lovers could realize that their different points of view are more important than the facts, they could begin understanding each others' reactions much more quickly. He may say, "She screams at me." Her version is, "I slightly raised my voice for emphasis." They have different viewpoints, stemming from their own family experience with anger.

### The Power of Empathy

The third part of the communication skill is empathy. This is understanding on a gut level what the other is feeling. It is not sympathy or even compassion, although these feelings may flow out of empathy. Empathy is simply understanding with a degree of trying to feel yourself what your partner is feeling. Using this technique can create miracles of understanding and help transform a relationship locked in a power struggle into something that works.

I asked Bryan to say another thought chunk to Paula about something that was important to him. "OK, I want you to know that I'm doing my best to juggle my work and our relationship, which I do value a lot. I want you to quit bugging me about my fear of commitment."

Paula mirrored this to his satisfaction and then looked at my white board in the office for the next step. "Now, I'm supposed to say that makes sense to me from his point of view?"

"Yes," I coached her.

"I guess I can do that; it does make sense from your point of view." Looking again at the board, she said, "and I imagine you feel overwhelmed and picked on and maybe unappreciated for your efforts."

Byran's face instantly got smoother, and the wrinkles around his forehead and his eyes softened. In a quiet voice he said that it was exactly what he was feeling.

Now it was Paula's turn to speak her mind and she began: "I feel that you are pushing me away and wanting me to keep some distance to make life easier for you. I feel that I got sucked in, and now I'm getting pushed away."

"This is hard," he said looking at me for mercy and permission to set her straight on all of these points, rather than simply mirror them. When I didn't move, he looked back at her and mirrored very well using most of her own words. She seemed to relax, finally having been heard rather than contradicted.

"What do you do when you're having a hard time validating?" Bryan asked me.

"People have difficulty validating for a couple of reasons. The most common one is that they are confusing validation with agreement. Are you doing that?"

"Yeah, I guess I am."

"OK, without agreeing or disagreeing, could her statement make sense from Paula's point of view?" I coached.

"I think so; I can see how you could see it that way."

"And how do you imagine that she feels having this view of it?" I prompted.

"Pretty scared and hurt, I guess."

Paula's eyes misted, and I could see that she was now struggling to hold herself together. Any feeling understood for the first time often spills tears. She nodded her head in silent agreement.

"How is this going for you both?"

"It's hard to not jump in, but we're talking and that's an improvement," Bryan responded and Paula nodded.

---

> Any feeling understood for the first time often spills tears.

---

## Transforming Conflicts into a Common Search for Solutions

I had Bryan and Paula continue the discussion and coached them through the steps:

- Thought chunks

- Mirroring without defending

- Validating

- Empathy

As they each took turns, the content deepened and began to turn into a common search for what this struggle was really about.

Paula mirroring Bryan: "So you're saying that this feeling of doing what you need to do in your own hectic life and also having to worry about whether I think I can trust you to stay committed is reminding you of being a teenager with your depressed mother who would interrupt your studying with her need to talk. Is that right?" After receiving his nod, she said it did make sense that he could feel that way, and she imagined he felt overwhelmed and scared of her demands, as well as feeling unappreciated. He agreed.

"But I do respect your work and don't want to be a drain on you, only a friend. But you don't let me in!" She entreated.

He ended his reflection with the step of empathy by saying, "You must be feeling pushed away, hurt, and confused."

"And panicked about getting hurt," she added.

This took about half an hour, and now they were beginning to try and understand that they each had reactions to getting closer and each had issues about intimacy. From there, they explored what all this new awareness reminded them of in their lives. Memories of childhood came up, along with fears and disappointments from earlier relationships. They immediately noticed that this was much more like the friendship they had earlier in their relationship when they trusted each other. They wanted to know where to go from here.

## The Technique of Making Positive Doable Requests

"I'm going to teach you how to make requests rather than demands and criticisms," I responded to their question of what to do next. "Keep the concept of ambivalence in mind once again. You now have a better understanding of your fears about getting closer and how early childhood fears have been triggered. You want closeness, but you're afraid of it. Learning how to respect your fears but not be ruled by them is a matter of learning how to take care of yourselves without isolating yourselves from each other. And that is where making requests comes in.

"When you were younger, you could choose to leave. You might have gone to a friend's, to your room, or simply refused to talk. But that doesn't work now because it doesn't help to keep you in the relationship. Momentarily, it gets you out of the attack or hurt, but it doesn't get you any closer to each other."

"It's the only thing I could do with my mother," Bryan said. "I had to hide from her for my own sanity."

I continued this same train of thought with Paula. "Paula, you seem to have learned to tug on your mother's apron strings to get attention. You felt scared and panicky when she left the house because she often wouldn't come back when she said she would. Is that the gist of what you were just exploring?"

"Yes, and I can hear now how this isn't working with Bryan. But what do I do now?"

"Before leaving today I would like each of you to make a request that you think would help you to feel a little safer in this relationship. But there are two rules; the request has to pass two conditions to be workable. One is that the request has to be positive and pass the corpse test. In other words, if a dead person could do it, it doesn't pass. If you say, 'I want you to leave me alone when I'm reading,' it won't pass the test because a corpse can do that perfectly. Or if you make a request about not making dates that get canceled later, it won't pass because it's negative and not positive."

Couples don't realize this, but if you make a string of negative requests, you're sending a message to your partner that you're happier when he or she isn't around to bug you. It's like saying, "Drop dead and I'll be happy." It's very important that your requests always give the other person something to do, rather than something not to do.

The second condition of request making is that it be a specific behavior. If you say, "I want you to be more affectionate or patient," it comes out too much like saying, "Change your personality." Nobody can do that, and it won't be received in a positive way. Instead, break down your desires into behaviors that can be seen and heard. If you want your partner to be more affectionate, ask yourself, "*What would it look like* if he or she were doing this for me?" This will help you get in touch with specific, positive actions that your partner can do to make you happy.

---

If you say, "I want you to be more affectionate or patient," it comes out too much like saying, "Change your personality." Nobody can do that, and it won't be received in a positive way. Instead, break down your desires into behaviors that can be seen and heard. Ask yourself, "*What would it look like if he or she were doing this for me?*"

---

"I'm ready with mine," Bryan said. "Paula, I want you to stop talking about my fear of commitment."

"But that doesn't pass the positive test or the corpse rule," she blurted out, looking betrayed and hurt.

"Oh yeah—OK—I want you to . . ." He looked at me and said, "I know what I want, but I can't make it positive. Help!"

"How about asking her to say something to you when she is feeling ignored that shows she understands a lot of what you two talked about today?"

"Well, let's see. It would feel much better to me if you could say, 'Honey, I respect your work and want you to succeed, but I also want to play with you' when you're feeling put off by me. I think I could hear that without getting defensive."

Bryan had made a great first attempt at taking care of himself, and Paula agreed to try it for the next couple of weeks as an experiment.

Then it was her turn. "How about if you only suggest things to do together that you know you won't cancel no matter what. Everything else would be on a last minute, catch-as-catch-can basis."

"But you'll feel like I'm not initiating much!" He argued, as if caught trying to escape his mother's demands and waiting for the pathetic lecture.

"Yes, but you won't be canceling on me!" He got her point and said he could see how it was a good idea. At this point it was clear to me that both of them had lightened up considerably. You could see the change in the way they looked at each other instead of looking only at me. Their faces had shed at least fives years from when they first walked into my office.

## New Communication Skills Are the Key to Better Relationships

You, the reader, may think that this is simplistic and doesn't reflect real life as you know it. While I can understand that reaction, I also want to confirm that over and over again, conflicts are resolved this way in my office. While every conflict doesn't always resolve itself this smoothly, these techniques work. They also serve as a launching point for renewed trust and hope that the problems can be worked out.

When couples begin to communicate in a positive, workable way, their relationships begin to move in much more positive directions. Having one's point of view understood, and then validated, creates a truce in the war between the sexes. This becomes a new experience that leads to further understanding and a glimpse of the hoped-for partnership that most people want so badly.

> Having one's point of view understood, and then validated, creates a truce in the war between the sexes.

These basic tools for dialogue and positive, doable requests work well in conflict situations. They also work well during quieter times when you need simple listening and support. They aren't magic, but they provide a way for working through situations that previously seemed impossible. However, they don't work unless they're used. Although I have never had a couple tell me that these skills didn't work, I have had plenty tell me that they didn't use them. Lovers often avoid using them because they don't want to be close in the middle of a conflict. They are afraid that if they use these tools, they will be pulled in the direction of more intimacy.

When closeness and understanding are wanted, these tools give couples the skill to negotiate through difficult topics and troubled times. The majority of couples can help themselves by practicing these skills until they are good at them. It's also important to be careful not to push closeness when both people are afraid of it. Later, when closeness is desired again, use the tools to get there.

When the cycle of blame poisons the joy of loving, it's a good indication that something is going on that neither partner is aware of. This is the time to pull these tools off the shelf and use them.

## Exercises for Understanding Each Other

I'm going to share another fundamental truth about relationships. When you're not getting along, you're also resisting getting closer. At those times, employing these tools probably won't work because you don't want them to work. Here is the next step at those difficult times.

First, take a look at what's going on with *you*. Why are you drawing back? Are you afraid of getting dependent? Are you afraid of losing your freedom or your own sense of self? What are you defending and protecting that is important to you? Whatever it is, it's usually taking place on an unconscious level and isn't easy to spot.

The exercises below will help you form a habit that will push you into first looking at yourself rather than at your partner when the relationship feels off or scary. Once you have acquired the habit of examining your own flights from closeness, and have stopped blaming your partner, the tools discussed in the previous section will be extremely useful.

The following exercises will help a sincere person see if he or she is digging in to protect him or herself or reaching out to understand what is going on underneath it all. Once the desire and commitment to attempt understanding is secure, the dialogue and request-making skills can be employed.

**Exercise 1.** Imagine what a really fine relationship with your partner would be like. Picture it in your mind with the detail of daily life taking shape in concrete form. Go through a day in this wonderful relationship with him or her. Then go through a week.

Now, ask yourself, are there are any disadvantages that you can notice in having this ideal relationship? Are there any fears about your own freedom being endangered? Any fears about getting dependent and then being left? Do you have any fears about losing yourself, losing your self-esteem, or losing the ability to make your own decisions?

Pick the fears that seem to be strong and list them in your book under "What Could Scare Me Out of this Relationship." Then use this list to have a good conversation with your partner. Don't try to solve the fears; simply talk about them as normal, human reactions, and use the mirroring, validating, and empathy techniques as you listen to each other. You won't have to take turns each time, but rather let one person talk out his or her fears and then switch to being the listener.

**Exercise 2.** When you are in the midst of a fight but away from each other, ask yourself what is your *intention* in this fight? Are you protecting your reputation, your image of yourself, or your view of the situation? Are you trying to be right? Are you getting back at your partner for a previous hurt?

Now ask yourself what would you lose if you stopped protecting yourself and attempted to understand your partner? Be honest with this question until you come up with something that you would lose. Maybe you fear losing your facade of looking competent. Maybe you fear having your own needs ignored if you fulfill your partner. Perhaps you are worried about being lost in your lover's dominating personality. Perhaps you have issues about not getting your way. Or perhaps you are feeling confused and out of control. Write this out under "How Understanding My Partner Could Turn on Me."

After you find out what you are protecting, weigh it against what you will lose by not moving to understanding. In other words, there's a fight going on. This is creating distance between you and your partner. Angry, blaming feelings have gotten in the way of loving and joy. This is the price you are now paying. Moving toward understanding would alter this. Would it be worth it to you? Again, use this information to have a good discussion. At this point, continue to discuss or trade experiences, rather than going for solutions.

**Exercise 3.** Begin to notice your body reacting to impending fights, criticisms, cheap shots at your self-esteem from your partner, or conflicts at work. Check for feelings of clenching or heaving in your stomach, tightening of your neck and shoulders, shooting pains in your back, aching in various areas of your head, fatigue and the desire to give up, or a flushed feeling in your face. These are your triggers. If you can learn to recognize them, they will let you know when you are getting ready to protect yourself. List these triggers in your notebook under "My Body Sensation of Getting Protective." Use these triggers to alert you to your knee-jerk reactions. This gives you a chance to decide if you like the defensive reaction or if you would prefer moving to understanding the situation, yourself, and your partner—especially if the discussion could feel caring and safe.

These three exercises are designed to help you make a decision that is crucial. When you are ready to listen and explore each other's differences without making them automatically wrong, you can use the tools described above and outlined below. The payoff for moving in the direction of understanding is the return to a more rewarding relationship.

## Active Listening Techniques at a Glance

Here is an easy-reference, capsule review of the techniques you have learned in this chapter.

**Mirroring.** Reflecting back exactly what you heard, like a tape recorder, or sometimes, a condensation of what was said. Do not add any interpretation or different language. When finished, ask if what you said was correct. Remember, the speaker talks in thought chunks.

**Validating.** Using expressions such as, "That makes sense from your point of view" or, "I can see that." You are validating your partner's point of view as sane and credible. It is his or her point of view, not yours. You don't have to share it or agree with it to validate it.

If you find you can't validate, there are two possible reasons. Either, you are mistaking validation for agreement, or you need more information. To correct the first, realize that you are not agreeing when you validate, only saying that your partner has a legitimate point of view. If you are trying to validate and it just doesn't make sense, ask for more information.

**Empathizing.** Using the lead-in, "I imagine you're feeling . . ." try to use one word for each feeling that comes up, for example, sad, hurt, angry, misunderstood, anxious, scared, unappreciated, unseen, loving, excited, and so on. Your partner can add or subtract feelings that are right for him or her after you say what you think.

Take turns doing these three steps for each other until you both feel understood and understanding of the other person. (I owe this beautiful process to Harville Hendrix, with whom I have studied.)

## Making Requests at a Glance

When making requests of your partner, follow these two rules:

1. Requests must be positive and pass the corpse test.

2. Requests must be behavioral and specific. That is, instead of saying, "Be more affectionate," say "when you greet me after having been away, give me a kiss and a hug."

I first learned this approach to making requests from Richard Stuart, author of *Helping Couples Change*. These tools have helped hundreds of couples learn a different way of talking and understanding each other to satisfy their mutual needs. Some people learn the techniques, use them, and feel good most of the time. Others need more coaching and the help of a third party to get to the underlying issues that invisibly but effectively keep them at odds.

We are all at a disadvantage in our relationships today. We want so much out of them, yet we have been so poorly trained in creating happy homes. We wouldn't let a mechanic near our car with as little training as we get to repair the tricky breakdowns of relationships. But now you have more information and better skills. Good luck!

# 14

# Letting Go of Being in Love

A great day for a wedding! I'm at Rick's marriage celebration in the spacious backyard, ringed with brilliant flowers, of his soon-to-be in-laws' house. I arrived early and am in a reflective mood since I've broken my usual policy of not going to weddings or parties of clients. Somehow being at this one seemed sufficiently special and right.

Rick, who is thirty-eight, hasn't come to my office for a year now. Since his last visit, I have received two lengthy and informative letters confirming that the therapy had been extremely productive. He was feeling pleased that all the pieces of his life were working so well. I identified with his struggle and his growth and was very pleased for him and about our work together. So here I was, on his wedding day, early and pensive.

In my memory, I can picture Rick in one of the beginning sessions—a dramatic one—after he had broken up for the umpteenth time with another "great woman who was really right." He was confused and hurt that after all of his efforts to please, the relationship still hadn't worked out.

I could have predicted this ending and was frustrated for Rick. I wanted him to look at the dead-end approach he was using: "Aren't you exhausted? All that shifting back and forth to try and please? You're like a chameleon! Why don't you just stop trying so hard to please, get clear about who you are, and start thinking about what you want for yourself from a relationship?"

> I wanted him to look at the dead-end approach he was using: "Aren't you exhausted? All that shifting back and forth to try and please? You're like a chameleon! Why don't you just stop trying so hard to please, get clear about who you are, and start thinking about what you want for yourself from a relationship?"

"Yes—I'm tired of it all," Rick had murmured with his head hung in defeat. "And it doesn't work anyway. No matter how hard I try to please, it all catches up with me sooner or later. When it's all said and done, women like chameleons. I can't always be what women want, and when I change to something that suits me more, they blame me for not being there for them. Now I'm feeling confused and angry."

"Why don't you try being yourself with no holds barred. What do you have to lose? Trying to please isn't working, and you're exhausted. Don't you think it would be exhilarating just to be *yourself?*" Knowing I had a window of opportunity here, my bulldog personality pursued. "You know, just say what you're really thinking instead of censoring it. Do what you want instead of checking everything out in those cautious ways of yours." Rick, changing his posture, brought me to an abrupt halt. "Look at how you change just thinking about it," I added.

Rick had straightened up. He looked lighter somehow, and his eyes brightened. I saw a hopeful smile breaking through the gloom. I can still see him clearly in my mind as he left that session—attempting a bright but tentative smile, broadcasting the fresh hope that a new concept inspires.

In the next few months, he attacked this new plan with a vengeance. He had hit bottom, like an alcoholic, and couldn't stand it any more. He was a man with a mission! He played at, in his words, "being more selfish and opinionated." It was fun, he reported, trusting his own view of things instead of the friend he was with or his current date.

Rick finally accepted that everyone wouldn't agree with him or even like him. That was the hardest hump to get over. In a number of sessions he talked about how foreign it felt not to focus primarily on whether what he was doing was going to make his date like him. Gradually, asking for what he wanted, stating his ideas without waffling, he began to see results. He was changing, and his life was changing with him. He was finally learning to like who he was on his own terms, and to his great surprise, a miracle had happened—others liked him that way too.

I knew he had made a radical shift when he gave me the "famous lecture," as we both referred to it later. "You know, I'm not a young stud just starting out. I have to face the fact that I have a lot of accumulated baggage in my personality. I like a lot of things about my life and what I do, and I want to honor them, not someone else's version of life. Also, I'm getting clearer about the kind of woman I want to be with. Some of my friends are saying that I'm being too picky, wanting perfection where it doesn't exist."

> "You know, I'm not a young stud just starting out. I have to face the fact that I have a lot of accumulated baggage in my personality. I like a lot of things about my life and what I do, and I want to honor them, not someone else's version of life.

He mimicked his friends voices: "'If you don't settle for someone, you'll be alone the rest of your life.' I'm sick of hearing that. I don't want to settle, and I'm not going to. I'm going to just keep on trusting myself and acting as if I know what's right for me. Who else can I trust if it isn't me?" He snuck a glance at me as if he had hurt my feelings for not being included in the list of "trustees."

"Christ, I know the kind of woman I want isn't going to be easy to find, but she isn't a figment of my imagination. She's probably around the block somewhere if I can just open my eyes." He was really on a roll now. "I want a woman who is comfortable with herself, and I'm simply not going to meet her until I'm comfortable with myself. If I want to be loved for who I am, I have to start loving myself first. I want a relationship of equals."

He then glared at me, like a prophet challenging me to refute any of the truths he had just proclaimed. Was he the new John the Baptist of equal relationships? I was in no mood to refute or caution. He had gotten the message; he was on fire with it.

The wedding music was starting, and it charmed me back to the present. After three bridesmaids carefully walked toward the minister with that peculiar wedding step, the woman he had held out for and knew he would meet came into my view. I had only heard of her in his letters; this was my first glimpse of the real person.

Ellen seemed comfortable with herself (he had told me this in his letters). Her father, walking at her side, certainly loved her. You could see it in his face. You could tell they had a genuine fondness and respect for each other. I also saw the burn scar on her left cheek that Rick wrote about. He wondered how it might affect him over the years.

As the bride and her father passed my row, my thoughts swirled back to another highlight in Rick's journey to this union. After the initial burst of experiments became routine, Rick began to assimilate new habits. He calmed down and began living a steady, less up-and-down existence. This quieter time invited certain feelings he hadn't expected. He had let go of a lifestyle, and there was bound to be some sense of loss and grief.

"How are you?" I asked at the beginning of a session when I noticed he lacked the energetic bearing I had grown used to.

"OK, life is calmer." He responded confidently but in tones that reminded me of a funeral. "I have a lot of joy at times. Other times are hard. I feel solid, but I miss the excitement that fantasies create. The hunt for the perfect woman may have been crazy, but it was exciting. Every day, I could wake up to the thrill of a possible new 'wonder woman'. I miss that excitement even though I know what a dead end it was."

"So you're liking being yourself, and missing some things too?" I asked.

"Yeah, I am."

"Any romance in view?"

He laughed, smiled, changed his position in his chair, and said, "Not really. It isn't going to be easy to find the woman I want. I've gathered quite a portfolio over the years and really want to be *met* by a woman. You know—a real partnership."

"So how are you dealing with that?" I asked. "Sounds real different for you."

"It's different, and it feels right. I'm handling it by developing myself. I'm beginning to find joy in being myself instead of finding excitement in the hunt. I've also discovered something that I heard you tell me months ago, but I'm just understanding it now. It's the idea that *expressing* myself is really different from *impressing* others.

"You know how I always used to think about impressing everyone? Well, now I'm into expressing myself. I'm offering more of my own ideas and suggestions at work, which is helping the flow of creative juices. I'm also back playing basketball with a group of guys I've gotten to know, and that feels great. This change to expressing myself is a lot more rewarding. I used to feel like a hamster running in a wheel trying to impress people. Now, I'm more relaxed, and I believe even more productive.

"You know, Al, I think I have experienced joy in myself for the first time in my life. It's a great feeling to have moments of truly enjoying myself. I'm willing to give up approval-seeking too. Right now, I'm feeling a little lonely, but I figure the woman I'm waiting for will come when it's right. I can wait. Actually, I'm enjoying myself."

My attention was drawn once again to the ceremony by a long silence after the minister asked if anyone had any cause to prevent this union between Rick and Ellen. A real jokester, he punctuated the silence with, "No one? Are you sure?"

My eyes misted a little watching Ellen take Rick's hand and read the vows that she had written. How different the vows would have been if he hadn't gone through the metamorphosis from chameleon to independent thinker! Rick's voice was strong and confident when he promised to respect Ellen as much as he respected himself. That reminded me of another one of Rick's statements about his change to a new, self-accepting being.

Three months after his "conversion," Rick came into my office full of purpose with a wide grin on his face and said, "It's working; in fact it's all falling into place. I'm finding a lot of satisfaction in what I'm doing. I'm especially enjoying trusting myself. I no longer watch for how I'm supposed to act or think according to the person I'm with. I can disagree with people, and it's fine. I never used to do that. I might have disagreed in my own mind but never would have been blatant about my differences in case they weren't acceptable. It took so much energy to be so vigilant and censor myself!

"I'm learning to be unapologetically me. I'm not keeping secrets about myself. There really isn't any longer a private me I'm ashamed of. Hiding secrets always made me feel like I wasn't good enough. It didn't occur to me that other people were probably hiding things too. Now the private and public me are the same. It feels great!"

"Are you lonely?" I asked.

"Sure, I'm lonely at times, but not the same way. I have myself to relate to now. I know it sounds weird, but there is a difference now, when I'm alone. I also have friends and even some warm and loving sex. I haven't met the right woman yet, but I'm patient. I'm really counting on my own judgment. My friends have been great in not getting on my case about it; most of them now enjoy my frank and honest statements. I just feel so much lighter and freer, and that's reward enough right now. But at times I wish I could be sharing this with someone special."

The newlyweds were now exchanging rings, and it was sweet. The photographer was edging in for the perfect shots, and the guests were feeling the bond that these two people had worked so hard to achieve.

They kissed for a long time and then turned to us all, beaming joyful smiles. Then one of Ellen's female friends began to sing "Loving You." The new couple went over to their parents for kisses and hugs. My thoughts drifted back to Rick in the final months before ending therapy, before he had met Ellen.

> The vows would have been different if he hadn't gone through the metamorphosis from chameleon to independent thinker.

"Something is happening," he said to me quietly one afternoon. "I feel very alone"—he was practically whispering—"and it hurts. I'm letting go of something. I feel weird. Whatever I'm letting go of, I've had for a long time. I'm sad somehow, and I know I can't hang onto it. I think I'm letting go of the need to be in love. Now that I know being in love won't fix me, I can't look forward to love to make me happy. The idea that I'm a puzzle with a piece missing doesn't make sense to me anymore. I used to think that when I found that missing piece, that perfect woman, I would be happy and complete.

"But now I feel lost." His eyes were closed, and he tightened his face in grief. It was difficult to sit there with him, helplessly watching his face register confusion, fear, and loss.

"Letting go of being in love leaves me with this great emptiness or, at least, a fear of being empty. I feel like a wanderer without a home."

"I'm here with you," I said quietly.

"I know that, and it's important," he added, attempting to take care of me now. "I also know I have the comfort of knowing who I am and what expresses me. I'm not exhausting myself trying to impress other people or hiding parts of myself."

"And," I added, trying to give him something to look forward to, "you have the future with all its mystery and richness. Of course, you can't control it, and that's what's scaring you."

"I can feel the need to be in love fading." He looked at me, full of worry. "It leaves me feeling shriveled, without any interest or passion. I was so turned on just last week. What happened?"

"You've lived with that hope and drive for a long time. Now it doesn't make sense, but you don't yet have a replacement or anything to lean on. You're grieving the loss of an old ally," I counseled.

"Sorry about all this sadness! I just can't believe that this is so physical. It actually feels like something is tearing away from my body. It's leaving me raw. I get teary easily these days. I'm sad about losing this hope, or whatever it is, of being in love."

"You don't know what's ahead," I cautioned. "You're following your own expression of who you are, and it has led you here. Looking toward being in love no longer can give meaning to your life as it once did. There was a time when looking for love could give you a sense of meaning and expectancy. Your new joy, from expressing yourself rather than impressing others, is a new and unfamiliar thing. Think of yourself as an evolving art piece!"

"I just realized something," Rick said. "I've given charge of my happiness to a future relationship! To a mythical, wonderful someone. In a way, I've allowed myself to be held hostage by the myth of being in love. I couldn't be totally happy until something from the outside happened to me. What a victim I've been! Now, I want to be in charge of my own happiness, relationship or not. I think I've been afraid of that responsibility." He looked down, deep in thoughts that needed silence to strengthen and coalesce.

"You know," Rick finally said, "this is probably the best way of inviting a great partner to come into my life—letting go." He spoke with the sudden burst of energy of the newly converted. "If I stop worrying about anything except being the me that I respect and enjoy, I'll be the most attractive and receptive I've ever been to the right woman. We'll meet each other without pretenses. No acting. No impressing. If we like each other, it'll be comfortable. It'll feel right and solid.

"I'll also be much better at holding my own in the relationship. I won't be a chameleon watching to see what color I'm supposed to be. Instead, I'll have my beliefs, my desires, and be able to ask for what I want. Maybe the most important difference is that I won't be sneaking or resenting not getting my way in those hidden, smoldering ways I've used in past relationships.

"But I have to give up holding my happiness hostage to the idea of the great romance. He looked at me with boyish charm and innocence. This could really work, don't you think?"

I smiled with him and said, "You never know. But for sure, you have what you have right now, and that's considerable."

Now, being here with him at the promising start of the equal partnership that he had wanted so badly, I was leaking out a few tears. I shook his hand and gave him a hug in congratulations. Introducing me to Ellen, he whispered, "You can thank him for my stubborn streaks and holding my own with you."

She laughed, hugged me, and said, "Well, mostly I like it, and at least he fights fair."

## Conclusion

I don't claim that Rick's story is for everyone or that he is the picture-perfect client. Indeed, I think that his journey, intense and dramatic as it was, would be terrible for many people. However, the stages of growth from the chameleon to a person who can find joy inside himself is inspiring. Relationships of this era demand people who are able to define themselves from inside, rather than from other people. Lovers want to be respected as equals by their partners. But first they have to respect themselves, and that may be the longer journey.

This book has presented a road map to that goal. I have woven theory and life-changing experiments together to produce the two qualities most needed for success: more self-acceptance and sharper judgment in selecting potential partners. I hope the trials and successes of the many people in this book can help light your way in adopting the same principles in your life.

I have also proposed dating as a valuable tool—a progressive therapy—used like stepping stones to achieve your highest potential.

Marriage—the goal of this book—is never a solution; it is simply a lifestyle choice. It has its own set of problems, joys, and terrors. It is, however, a lifestyle that has the potential to shape us into full, healthy, satisfied, and giving people. This potential for growth is enmeshed in the struggles of two people who are wounded and fallible. These struggles,

> I have woven theory and life-changing experiments together to produce the two qualities most needed for success: more self-acceptance and sharper judgment in selecting potential partners. I hope the trials and successes of the many people in this book can help light your way in adopting the same principles in your life.

instead of producing richer lives, can also cripple the partners, turning them into sour and hurt enemies seeking revenge for all the wrongs they have suffered.

This book is intended to help you begin a journey to commitment in love on the wisest path. Prepared with the best skills possible, I hope you will turn the trials of relationship into a beautiful process for yourself—like a tumbling machine turning a rough stone into a polished gem. I ask you to supply the courage to keep at it, to keep looking at yourself as the only person you can change, and to get extra help if you need it.

May you stand at your wedding next to a person who loves you as you are.

# Appendix

# Exercises for Discovering Your Childhood-based Fears of Closeness

This appendix has two parts. Part One helps you explore your hidden fears of relationship and learn how you can take these fears into consideration in finding a mate. Part Two helps you discover the qualities to avoid and the qualities to search for in a mate.

## Part One

When you understand your hidden fears of relationship, you are less likely to let them sabotage your efforts and, instead, let them become advisers to guide you to a relationship that works and is fulfilling.

Ask yourself these questions about past relationships:

1. Which of the three major fears about getting in a serious relationship do you think relates to you the most: (a) being abandoned,

(b) being engulfed or taken over, or (c) losing your self-esteem? Answer the questions below for additional help with this question.

2. Why do you think past relationships ended?

3. What issue or complaint in the relationships did you struggle with the most?

4. What, in the relationship, made you want to flee or fight?

5. Is there any fear or dread, even if small, that you feel when you visualize yourself in a lifelong relationship? Which of the three major fears from question 1 might it be part of?

6. List these fears or dreads from question 5 and see how they relate to your answers in the first four questions.

If possible visit your parents as a field trip and answer these questions about early family influences.

7. What do you think of your parents' relationship? Would you like to be in one like theirs?

8. What, if anything, do you hate about your parents' relationship?

9. Relate the three major fears (from question 1) to these observations about your parent's relationship. Which might you be most afraid of if you were in their relationship?

10. You may find that your parents can talk more freely to you about your early years now that you're older and more understanding. Take advantage of this and ask them about your first few years of life and what was going on in the family, especially around your first to third birthdays.

    If your parents are unavailable, take a fresh look at your memories. Look at pictures of your childhood, paying attention to your thoughts, memories, and intuitions about possible events that could have shaped your attitudes about getting close to someone.

    Ask aunts, uncles, cousins, grandparents and friends of your parents about what was going on in your parents' lives when you were two. You'll get a lot of rich psychological material from this process.

11. What might be your greatest fear about trusting others from your early childhood experiences that you have just examined?

12. Relate what you learn from this detective work to question 5 about any dread you may have of a committed relationship and the three major fears (from question 1).

Ask yourself the following questions about friends and work:

13. What things about you bother your friends? What do you get teased about or confronted about? (Late for appointments, critical, selfish, demanding, judgmental, depressed, and so on.)

14. At work, what are your boss's and subordinates' complaints about you? What are your complaints about them?

15. Keep relating these pieces of information to question 5 to determine what your main area of friction, and therefore resistance to being in a relationship, might be. If, for example, you are learning that you have a hard time dealing with a bossy boss, and your friends tell you that you are stubborn and opinionated, you might look at fear of being taken over as your primary fear. If you are discovering that you fear disapproval and not being liked, both at work and with friends, you could relate that to fear of being abandoned. If you are struggling with friends and at work over issues of being judged and found wanting, it may relate to a fear of losing your self-esteem in a relationship.

What you will learn from this first section is the area of fear that you need to respect about yourself in relationships. You are particularly vulnerable in that area. If you disregard it, your unconscious will sabotage relationships to keep you from getting hurt. If you take your fears into consideration and give them voting privileges about good mate selection, you will find safer and therefore more satisfying partners. For example, if you have found that you are worried most about self-esteem, you would sort most especially for a less critical, accepting person, instead of a fun-loving, brilliant, critical, and impatient one. Sound familiar?

## Part Two

Discover the qualities to avoid and the qualities to search for in a mate. To start on this exploration, do this short guided imagery exercise with a piece of paper and pen handy.

Take yourself on a guided imagery session back to your early years into the house of your youth. Take some time to examine all the rooms, including where your dresser, bed, and closet were in your bedroom, as well as the main appliances and furniture in the kitchen and lounging areas of your house. Now, find your father or male caretaker. Observe him from a distance and notice his qualities—the good and the bad. After you have done that to your satisfaction, go up to him in this totally safe vision and tell him what it was like to grow up with him. You might even tell him something that he should know but you have been afraid to tell him, such as what you wanted from him or feared in him.

Repeat this with your mother or female caretaker and older siblings or major players in your early life.

*Warning:* the following exercises sound more complicated than they are. If you do them step by step on paper, it will work out fine.

**Exercise 1.** After you have taken your imaginary journey, write down all the qualities that you can remember, both good and bad, of both your male and female caretakers. One-word qualities like warm, gracious, sharp, cold, judgmental or the like will be best. Also write out what it was like to live with that person as parent and the thing you said that you had always been afraid to say.

**Exercise 2.** Now make a list of the qualities you would like in your ideal partner.

**Exercise 3.** Ask yourself which of these four word categories presses your buttons the most if said about you in a critical way: (a) lazy/responsible, (b) crazy/sane, (c) stupid/smart, (d) bad/good? To help this process, ask which criticisms bother you the most. What categories would they be represented in? Are they represented in more than one?

**Exercise 4.** Look back on the list of qualities you are looking for in a mate and the ones you have concluded you possess. Try and match one of the four word categories in exercise 3 to each of the qualities on the list. For example, the quality, smart, gets assigned into the category of stupid/smart; the quality, caring, gets assigned to bad/good; the quality, sexy, might get assigned to crazy/sane; and so on.

**Exercise 5.** Underline qualities on the list that you think *you* possess. Have a friend check this list to see if he or she agrees with your assessment. This may test your friend's honesty and your humility, but it will provide valuable self-knowledge. You may have underlined understanding, clear about feelings, giving, sexy, and smart. Now think about friends' comments. You *want* to be understanding, but some people may find you abrasive and critical. You *want* to be clear about feelings and think you are, but some people have accused you of being angry and not expressing it or hurt and not showing it. Take everything into consideration and do your best in listing which qualities you possess.

**Exercise 6.** Which of the four word categories appears the most on the list? Lazy/responsible, bad/good, crazy/sane, or stupid/smart? Use this information in two ways:

1. Make sure that you pick partners who take care of this category that you are most aware of and vulnerable to. For example,

   - If crazy/sane, you will need a good communicator and a person who is willing to work things out.

   - If lazy/responsible, you will need a person who stresses living over success, enjoying life, people, or spiritual qualities over efficiency and success in the workplace.

   - If bad/good, you should go for qualities of understanding, caring, supportive, and warm.

   - If stupid/smart, find a person who is comfortable with his or her intelligence, is nonjudgmental and patient.

2. Next, make sure you give what you want to receive. If you want gentle, learn what it is to be gentle yourself; if you want interesting, take a good look at yourself and see if you are interesting. This is an extremely important point because if you are looking for a quality that you do not possess, you are looking for another person to make you complete and acceptable. The problem with that is it just never works. People complement each other but don't complete each other.

**Exercise 7.** You still have a list of your parents' qualities that we haven't worked with. Look at that list now and see the negative qualities of both your parents. Again, let that push you into making sure that the qualities you look for in a mate are ones that don't repeat the worst of your parents' negative qualities.

By looking at these qualities, you can get beyond the external things that you may have been attracted to in the past, such as dress, looks, sexiness, strength, confidence, and so on. By pushing yourself in this direction, you will be emphasizing loving qualities that will become more and more satisfying to you. Ultimately, a great relationship is made up of feeling accepted, validated, and prized for who you are and giving the same to your mate.

This is not to say that other qualities like attractive, fun, and interesting aren't important. They will also be included in your search. Using chemistry as a necessary but not all-inclusive tool will ensure that you are sufficiently interested in any potential mate. The main thing to learn from these exercises is how to identify the softer, deeper qualities that will help you feel accepted and loved. People often hold the mistaken ideal that most people, when in love, will have these kind, warm, communicative, and caring qualities when, in reality, you must search out these qualities in potential mates.

May your mind and your heart be open in your search.

# Further Reading

## Books

Gendlin, Eugene. *Focusing*. NY: Bantam Books, 1981.

Harville, Hendrix. *Getting the Love You Want: A Guide for Couples*. NY: HarperCollins, 1990.

————. *Keeping the Love You Find: A Guide for Singles*. NY: Pocket Books, 1992.

Love, Patricia. *The Emotional Incest Syndrome: What to Do When a Parent's Love Rules Your Life*. NY: Bantam Books, 1990.

Paul, Jordan and Margaret Paul. *Do I Have to Give Up Me to Be Loved By You?* Minneapolis, MN: CompCare Publishers, 1983.

Scarf, Maggie. *Intimate Partners*. NY: Random House, 1987.

Stuart, Richard B. *Helping Couples Change: A Social Learning Approach to Marital Therapy*. NY: The Guilford Press, 1980.

Tan, Amy. *The Kitchen God's Wife*. NY: Ballantine Books, 1991.

## Tapes

Crowell, Al. "Verbal Aikido." Send $10 to 643 Green Ridge Drive, #3, Daly City, CA 94014. (See Chapter 11.)

George, Dawn. "Focusing: Unlocking Your Body Wisdom." Send $29 to 888 San Ysidro Lane, Santa Barbara, CA 93108.

# Other New Harbinger Self-Help Titles

*Preparing for Surgery*, $17.95
*Coming Out Everyday*, $13.95
*Ten Things Every Parent Needs to Know*, $12.95
*The Power of Two*, $12.95
*It's Not OK Anymore*, $13.95
*The Daily Relaxer*, $12.95
*The Body Image Workbook*, $17.95
*Living with ADD*, $17.95
*Taking the Anxiety Out of Taking Tests*, $12.95
*The Taking Charge of Menopause Workbook*, $17.95
*Living with Angina*, $12.95
*PMS: Women Tell Women How to Control Premenstrual Syndrome*, $13.95
*Five Weeks to Healing Stress: The Wellness Option*, $17.95
*Choosing to Live: How to Defeat Suicide Through Cognitive Therapy*, $12.95
*Why Children Misbehave and What to Do About It*, $14.95
*Illuminating the Heart*, $13.95
*When Anger Hurts Your Kids*, $12.95
*The Addiction Workbook*, $17.95
*The Mother's Survival Guide to Recovery*, $12.95
*The Chronic Pain Control Workbook, Second Edition*, $17.95
*Fibromyalgia & Chronic Myofascial Pain Syndrome*, $19.95
*Diagnosis and Treatment of Sociopaths*, $44.95
*Flying Without Fear*, $12.95
*Kid Cooperation: How to Stop Yelling, Nagging & Pleading and Get Kids to Cooperate*, $12.95
*The Stop Smoking Workbook: Your Guide to Healthy Quitting*, $17.95
*Conquering Carpal Tunnel Syndrome and Other Repetitive Strain Injuries*, $17.95
*The Tao of Conversation*, $12.95
*Wellness at Work: Building Resilience for Job Stress*, $17.95
*What Your Doctor Can't Tell You About Cosmetic Surgery*, $13.95
*An End to Panic: Breakthrough Techniques for Overcoming Panic Disorder*, $17.95
*On the Clients Path: A Manual for the Practice of Solution-Focused Therapy*, $39.95
*Living Without Procrastination: How to Stop Postponing Your Life*, $12.95
*Goodbye Mother, Hello Woman: Reweaving the Daughter Mother Relationship*, $14.95
*Letting Go of Anger: The 10 Most Common Anger Styles and What to Do About Them*, $12.95
*Messages: The Communication Skills Workbook, Second Edition*, $13.95
*Coping With Chronic Fatigue Syndrome: Nine Things You Can Do*, $12.95
*The Anxiety & Phobia Workbook, Second Edition*, $17.95
*Thueson's Guide to Over-the-Counter Drugs*, $13.95
*Natural Women's Health: A Guide to Healthy Living for Women of Any Age*, $13.95
*I'd Rather Be Married: Finding Your Future Spouse*, $13.95
*The Relaxation & Stress Reduction Workbook, Fourth Edition*, $17.95
*Living Without Depression & Manic Depression: A Workbook for Maintaining Mood Stability*, $17.95
*Coping With Schizophrenia: A Guide For Families*, $13.95
*Visualization for Change, Second Edition*, $13.95
*Postpartum Survival Guide*, $13.95
*Angry All the Time: An Emergency Guide to Anger Control*, $12.95
*Couple Skills: Making Your Relationship Work*, $13.95
*Handbook of Clinical Psychopharmacology for Therapists*, $39.95
*Weight Loss Through Persistence*, $13.95
*Post-Traumatic Stress Disorder: A Complete Treatment Guide*, $39.95
*Stepfamily Realities: How to Overcome Difficulties and Have a Happy Family*, $13.95
*The Chemotherapy Survival Guide*, $11.95
*The Deadly Diet, Second Edition: Recovering from Anorexia & Bulimia*, $13.95
*Last Touch: Preparing for a Parent's Death*, $11.95
*Self-Esteem, Second Edition*, $13.95
*I Can't Get Over It, A Handbook for Trauma Survivors, Second Edition*, $15.95
*Concerned Intervention, When Your Loved One Won't Quit Alcohol or Drugs*, $12.95
*Dying of Embarrassment: Help for Social Anxiety and Social Phobia*, $12.95
*The Depression Workbook: Living With Depression and Manic Depression*, $17.95
*Prisoners of Belief: Exposing & Changing Beliefs that Control Your Life*, $12.95
*Men & Grief: A Guide for Men Surviving the Death of a Loved One*, $13.95
*When the Bough Breaks: A Helping Guide for Parents of Sexually Abused Children*, $11.95
*When Once Is Not Enough: Help for Obsessive Compulsives*, $13.95
*The Three Minute Meditator, Third Edition*, $12.95
*Beyond Grief: A Guide for Recovering from the Death of a Loved One*, $13.95
*Leader's Guide to the Relaxation & Stress Reduction Workbook, Fourth Edition*, $19.95
*The Divorce Book*, $13.95
*Hypnosis for Change: A Manual of Proven Techniques, Third Edition*, $13.95
*When Anger Hurts*, $13.95
*Lifetime Weight Control*, $12.95

Call toll free, 1-800-748-6273, to order. Have your Visa or Mastercard number ready. Or send a check for the titles you want to New Harbinger Publications, Inc., 5674 Shattuck Ave., Oakland, CA 94609. Include $3.80 for the first book and 75¢ for each additional book, to cover shipping and handling. (California residents please include appropriate sales tax.) Allow four to six weeks for delivery.

*Prices subject to change without notice.*